D1084441

SYLVESTER JUDD'S
NEW ENGLAND

Sylvester Judd
1813-1853

SYLVESTER JUDD'S
NEW ENGLAND

Richard D. Hathaway

THE PENNSYLVANIA STATE UNIVERSITY PRESS
UNIVERSITY PARK AND LONDON

Dedicated to the memory of
Elizabeth Judd Micoleau
Jeannette Whipple
Louise Harris Beach

Library of Congress Cataloging in Publication Data

Hathaway, Richard D.
  Sylvester Judd's New England.
  Includes bibliography and index.
  1. Judd, Sylvester, 1813-1853. 2. Unitarians
— New England — Biography. 3. New England —
Biography. I. Title.
BX9869.J8H37   288'.3 [B]   81-17854
ISBN 0-271-00307-3   AACR2

Acknowledgments

This study began with Kenneth Murdock, whose advocacy brought Sylvester Judd first to my attention, and with Perry Miller, who once said to me about Judd, "He's my pet." I am grateful to Oscar Handlin, Carl Wittke, George Kummer, and Rolland E. Wolfe for encouragement, and especially to Lyon N. Richardson for guiding my writing with his combination of skill and caring through the first and second drafts. To Charles L. Sanford I owe an intellectual debt for ideas he first published in 1952 concerning the "Edenic myth" in American culture. He and Robert Thornton made useful comments concerning the pages of my manuscript that I showed them.

Sylvester Judd's granddaughters, Elizabeth Judd Micoleau and Jeannette Whipple, and his granddaughter-in-law, Louise Harris Beach (Mrs. Sylvester Judd Beach), encouraged and assisted my work with unusual interest and warmth. They treated me as a friend, invited me several times for visits, and for my use entrusted the large body of manuscripts now known as the Judd Papers into my hands. From there these went as a gift to the Houghton Library at Harvard University. These papers are in two parts. The first was unearthed when Louise Beach and I worked together and found in her home part of a large collection that she thought had been destroyed. The second, now numbered 55M-2, I took to the Houghton Library from the then-dormant Kennebec Historical Society in Augusta, Maine, as authorized by its president, Merton Bailey, and the heirs of Sylvester Judd named above. The Judd Papers are quoted with permission of the Houghton Library.

Acknowledgments

Other manuscripts are quoted with permission of the trustees and/or staffs of Forbes Library, Northampton; Northampton Historical Society; Maine Historical Society; Massachusetts Historical Society; Harvard University Archives; Yale University Library; Columbia University Libraries; Boston Public Library; Westhampton Congregational Church; and First Church of Christ, Northampton. For permitting me to use other manuscripts in private collections, I am grateful to Robert Young, Richard and Caroline Hamlen, and Henry W. Fuller. Among the scores of people who have given me information or shown me manuscripts at their homes are Reuel Williams Beach, Miriam Titcomb, Marguerite Brooks, John T.G. Nichols, Joseph Mellen, Marian H. Judd, Mrs. Fred Singleton, Cornelia James Cannon, Jennie Cochrane, Beatrice G. Slocombe, Katherine H. Newell, and Norman Holmes Pearson. As librarians, Kathleen Doland, William H. Bond, Ruth Briggs, Mrs. Alfred Gammon, and Juliet Wolohan provided extraordinary assistance. Ruth Briggs, Merton Bailey, and Joseph Beck gave me access to scarce books from the Lithgow Library's collections on unusually generous terms.

The Research Foundation of the State University of New York through a grant gave me time and clerical assistance. Typing and other expert services were provided by Alice Wendover, Shirley Hathaway, Susan and Ray O'Connor, Edith Hathaway, Haig Shekerjian, Leo Spies, and Andrew K. Ellis. Viola Hale Hathaway not only prepared the index but lavished upon the final revision of the manuscript her skill as a professional editor and writer.

Richard D. Hathaway

New Paltz, New York

Contents

A gift of property and cash from his father-in-law allowed Judd to build this house in 1846. Family and friends called the house "Riverside," a reference to its location on the eastern bank of the Kennebec River, but its official name, always used in church-related business, was Christ Church Parsonage.

Introduction

"The world globes itself in a drop of dew," wrote Ralph Waldo Emerson. "The whole of history is in one man." That a single man may be thus a microcosm of his times is open to some doubt, Emerson notwithstanding; but if one were to look for a representative figure, one whose life and works illustrated the intellectual and religious tensions of Emerson's day, it would be hard to find a more interesting one than Sylvester Judd (1813-1853). A convert from Congregationalism to Unitarianism, Judd flirted next with transcendentalism, touching on as many points of the New England compass, in his intellectual odyssey, as any person we could easily name. He became a Unitarian minister, a novelist, a poet, and one of those universal reformers who made the 1840's lively.

Judd started life in the back country: Westhampton and Northampton, Massachusetts. There the orthodox world of Jonathan Edwards had seemed rock-solid in 1820, but then it began cracking, and Judd's apostasy was a symptom of what was happening. Alienated, uprooted, on the move, Judd made the leap into what he thought was the future, across the symbolic gaps that separated Northampton, Cambridge, and Concord. But the tension pulled both ways. It kept drawing his imagination back toward his childhood

1

world. Judd's effort to untangle the meanings of his origin finally started him writing a novel. The Emersonian oracle, sphinx-like, told him that if he could understand the unique and particular—the place he had come from, for example— he would have the cosmic clue with which to understand the Universal. He would know his Self. Judd thought he would give it a try.

Judd's Margaret

Judd's novel *Margaret* (1845)[1] begins with the real world, the countryside and country people of New England: gritty, granitic, somewhat angular and often amusing, but beautiful. The freshness of nature is in the air. Margaret, a nine-year-old nature child, frisks in a pond, sozzling her feet. Or in winter she brustles and bumps downhill on a sled, Judd's prose sending up a spray of verbs: "Some of the boys were doused into each other, some were jolled against the tree, some sent grabbling on their faces down the hill, some plumped smack on the ice." *Margaret* is Judd's celebration of the resources of language, rooted in folk culture; and it is also his celebration of his roots in nature, the woods and ponds he loved, the village he had left.

Margaret lives in the woods, safe from the strictures of society, attending neither church nor school. In the village, nearby, is the canker of Calvinism. Judd satirizes the old, the orthodox, the rigid; he cries up everything tender, growing, and untried: "The Newness," as it was called. *Margaret* is ostensibly about growing up, about rebellion, transformation, and progress; but an undertow of atavism is there, the real drift of the book being backward, toward Nature.

Judd senses that getting back to roots can reinvigorate a person or a culture. "Children that germinate with a plenty of mother earth about them, come out in the fairest hues," he says, contemplating the rose-gold of a rhubarb root in the spring. Judd sifts through his past, turning over the mother earth, rejecting and brushing away what he cannot use, to disclose the rich colors at the roots. Neither a Puritan nor a rationalist in his emotional center, Judd is attracted to richness and variety. Like other romantics, he likes rainbows, but he keeps searching for the point at which they intersect with earth. The closer to the soil, to the Folk, the more vital. When Judd comes upon inelegant words like "bellygut," to describe a way of flopping on a sled, he does not wince, at least not in the first edition; and he flaunts the real language of real people in the faces of the genteel—in a way that Wordsworth never did—as if discovering a source of his own aliveness. One might say that the energy of *Margaret* derives from Judd's nostalgia for home, for mother earth, for childhood.

Judd's earthiness and realism was in tension with his idealism. *Margaret* was subtitled "A Tale of the Real and Ideal, Blight and Bloom." Judd saw surfaces as symbols of inner depths, nature as an extension of the human mind and a revelation of God. Judd used fiction, as did Hawthorne and Melville, to seek the meanings behind the symbols of nature, the reality behind the masks; he sought to illumine the mystery behind his dreams, believing that real and ideal were correlative, aspects of one Unity.

Judd was a man to dive, and images of water expressed this relationship between depths and surfaces. Judd opened *Margaret* with dream-images, moving like mist or water, phantasmagorically, then focused more realistically upon Margaret, eight or nine years old, swimming, canoeing, wading. She "sozzled her feet in the foam" as a sandpiper "glided weet weeting along the shore." Seeing images reflected in the water, she dived to the bottom to "tread on the clouds," prefiguring her later dream-searches for God; then she came up to watch a blue jay "hustling the water with its wings."

One thinks of other images in romantic literature, oneiric ones, of children of light seen against the shimmer of lakes, rivers, seas: the boy William Wordsworth in his boat, pursued by the mountain; Thoreau, in Walden Pond up to his neck; the maidens of Typee, sporting like dolphins. Push not off from those innocent islands, warned Melville: you cannot return. Judd's pond was not an ocean, but it was deep enough. For Judd, as for Melville, water was a gateway into plenitude.

But Judd, trying to reconcile the usually static vision of innocence with his concern for progress, reversed the direction of ravaging time. Not wanting a mere noble savage or eternal child, a static image like Melville's Fayaway, Judd imagined Margaret as a person who would triumph over time, who would grow up and transform the world into the likeness of herself, into nature's purity. Judd, like Ahab or Taji or Pierre, was pursuing the impossible dream; and Melville persistently warned that that led to drowning in the Infinite. Judd—for all his earthiness and rude vigor of language and metaphor that rasped on some of his early critics the way Melville's writing rasped—was more than an idealist; he was that whipping boy of modern criticism, a sentimentalist. He was one of those persons who, in Emerson's phrase, "see the sun." Judd kept imagining that the sun was only a short flight away, that wings and persistence were all he needed to reach it.

Despite his idealistic faith in harmony, Judd was involved in paradox, perhaps we could even say contradiction, at the heart of his book and his life. For example, his feelings were curiously mixed about childhood and change, two of the central concepts of *Margaret*. Childhood is an age of innocence. It is also associated with his early Calvinism, full of guilt-mongering and fear of hell. Romantic nostalgia summons up the specters of childhood, the nightmares along with the warmth. There is a certain desperation therefore as Judd writes on, and seeks to lay his ghosts.

To dispel the phantasms, Margaret must change, must grow up. As a child of nature she is attractive but has no power to enact. Judd wants to solve the problems of life by utopian idealism, by bringing the eternal into time, somehow reconciling Eden with civilization. Margaret must triumph, unspoiled despite the efforts of "the world" to corrupt her with the wrong kind of knowledge. She takes a job as a teacher and loses it for standing firm against the heresy-hunters; she shakes off an attempted seduction; she sees further injustice in the execution of her foster-brother Chilion for what would be today adjudged manslaughter; she emerges unspotted from a stay in the city, the traditional labyrinth of evil in romantic literature. Another cliché of romantic novels brings her trials to an end. She is found to be a missing heiress and marries the cultured gentleman who has been for some time busily converting her from natural innocence to the Christian innocence of Unitarianism. With money and married respectability firmly in hand, she and her husband take over the village. Margaret ends as a feminist yet feminine saint, building a new society. The lion and the lamb lie down together; universal harmony once again reigns over all, though without stagnation, without Puritan austerity. Art flourishes, militarism withers, retributive justice vanishes. Sectarianism dissolves in a kind of Christian jubilee.

The utopian vision is of course not very convincing, even as a novelist's fantasy. Not only do we doubt that the transformation is possible, but we even wonder whether it is desirable. Our doubts begin in the middle of the book when Margaret's future husband, Mr. Charles Evelyn, appears in the village. He is impeccably sophisticated. In this theological opera he sings a kind of Unitarian aria to Margaret, while little Job Luce—the hunchbacked boy who is Margaret's friend—intersperses a haunting, mysterious obbligato about "Whippoorwill," the voice of nature: "I shall die of Whippoorwill."

At first the voices of nature and culture seem to harmonize; ultimately they become discordant. Mr. Evelyn is singing sharp. He has not had the important advantage of beginning as a child of nature, like Margaret and Job. The very name "Mr. Evelyn," which Judd uses more than "Charles," sounds effete, as if even Judd subconsciously feels there is something not quite right, something lacking, in the smooth, genteel world that Judd's youthful radicalism seems to result in. In the afterglow of romantic ecstasy comes domesticity; after rebellion comes Victorian contentment. Judd and Mr. Evelyn deliver Margaret into the promised land that Judd had longed for in real life and had by that time in fact achieved: the world of tinkling pianos, the literary graces, carpeted drawing rooms with chaste works of art, Sunday school picnics, pastoral power over a flock, and respectable radicalism. The reader is uncomfortable, perhaps feeling that Judd has betrayed the primitivistic premise—the Whippoorwill—that has been the source of the book's power; and Judd seems embarrassed too, not quite at home in this world. He does not belong. He was not raised there.

Judd's Life

Sylvester Judd, the third of that name, began life in the tiny village of Westhampton, Massachusetts, where carpets, pianos, art works, Unitarians, and novels were regarded as not only unnecessary but downright unwelcome. It was perhaps the most solidly unified and orthodox village that he could have been raised in; the time, 1813 and the nine years thereafter, the most idyllic of all possible times. The Revolution was over, the church secure. The people were unitedly Federalist. Unitarianism and Jeffersonian liberalism, though creeping in stealthily elsewhere, even in nearby

Northampton, did not have a chance with parson Enoch Hale and "Squire" Sylvester Judd, the novelist's grandfather, in charge of the spiritual and temporal affairs of the town.

In 1822 the Judd family moved to Northampton. It was like a loss of innocence, an entrance into a more complex world. The times were turbulent. The Federalist party evaporated, and suddenly a man did not know anymore what to believe or whom to believe and might in the confusion end up voting for the Democrats. The town was torn by religious dissension. The very church of Jonathan Edwards split into fragments, its members distrusting each other and no longer tolerant about differences of theology. New churches appeared suddenly: Unitarian and Baptist and Episcopal. The "era of good feeling" was indeed over. As Sylvester Judd heard people saying, it was enough to make a mud turtle jump. Even staid Westhampton caught the frenzy and split asunder with an audible rip, not because of Unitarianism but because of an excess of revivalist fervor.

Two waves of revivalism swept the area during the decade. Sylvester Judd's personal insecurity perhaps made revival conversion an especially urgent need for him. In Westhampton he had been secure. In elegant Northampton he was a country cousin and did not really belong, even though his father was editor of the newspaper. We can surmise that young Judd had conflicts with his father about education and a future career, plus inner conflicts as he waited on the anxious seat for the lightning of God's grace to strike. Finally, tossed by the alternating and interconnected waves of dissension and revival, he "secured a hope" of conversion, felt a call to the ministry, and went to Yale to prepare.

The conversion experience involved a pattern of agonizing self-doubt, swept away by ecstatic assurance. Soon after his graduation in 1836 from Yale College, where he should have been quite sheltered from heresy but where doubts actually began to come in on him, Judd went through the conversion pattern again, this time finding himself delivered over to the enemy, Unitarianism. A special irony of his life is that these cataclysms of conversion played so large a part in his development and that he then went on to preach the idea that conversion experience was neither a necessary nor a desirable part of the religious life. He felt that children were naturally religious. All a church had to do was water the seed and pull out a dandelion here and there. The naturalness of religion became a central idea in Judd's later ministry and in *Margaret*.

Ending up at Harvard Divinity School in 1837, Judd arrived just in time to hear Emerson deliver his "American Scholar" address and the one at the Divinity School a year later. Judd became a friend of Jones Very, the transcendentalist poet. Respectable Unitarians such as Judd's professors united in condemning the Emersonian heresy, but the young rebel was too romantic, too much on the side of nature, to toe the rationalist, respectable line. Unlike Emerson, however, Judd continued to insist on his Christianity, the centrality of Christ. His orthodox heritage still influenced him.

Further trouble lay ahead. Installed in 1840 as a Unitarian minister in Augusta, the bustling young capital city of Maine, Judd married the next year the daughter of Reuel Williams, a U.S. Senator and the richest man in that part of the state. Then he began to stir up a storm. He preached his bundle of assorted "isms," including pacifism, to an audience that included the governor and some state legislators from time to time, as well as Reuel Williams. In 1842 Judd gave a Sunday evening lecture in his church, showing the "moral evils" of even so sacred a war as the American Revolution. After a furor, during which he explained in print that he was condemning all war, not just the American

Revolution, the young minister retained his pulpit, though not his role as one of the chaplains to the state legislature. He had a glowing, sometimes Emersonian eloquence and an erudite command of facts. He had love and good will, superabundantly. He had little tact. He had connections, and Reuel Williams stood behind him.

In 1843, barely launched in life, Judd began his last decade. He sat down to write a novel, an indiscretion a minister was traditionally not supposed to commit. He swore the publisher to secrecy before permitting him to look at the manuscript, and published anonymously. The Puritan prejudice against fiction still had some force among the high-minded. Henry David Thoreau, in *Walden,* would say that reading a typical modern novel led usually to "dullness of sight, stagnation of the vital circulations, and a general deliquium and sloughing off of all the intellectual faculties." "The next time the novelist rings the bell I will not stir though the meeting-house burn down." Other discriminating readers stirred to the bell, however. *Margaret* was privately praised by Hawthorne, publicly championed by James Russell Lowell. Transcendentalists like Margaret Fuller and Theodore Parker gave it their approval, and Parker, as Lawrence Buell points out, could be as sarcastic about novels as Lyman Beecher, who called religious-novel readers "effeminate." When the secret of his authorship came out, Judd achieved a minor celebrity.

Judd never wrote another work with the vitality of *Margaret.* His mask of anonymity gone, he had to look to his reputation for respectability. The very strength of *Margaret,* its use of back-country vocabulary, was being attacked by some critics as "vulgar." Judd's next books, both published in 1850, have all of *Margaret*'s faults—dull plots, chaotic structure, sentimentality, inconsistencies of tone and style—and few of its virtues. *Philo: An Evangeliad* is a long dramatic poem with rhythms that make Emerson's look polished by comparison. Philo is taken, not by Mephistopheles but by the angel Gabriel, on a guided tour of the world's imperfections, ending up with a somewhat Shelleyan (though Christian) extravaganza: a utopian transformation of the world by the Advent of Christ, the world being freed of war, slavery, imprisonment, and poverty. As is usual in theological poems, the presentation of the good looks pallid by comparison with the presentation of evil. Judd's attack on the Mexican War and his characterization of the Devil provide the book's most vital passages. His Devil is humorously vulgar and even appealing; ultimately he is converted into a reformer. Evil, for Judd, is inside man, not outside him as a supernatural agency: Judd creates a Devil only to dispose of him. He creates a millennial vision only to illustrate his idea that the true millennium is already in process of becoming, that it begins in the hearts of Christ's followers, that it is brought about through choice: the human acceptance of divine judgment upon evil institutions and actions, the embodiment of Love in the world.

Richard Edney and the Governor's Family[2] is a less pretentious work. It is a determinedly cheerful novel of a young man's rise in the world. Judd essays Dickensian touches of whimsy, Pickwickian stagecoach driver and all, with a talking bridge thrown in for good measure. He satirizes the game of politics good-naturedly as a rivalry between dog lovers and cat lovers; he explores the city's evils in back lanes like a social worker looking for opportunities to organize the slums and do good to people. On his way up the social ladder, Richard Edney, like Benjamin Franklin, is beset by a femme fatale; but unlike Franklin he escapes without *erratum.* Richard's marriage to the governor's daughter, like other elements in the book, such as the great attention paid to the antics of little children, is of course a sentimental cliché, and no less so because fashioned from the very stuff of Judd's life. By 1850, Judd had not only married the senator's daughter; he had surrounded himself with children and chickens.

Judd was, after all, a Unitarian minister, a nonconformist but trying to belong, somewhat uneasily, in his adopted society, in his case a wealthy one in Augusta that had minimal use for rough edges or rebels, although it was liberal and tolerant. Torn between the opposite attractions of rude nature and polished civilization, Judd wrestled with one of the principal dilemmas of his time. The modern reader, contemplating the progress, the devastations, and the alarums of our day from a retreat in the Catskills or the Berkshires can find some bond of feeling with him, no doubt.

Neither romantic primitivism nor genteel culture, neither transcendentalism nor Unitarianism gave Judd the final resting place he was looking for. A cloying Victorian odor of respectability emanated from the latter part of *Margaret* even, and Judd's utopian fantasy there included a strangely un-Unitarian version of the church, with bishops in the background. Judd was ready to rise above Unitarianism and unite tradition with utopian yearnings for a Church Universal. He spent his last years trying to reunite the splintered Church, trying to bring the Unitarians of Maine together, trying to bring the competing sects of Augusta together. He tried to lead Unitarians back to a sacramental sense of The Church, one to which everybody, even children, belonged and in which everybody partook of baptism and communion. But Judd was spitting into the wind, against everything Congregationalism stood for and against the direction Unitarianism was going.

To Judd, his ideas were all very consistent. If Wordsworth's Lucy or Judd's Margaret or Henry David Thoreau were already trailing clouds of glory in the untrodden ways beside the springs of Dove or the ponds of New England—

if natural goodness was the child's birthright—then the churches should not quarrel with each other or get in the way of holiness with quibbles about church membership or conversion experience being the prerequisite of one's taking communion. Sylvester Judd had been through all the conversion experiences that a New Englander could conveniently have, and he thought he knew whereof he spoke. But to almost everybody besides Judd, his strange collection of radical and conservative enthusiasms constituted a very mixed bag. On the issues of the sacraments and the Christocentric church, Emerson, for one, was leading in the direction exactly opposite to the one Judd was taking; and in the Unitarian church Emerson, not Judd, represented the wave of the next hundred years. Judd, in his lifetime, could not even persuade Reuel Williams to undergo baptism; only Judd's death, in 1853, sufficiently moved Williams to make him take that step.

Criticism of Judd

Judd has never attracted a large audience, and his faults have always been evident even to his admirers. But in 1846 Margaret Fuller, in her *Papers on Literature and Art* (II, 137), gave more unreserved praise to *Margaret* than she did to the works of either Cooper or Emerson. She welcomed Judd's book as "a harbinger of the new era," a "work of great power and richness," an "aviary from which doves shall go forth to discover and report of all the green spots of promise in the land." Considering that she had just dismissed Longfellow as "artificial and imitative" and Lowell as "stereotyped," "absolutely wanting in the true spirit and tone of poetry," it was significant that she found *Margaret* to have "originality and genuineness" and "beautiful simplicity of action upon and within the mind of Margaret, Heaven lying so clearly about her in the infancy of the hut of drunkards." She concluded by calling Judd's book "this one 'Yankee novel,' " a note picked up by Lowell in *A Fable for Critics*, where he hailed *Margaret* as

> the first Yankee book
> With the *soul* of Down East in't, and things farther East,
> As far as the threshold of morning, at least.

Lowell went on, in the *North American Review* of July, 1849, to call *Margaret* "the most emphatically *American* book ever written." He added that even its turbulence and disorder of form partook of the frontier spirit. Lowell's approbation of Judd's backwoods roughness—his use of dialect and folklore, his creation of at least one truly Yankee character, Deacon Ramsdill—was not shared by everybody. Lengthy reviews of Judd in the *North American Review* of January, 1846, and April, 1850, by the Unitarian ministers W.B.O. Peabody and Andrew Preston Peabody, strongly criticized *Margaret* and *Philo* for vulgarity. When such critics as these managed to find something in Judd to praise, it was often the wrong thing: something didactic or sentimental, something genteel with no rough edges.

The weakness of *Philo* and *Richard Edney* has been obvious to almost everybody—Longfellow for instance—but *Margaret* has through the years found a few enthusiastic readers. In the January, 1855, issue of the *North American Review*, J.H. Morison wrote, "No American writer surpasses Mr. Judd, we know of no one who equals him, in the lifelike delineation, or rather the fresh creation, of natural scenery and events." In 1856 Felix O.C. Darley created an oversized book of drawings illustrating *Margaret*. Nathaniel Hawthorne, asked in 1854 to send to R. Monckton Milnes a few books that were most "characteristic" of American writing, chose *Walden, Margaret,* and a few others. One might infer from his letter that Hawthorne regarded *Margaret* more highly than *Walden;* yet he doubted that any Englishman could appreciate Judd's book, it was

so "intensely" American.[3] Similarly, Theodore Parker hastened to send *Margaret* to his English correspondent James
Martineau, assuring him "that it was the most original and
characteristic book that would appear here for twenty
years to come." And as Samuel Bowles' *Springfield Repub-
lican* commented in telling this story on October 21, 1870,
"This prediction was probably true, for, although Hawthorne's romances, and Lowell's 'Biglow papers,' Thoreau's
volumes and Walt Whitman's verses came out in the inter-
val, none of them were so truly characteristic of all sides of
American life as is this book of Judd's." In November,
1873, writing in *The Atlantic Monthly,* Clarence Gordon
went so far as to list *Margaret* second only to Hawthorne's
works among American novels.

By 1911 Judd's reputation had declined to the point
where, by one standard, it was as low as Melville's: the
Encyclopaedia Britannica of that year gave Melville thirty-
three lines and Judd thirty. But in 1921 Carl Van Doren,
in *The American Novel,* wrote of *Margaret*'s having "a kind
of spiritual ardor which pervades it throughout," lifting it
above the best-sellers of its day, that "ruck of smaller
undertakings which swarmed over the literary scene, coloring the world with pink and white, scenting it with the dry
perfume of pressed flowers." Perhaps the odor of pressed
flowers emanating from *Margaret* accounts for the fact
that in the 1940's the pontifical *Literary History of the
United States* mentioned Judd only in the bibliography
volume. But Van Wyck Brooks found Judd's book still
fresh. In *The Flowering of New England, 1815-1865,*
Brooks wrote, in 1936,

> His best scenes were almost as good as Hawthorne's. There was a
> touch of ecstasy in some of his descriptions, the thunder-storm,
> the winter scenes, the snow-storm, the sunny clearing in the sum-
> mer forest, the coming of the flowers in spring, the horse-tails
> with their storied ruffs, the fleecy mouse-ear buds, the straw-

coloured blossoms of the bell-wort, the little polypods with their feathery fronds and the young mulleins, velvety, white and tender.

Brooks also found the book "obscure and confused," though often "vividly picturesque," and he felt that "this Fourieristic fantasy, more than a little drawn from *Wilhelm Meister,* with a heroine often suggestive of Mignon, was quite in the Brook Farm spirit."

Also in the 1940's, Philip Judd Brockway wrote the first book about Judd since 1854, the year when Judd's aunt, Arethusa Hall, had published *Life and Character of the Rev. Sylvester Judd,* containing copious extracts from Judd's letters and journals. Brockway's *Sylvester Judd (1813-1853): Novelist of Transcendentalism* (1941) develops in brief compass the thesis that Judd was influenced by Emerson. Kenneth Murdock, in contrast, was more interested in Judd's relation to the symbolic novel. In the 1950's Murdock was in the habit of beginning his discussion of Melville and Hawthorne, in his Harvard course on the nineteenth-century American novel, with an hour or more on Judd, his use of local color, his Elizabethan gusto of language, and his symbolistic projection of the inner mind. Still, *Margaret* was for over seventy years out of print and was available only at a few major libraries; until its reprinting in 1968 it was almost unread. Now, with the recent appearance of a sprinkling of critical articles and references to Judd, a modest renewal of interest may be stirring. The appearance, fourteen months apart, of this present study and another one by Francis B. Dedmond in the Twayne United States Authors Series* may be taken as

---

*Readers are referred to Francis Dedmond's *Sylvester Judd* for the detailed summaries of Judd's published works and the review of criticism that make up the bulk of his book. Francis Dedmond read an earlier draft of my book in 1978 and borrowed from it, with permission, some facts and quotations from manuscripts I had unearthed; but he has been careful to make his book quite different from mine. He gives little space to what has been my main interest: Judd's development, viewed in relation to his New England heritage and to *Margaret.*

evidence that publishers no longer regard Judd as a man to
be ignored.

Margaret is certainly our best, almost our only, novel influenced by transcendentalism. Lydia Maria Child's *Philothea* (1836) challenges it for that distinction, but its setting
in ancient Athens robs *Philothea* of that "smack of the
soil" which is *Margaret*'s special flavor. Yet, *Margaret* is
lacking in many of the qualities that readers expect in a
novel. Judd had genius but not talent. He overloaded his
books with a freight of ideas, words, and psychic tensions
that proved more than he could master. He was inspired,
but only in flashes. His sense of structure, plot, and proportion was poor. His style was often clumsy, though
emanating frequently a lovely aura of freshness. He had a
passion for enumeration—wildflowers, birds, folklore,
bookish oddments—that outstripped the reader's interest.
He strewed his pages with Anglo-Saxonisms that brustled,
bumped, skewed, skittered, wabbled, and warped across
the page like the rickety crate-sleds in the race that he was
describing. *Margaret* at times resembled a junk shop, a
tangle of miscellaneousness in which only the fittest readers could survive. Like Melville, Whitman, Wolfe, and other
"Putter-Inners," Judd wrote one of those gigantic catalogue-
books into which he poured everything he could lay his
hands on. His popularity would probably increase if someone would publish his best passages in an anthology. His
plots did not matter anyway. Like those Druids and terri-
ble Berserkers from whom Emerson traced Shakespeare,
Judd was a piece of "unhandselled savage nature," rising
to inspired heights but flawed.

In presenting Judd's life, I am more concerned with
where he came from than in where he arrived. This seems
to me appropriate: *Margaret* is perhaps the first American
novel to be so centrally concerned with inner life and with

the development of a child into an adult. In this respect it can be compared with Wordsworth's *The Prelude*, written earlier but published later. My title, "Sylvester Judd's New England," implies, first of all, the inner New England of Judd's imagination. What his childhood heritage did to him and what he did with it are my main subject.

As symbols of the orthodox heritage that Judd later repudiated, I have begun with three ministers who maintained their allegiance to the closed society of the New England village: Dorus Clarke and Enoch Hale of Westhampton, and President Timothy Dwight of Yale College. Judd's life can be viewed as a prolonged argument directed against such stiff-necked men as these. Timothy Dwight was one of the creators of the revival waves that buffeted the Judd family. Enoch Hale was Judd's minister during his earliest years. He also was the grandfather of Judd's friend Edward Everett Hale and the brother of the Nathan Hale who gave his one life for his country. Dorus Clarke is the man we begin with, chiefly because he is a nostalgic reporter, a camera eye upon the Westhampton of Judd's childhood. Because much of *Margaret* is a motion picture, through the lens of romanticism, of the society of Judd's youth, passages from that book will be used as source material for recreating the flavor of Judd's environment. The reader will of course bear in mind that these later memories by Judd represent his attitudes in the 1840's, when he regarded Westhampton with a mixture of nostalgia and rejection.

Judd lived intensely. Every feeling was a pang, and he was often a man possessed. Though he was, emotionally and intellectually, at the opposite pole from Clarke, Hale, and Dwight, he was a product of their world, and he could never escape it. Judd was half in love with the society he satirized. He had a lover's quarrel with it. His symbolic slaying of the Father, while on the road to self-discovery, was accompanied by much inner conflict that threatened at times to tear him irreparably. This was ironic: Judd longed for unity and peace above all else. But he could rest neither in primitivism nor in progress, neither in Westhampton with its sand-strewn floors and Calvinism nor in Cambridge and Augusta with their deep carpets and rationalistic Unitarianism. He tried antislavery, pacifism, transcendentalism, but found little rest in them, only trouble. He searched for innocence and eternal childhood, but the gate leading backward was barred. He took the long way around, pushed down the river to Yale, Harvard, Augusta, in order to find the way back to Westhampton.

For Judd, "Utopia" was a way of saying "Home."

Part I

The

New England

Heritage

1

Golden Westhampton

The Reverend Dorus Clarke, D.D., still peppery at eighty-one, stood up for what he thought would be the last time, December 4, 1878, to address the New England Historic-Genealogical Society in Boston. He was best known as editor, since 1844, of the *Christian Parlor Magazine,* a potpourri of Calvinism, soulful steel engravings, warnings against the iniquity of novels, and color plates of wildflowers. As one of the more hoary-minded members of the Society, he had contributed dozens of memoirs of departed members. Now he would preach them a sermon, a *l'envoi.* His subject was the past, but he had a warning about the future.

Behind him in memory lay the Golden Age of New England history, epitomized by his boyhood in Westhampton, Massachusetts, a tiny village near Northampton where the ghost of Jonathan Edwards still held sway in 1828, indeed in 1878. Around this memory, the subject of his address, the words grew luminous.

Before him in the large audience were a half dozen living relics of that age of innocence and of that particular garden spot in the Hamptons. Prominent among them was the Reverend Enoch Hale's daughter, whom Clarke recalled as his chief adversary in spelling bees seventy years before.

Hale had been Westhampton's only minister from 1779 to 1827.

Chauncey Parkman Judd was also there, wealthy Boston lawyer, railroad promoter, and associate of Rufus Choate and Charles Sumner. His brother, the Reverend Sylvester Judd (1813-1853), few would recall. Clarke, who had been a boy of fifteen at Sylvester Judd's birth in 1813 and who had gone away to Williams College that year, would scarcely have known Westhampton's only novelist and poet. And Clarke did not like to read novels. What could you expect from a *Unitarian* minister like Judd, Clarke might have asked.

All around his assembled audience, this solid, comfortable, proper segment of Boston, in Dorus Clarke's imagination, lay a hundred besetting evils. His voice rose earnestly in peroration:

> We live in a day, ladies and gentlemen, which presages unusual changes in the country and the world. . . . The unsettled relations between capital and labor, all over the civilized world, is the most portentous social problem of the present. . . . In the United States, "universal suffrage" seems likely to be an universal danger. Communism, which has already given France a taste of its quality, is threatening the stability of the governments in Germany, Russia, and Italy, is menacing the property holders in England. . . . The more intelligent and farseeing among us frequently refer to the subject, but with bated breath.[1]

The stirrings of the turbulent masses could be felt like the "initial heavings of the earthquake." A secret foreign communist conspiracy and spirit of violence was afoot. Labor riots in Pittsburgh; the sacking of the Tuileries; assassination attempts on the Emperor of Germany, the King of Italy, and high officials in Russia; Molly McGuires terrorizing the coal fields—all were evidence of a "communistic" and "atheistic" plot, formless and terrifying in its ramifications, a mass uprising of the devil, always lurking just beneath the surface, against the world of Jonathan Edwards, John Adams, and parson Hale.

The cry of foreign conspiracy was nothing new. The New England clergy had been fighting the popery and atheism of Europe for generations. From the period of the colonial wars against France and the Jesuits, to the Federalist battle against French infidelity and Jacobinism, to the Know-Nothing movement that met the foreign tidal wave of the 1850's, the Yankee clergy had been defending New England against outside influence. For two centuries they had been preaching their jeremiads, denouncing the clear signs of degeneration in the body politic, urging the people to repent and return to the pure faith of the founding fathers lest divine wrath overtake a fallen nation.

So Dorus Clarke, Josiah Strong, and all their friends instinctively knew how to react and where the infection was coming from. What came to be called Rum, Romanism, and Rebellion was in their minds but part of a larger and more complicated image, a configuration of evil, that included corruption and sin in the cities, immigration, soft money, labor agitation, atheism, and perhaps even modernist theology. Angered and bewildered by the great hangover from the crusade against slavery—turbulence, corruption, the fever of speculation, industrial boom and a great depression—they needed the convenient scapegoats that they found in communism and the foreigner. Even more than that, however, they needed a rock, a solid reference point. Dorus Clarke had that to offer them. His words, though a bit hysterical, were at once a comfort and a call to battle:

Rufus Choate said, that the days of our fathers were "the heroic age of New England." We need now another "heroic age." The preservation of our country from domestic violence; of our property from communistic confiscation; of our cities and towns from riots and incendiaries; of our persons from assassination; of our remains, after we are gone, from being exhumed by night and carried away to extort money from our children to recover them, and, if recovered, only perhaps to go round through the same process again,—our safety, I say, from all these perils lies primarily and principally in the *Christianity of the Bible.*

Christianity was the answer. Old-fashioned Calvinist Christianity. Westhampton and Enoch Hale were proof enough of that. The argument was simple. Westhampton had been fed straight Christianity for fifty years, and to-day there was as much solid virtue there per capita as in any other spot on earth. Perhaps more.

For fifty years parson Hale had stood like a rock in Westhampton, preaching the plainest of gospels. For fifty years every child in Westhampton had sat under the high pulpit, unable to see the parson's head, but only the warning finger that divided grace on the one side from eternal damnation on the other. There were no tender-minded Sunday schools for tired toddlers then. Parson Hale had taught no "lavender religion" of "fashionable sentimentalism." Instead, every child in town had been force-fed with the stern "moral pabulum" of the Westminster Shorter Catechism. "In my childhood and youth, we had it for breakfast, we had it for dinner, and we had it for supper."[2] Every child between eight and fifteen was required to "say" it in an annual ritual before the assembled church, and woe to him who did not know it "*verbatim, et literatim, et punctuatim.*" The results? A rock-ribbed solidity, a unity, a sobriety, a piety such as this troubled world sorely needed and seldom found. Dorus Clarke had resided in eight different Massachusetts towns and cities in his eighty-one years, and not one could match Westhampton. In none had he found such profound reverence for the name of JEHOVAH, the Infinite and Personal GOD; such unquestioning faith in the Divine authority of the Holy Scriptures; such conscientious observance of the Sabbath; such habitual practice of family prayer; such respect and anxiety for revivals of religion; such serious determination to enter into the kingdom of heaven.

Unmentioned among other results was the fact that such stern "moral pabulum" had caused spiritual stomachaches among countless New Englanders, so that by 1878 there were few indeed who could endure the old-fashioned bran diet. Sylvester Judd, for example, after attempts to swallow the prescribed dosage, developed such a revulsion that he ticked off the Puritan Sabbath with a vengeance in his novel *Margaret.*

But most conclusive proof of Clarke's argument was the town's gift to the world between 1800 and 1865 of thirty-eight college graduates, twenty-three of whom had become ministers, missionaries, or even college presidents. And this, too, was in a town that in its "palmiest days" never numbered much over 900 souls. No other town "in this or any other Commonwealth" could boast so large a percentage of "educated men, of Christian men, of useful men," claimed Clarke. For example, there was parson Hale's son Nathan, moving spirit for fifty years of New England's first daily newspaper, the *Boston Daily Advertiser,* and the man most responsible for bringing railroads and municipal water to Boston. Clarke did not say that Nathan Hale was father of two fiction writers, Lucretia P. Hale and Sylvester Judd's friend, Edward Everett Hale. As Dorus Clarke concluded his eulogistic roll call of Westhampton worthies, discoursing at length of those figures he approved of, he passed over Sylvester Judd with a bare mention.

If Clarke was merely an amusing anachronism, an affront to the Unitarian sensibilities of many of those in his audience, they evidently suffered him gladly and printed his address. This was the great age of nostalgia, the search for security in the past. America was Promise, America was Progress. But progress implies change, and the changes that dashed the hopes of the 1840's and of such a utopian as Sylvester Judd made the 1870's ugly, bewildering, even frightening. Anglo-Saxon, Protestant, native New Englanders were surrounded; and they banded together for mutual support. The centennial celebrations; the class reunions and town reunions, such as the Westhampton reunion of 1866; the enthusiasm for tracing genealogies; the founding, before the century's end, of the Daughters of the American Revolution, the Society of Mayflower Descendants, the New England Society of New York, the historical societies—all were evidence that New England people were among those looking backward. Respect for the Fathers was being encouraged all over New England in the Gilded Age by just such solemn rituals as that of the Historic-Genealogical Society on the day they listened for two hours to Dorus Clarke. Even those who could smile at Clarke's enthusiasm and his theology, those who felt that the world had somehow passed him by, could feel a bond of sympathy with him.

Nostalgia pervaded the literary expression of the times as well. English writers from Scott and Carlyle to Tennyson and Morris had made their various forms of medievalism fashionable; the American South turned to magnolias and mandolins and the Faithful Negro. Sylvester Judd was, in 1845, but one of the first to exploit the regional folklore, local color, in his novel of New England life, *Margaret*; after the Civil War the presses groaned with fictionalized dialect studies. *The History of Hadley,* by Sylvester Judd's father, was one of the earliest and best of the fat volumes of local history appearing everywhere. There was a sense that an era had passed; men and women rushed to capture its remnants before they faded beyond memory. West-hampton, Massachusetts, then, was for Dorus Clarke a symbol of a past still alive in the present—changeless, eternal.

*   *   *   *   *   *   *

In 1863, Enoch Hale's son Nathan lay dying in Boston, and his mind began to wander. He mused upon the past and upon the annual summer vacations at the Hale parsonage in Westhampton. With his mind already half in the other world, he could think of no better way to wish his family and friends an affectionate good-by than to say that he was going to Westhampton.[3]

Westhampton even today has something of another world about it. Climbing steadily from Northampton up toward the Berkshires, one turns back for a magnificent view of the Connecticut Valley, Mount Tom, and Mount Holyoke. Then the town center, white in the morning sun, tilts into view to the west, framed by huge maple and ash trees. Westhampton is not on the road to anywhere; it is the end of the line. It has no future except as an exurban retreat for commuters to Northampton; it has little past, for it was settled late, in the 1770's. It has always been about the same, a bit more bustling then than now, a garden in the midst of time's changes.

Frame houses, perhaps thirty or more, straggle from three sides toward the town center. There, the white library and the white town hall, with its Doric columns, are dominated by the startlingly large, steepled church. The Judd homestead across the street, like the church, is green-shuttered, white and simple. In the distance are two schools, farms, woods, and a scattering of modern houses.

And that is all. No store, no filling station, no restaurant. No post office. From the distance come vague intimations of a sawmill. Trees, along with grass and people, are Westhampton's chief natural resource. The distilleries, along with the town's abortive one-horse industries—the potash works, the lead mine, the tanneries, the grist mills—disappeared long ago. The town has never passed the peak of population it hit about 1820.

Actually, Westhampton is three villages, or not even a village at all. But under the New England system the scattered farms and the three or four crossroads more thickly sprinkled with houses are all considered part of the one town. The town center, properly, should never have been there at all. Perhaps we might call it the least of three evils. It existed, originally, only as the resultant of two competing forces, to the south and to the north.

Back in 1779, having just organized as a town and having attended to the essential business of settling Enoch Hale as their first pastor, the few-score inhabitants started assembling materials to build a meeting house. For five years the competing settlements to the south and the north played tug-of-war with the lumber, hauling it back and forth three times past the door of the parsonage. The award of an arbitration committee was never honored. It was even seriously proposed to locate the church in the exact geographical center of the town, which would have put it on top of Tob Hill. Finally the patient mediation of the pastor resulted in a church not far from his doorstep. In the midst of the primeval forest with no other houses nearby except a log hut, the church was midway between the contending parties and on the spot first proposed five years before.[4]

The methodical, steady patience and persistence shown in this dispute by the parson set the tone of the town for the next fifty years. Nurtured in Connecticut, "the land of steady habits," Enoch Hale was true to his birthright. His brother, Nathan Hale, though he had but one life to give his country, in 1776, gave it all in one moment of daring. Enoch proved that living, though not so dramatic as dying or so productive of fame, could also leave its mark. Drop by drop, steady on the stone: that was Enoch Hale's way. If he ever did anything daring, or different, or that could not have been perfectly predicted by correct logic from his past behavior and his moral principles, no one ever bothered to record it, startling as the event would have been. The orbit of his career was plotted to the last degree and minute. God said, Let Enoch be, to prove that Newton's right.

The unpredictable Sylvester Judd, whose brief career was meteoric and full of surprising conversions, might have profited, had he been temperamentally capable of stability, by Enoch Hale's example. Hale was not only the chief source of stability in that most stable of all possible towns, he was also its chronometer. When he arrived a minute late or a minute early for Sunday services, the townsmen reset their watches. Hale prayed and preached with his eyes open and his timepiece on the pulpit before him. When the time for closing came in the middle of a sentence "the remaining part was sure to be despatched in short metre." Dorus Clarke told a story that typified the man. Hale, for many years scribe of the General Association of Congregational Ministers in Massachusetts, was expected at a certain hour to open the annual meeting of that body, seventy-five miles from Westhampton. Five minutes before the appointed hour Enoch Hale was nowhere in sight. The ministers were quietly speculating about the probability of his arrival on time.

> One clergyman, who knew him better than the others, remarked, that the town clock may be wrong; that, if Mr. Hale should not be there when the clock struck, it would only prove that the clock was out of repair. . . . As minutes and half-minutes wore away, curiosity became intense and intenser; but, before the last

minute expired, Mr. Hale drove up in his "one hoss shay," entered
the church, and called the meeting to order.

Life in Westhampton was uneventful, with each day
much like the next. Each morning, noon, and evening Hale
carefully recorded the temperature and the condition of
the weather as a record of God's memorable providences.
At the end of the year he summarized on a page the major
events recorded that year in his journal. One such summary, for the year 1827, was typically brief:

July 10   Mr. Hunts goods carried to N
Aug.20   Clock cleansed
     25   Woodhouse addition raised
Sep. 5   Com. Dea Sikes &c
Nov. 9   Road Comm lay road thro my land & yard

The only other events worth this special notice were his
pulpit exchanges with other ministers, the leafing out of
the trees, planting of potatoes, killing of vines by the frost,
a snowstorm that impeded travel, and a special singing
meeting at the church, led by the Reverend John Truair. So
much for 1827.[5]

In such a life, it was possible not only to be predictable
and exact, but to be forehanded. Enoch Hale was that. On
September 22, 1780, newly settled as minister, with no
barn, no house, no livestock, no wife as yet secured, he
walked to the newly cleared spot marked out for an orchard and there "planted peach and plum stones."[6] One
had to look ahead. All his life Hale kept by his elbow
twenty extra sermons, unpreached, to be drawn upon in
case of emergency. In 1816 the emergency occurred: his
house went up in flames—but the sermons went up with it.
Unshaken, Enoch Hale worked until he had made up the
deficit and twenty new unpreached sermons stood on the
shelf.

In his sermons it was not necessary that Hale embellish
plain doctrine with the decorations that a later age, with its

lusting after excitements, demanded. A few simple defini-
tions and premises with logical deductions therefrom, a
liberal sprinkling of scriptural texts, that was enough. The
constant iteration of cardinal doctrines was studded with
such safe observations as, that "walking is a way of going
forward." If walking was a way of going forward for those
on the road to salvation, that sober light ought not to be
hid under a bushel.

The necessary doctrines were, after all, few and simple,
although sinful man could never seem to get them through
his head and heart. Hale repeated them unwearyingly for
fifty years, while three generations of Judds nodded. God's
predestinating decree has divided men into two classes, the
saved and the damned. Man is corrupted by the taint of
Adam and cannot attain virtue or salvation by unaided effort. No Benjamin-Franklin virtue-gadgetry can teach us
the mystery of love. Only God's Sovereign Grace can snatch
a man from the burning hell of his own self-centeredness.
Though man's efforts to crawl from the pit are useless,
nonetheless he must try, for the further we are from loving
God the more we are to blame, and He will not excuse us
from our responsibility.

Many a stronger, and weaker, mind than Hale's gagged
on such paradox. But the doctrine carried with it the authority of the ages, and before 1825 scarcely anyone could
be found in Westhampton to oppose it openly. Of course
there would have to be a village deist just as there would
have to be a town Democrat and a town drunk.

But deism and Jeffersonian liberalism broke harmlessly
on the rock of Westhampton stability and were routed by
the authority of its elders. Although they supported the
Revolution and made the town too hot for its one Tory,
Westhampton's citizens had no use for the Shays' Rebellion, and the Shays' men were afraid to march one of their
captives through Westhampton. Ethan Allen, whose *Reason*

the Only Oracle of Man (1784) is one of the yeastier documents of backwoods deism, was once in Westhampton dig-
ging for lead and silver, probably in the 1780's. The Rev.
Jonathan Judd, great-grandfather of the novelist, who was
to neighboring Southampton what Enoch Hale was to Westhampton, met Allen at the mine. Unawed by the general's
status as a war hero, Judd "took occasion to gently rebuke
Allen for his profanity." Allen, who despite his roughness
was a nimble man in a debate, slyly pleaded innocent "on
the ground of the depravity of human nature in general," a
doctrine that deists did not notably support. Nevertheless,
Allen was not heard to swear "for several days afterward."[7]
In those days ministers were regarded with awe.

When Allen died in 1789 and when in that year Federal-
ism and stability triumphed in the nation's affairs, to the
delight of Westhampton, the town was coincidentally
visited by its first major revival of religion, an outpouring
of grace that added fifty converts to the visible church. The
same year saw the birth of Sylvester Judd, the novelist's
father. Revivals were ever a powerful stimulus to the birth
rate. *Annus mirabilis.* The bumper harvest was to be repeated, but, under Enoch Hale's tutelage, always with
proper sobriety and decorum, in 1800, 1806, 1816, and
1823.[8]

Enoch Hale did not rule Westhampton single-handed.
The New England churches and towns were run by democratic methods. But the Constitution, not the Declaration
of Independence, expressed Westhampton's political philosophy, and deference to elders and "established men"
was a cardinal doctrine of morality. Forms and rituals were
important, and a boy was always expected to bow courte-
ously to any older person of consequence.

The ones who were remembered at the reunion of 1866
as the town's chief men were three: the doctor, the parson,
and the squire. This trinity led the Westhampton theocracy

with benevolent firmness and brought her safely through the surrounding waters of political and religious controversy. All three were sons of ministers, a fact in itself sufficient to make them venerated. All three lived eighty or more years and held sway with the authority of accumulating age for the fifty years from 1780 to 1830. While they were there things changed as little as possible; the young and energetic, the ambitious who wanted to get ahead, to question, to overturn, got out of town; Unitarianism never had a chance to get started. The parson, the doctor, and the squire saw to that.

Sitting on parson Hale's left hand was Doctor William Hooker, son of the Reverend John Hooker, Jonathan Edwards' successor in the Northampton church and a man who had quieted the troubled waters of Northampton.

On Hale's right hand sat "Squire" Sylvester Judd (1752-1832), son of the formidable Reverend Jonathan Judd, and grandfather of the novelist, Sylvester Judd III (1813-1853). Squire Sylvester Judd had hewn his farm from the wilderness in 1774. Squire Judd, thus called by common consent, symbolized civil authority. Division of labor had not proceeded very far, and the early stage of social development was reborn on the frontier: to his occupation of farmer, livestock merchant, and country storekeeper he added that of maker and expounder of law. He was no lawyer—no one was in Westhampton—but he had helped frame the Massachusetts Constitution and, as the town's first citizen, was elected year after year to the state legislature, fifteen years in all. As justice of the peace, Judd made and enforced what common law the simple affairs of the town required. Small boys, who stood in danger of being hauled before him for some disturbance in the meeting house or other breach of the Sabbath peace, regarded Squire Judd with a veneration not unmixed with terror. Their position on the brink of hell, into which they might slide at any time, was perhaps less awesome than those eyes and that massive brow. At the town reunion, forty years later, the brow and head magnified in their memories, they cried in a hushed chorus, "Venerable man!"

In the hands of such a man and of the white-haired council of elders, the affairs of Westhampton seemed safe enough and Westhampton's claim on Eternity, secure. But the generation which had settled the town as young men would not last forever. If one thing was certain in this town of certain certainties, it was that sometime between 1820 and 1830 would come a major readjustment and a sharp generation leap, a changing of the guard. Time could no more be evaded than Eternity. They had all come together to Westhampton as young men; now they would all be old together.

Though accentuated in Westhampton by the circumstances of its settlement, this phenomenon was not peculiar to her. Chief among Enoch Hale's generation as defender of orthodoxy was Timothy Dwight, since 1795 President of Yale College. In Northampton was Caleb Strong, whose frequent reelection as Governor of Massachusetts made him undisputed lord temporal of Hampshire County; in Northampton was the Reverend Solomon Williams, whose pastorate of over fifty years coincided in its tone, temper, and duration almost exactly with that of Enoch Hale. The ministers of six other towns in the area surrounding Northampton had also enjoyed long, uninterrupted pastorates and were now growing old together.[9] These men, the generation of John Adams and Thomas Jefferson, were destined to disappear with a rush, along with such symbols of the courtly past as knee breeches and property restrictions on the suffrage. Timothy Dwight and Caleb Strong were to be the first to go. Every one of the others would, in the course of Andrew Jackson's first four years or so in office, make a decisive exit, and Enoch Hale would find those years strange indeed.

Sylvester Judd, novelist, Unitarian, and utopian, was thus a product of the most solidly Calvinist and Federalist society to be found anywhere in the United States. But he was also a product of the discrepancy between the piety of the founding fathers and the backsliding of the second generation, a backsliding which is the subject of our next chapter. Sylvester Judd inherited not only Dorus Clarke's ideal world of perfect stability and unity; he inherited the real world of change. His novel *Margaret* bubbled with restlessness, tension, and revolution.

Of all this and of its consequences, as the year 1813 approached—a year decisive for this story—the doctor, the parson, and the squire were unaware.

2

Return Into Time:
The Baptisms of Water and of Fire

The day of July 23, 1813, a Friday, dawned cloudy in Westhampton. That fact the Reverend Enoch Hale duly noted in his journal and in a separate record the morning, noon, and evening temperatures. He had been keeping the same records for years, and always in the same little hand-sewn booklets that he used for his sermon manuscripts, always the same size. The other notable event of the day was the birth of a boy in the Judd house a good stone's throw down the road. Enoch Hale did not think the birth of Sylvester Judd, the future novelist, worthy of note in his methodical journals, but he did not fail to record that the clouds turned to rain towards evening. Sometime during the day he must have called, after Dr. Hooker, to offer a prayer for the baby's future. And of course, Squire Sylvester Judd and his eccentric wife, Hannah Judd, would turn up to look at their new grandson.

Thus in that room just west of the church the three generations of Judds who were named Sylvester came together for the first time. The benediction to be pronounced on this occasion was as predictable, by long usage, as the name to be bestowed. There was promise of the same blond hair and well-shaped brow. The birthright of the name always seemed to be reserved, by some providence, for the child destined to distinction as a writer —a circumstance later causing much confusion among librarians and historians. The infant of 1813 would become in the 1840's the Reverend Sylvester Judd III (1813-1853), novelist and poet; his father, Sylvester Judd II (1789-1860), would become in the 1820's editor of the *Hampshire Gazette* and later would become the historian of Hadley and Northampton; in the fourth generation Sylvester Dwight Judd would write numerous works on ornithology; and in the fifth Sylvester Judd Beach would write noted works on opthalmology. Had Squire Judd known of the vicissitudes to which his name would be subjected, particularly in the person of his novel-writing Unitarian grandson, he would not have approved. But at the moment, on July 23, 1813, there was no apparent occasion for anything but rejoicing.

Or if there were anxieties among those gathered to see young Sylvester, they were about things more immediate. Parson Hale was perhaps thinking about the question of whether his salary would be paid on schedule the next day. This was not one of the certainties in Westhampton life, we may surmise, and Hale had been careful in negotiations with his parishioners to spell out the agreement in proper legal form, down to the last load of wood. And with reason, for the next day, July 24, Hale's laconic entry read, "Salary paid—last pay^t supposed but not settled."

Or possibly the parson, the doctor, and the squire shared another ground for apprehension if they took their doctrine as seriously as they said they did. The Pit, into which one could slip and slide at any time, yawned for the infant as well as for the hardened sinner. Casuists from Yale would not learn for several more years how to exorcise this possibility. And the chances of young Sylvester's reaching the age when he could become a hopeful subject of conversion were, in that day, perhaps a little better than fifty-fifty. What could a concerned church and parent do in the meantime to increase his chances of being sealed among the Lord's elect?

Nothing, really. The Lord moved in his own mysterious ways, and there was nothing, theoretically, that any merely human agency could do. But in practice there were grounds for hope that, if the child could be properly baptized and preached over and prayed over, then a reasonable and a covenanted God would not choose to cast him aside. He would shuffle the accounts a bit and perhaps credit to the child some of the grace earned by the corporate body, the saints of the church and the child's parents. Of course it would not do to talk openly about "earning grace." That was dangerous heresy, smacking of popery and Arminianism. Yet the ordinances of baptism and the rest, if properly administered in a society as clearly the subject of divine concern and grace as Westhampton, if not efficacious to salvation in themselves, were at least worth something. One could then be satisfied that what human power could do had been done.

But the problem was precisely this. Young Sylvester was not going to be baptized. The stumbling block was father Judd, the Squire's unregenerate son.

It was not that there was anything scandalous about the life of father Judd. He was not openly a heretic and he regularly attended church. Politically he was safe, though perhaps inclined to raise questions, to dispute with his friends, and to grant too much virtue to the Jeffersonian enemy. But when, four years earlier, at the age of nineteen, he had confided his religious creed to his notebook, it was disconcertingly brief. He believed the Scriptures divinely inspired, he believed that both future salvation and happiness on earth were best achieved by conformity to Scriptural precepts, but here he stopped. As he surveyed "the peculiar doctrines of the different sects of Christians, as the Calvinists, Arminians, Unitarians, etc.,"—a playing with fire that

Enoch Hale might well have warned him from—his astounding confession was, "I am not determined which is right and which is wrong."[1]

This would not do at all. No such man could baptize his children in Westhampton: for that at least one parent must have experienced a conversion. Young Sylvester and his older brother, James Walker Judd, had to be left unbaptized while the elders shook their heads.

Seventy years before in New England there would have been no problem. The Puritans had faced the question of what to do with unregenerate children and had, in the Half-Way Covenant of 1662, solved it for what they thought would be all time. They had decided that if the sons were spiritually bankrupt, they could then draw on the spiritual capital of their fathers. All a child needed to have, to be baptized, was one visibly elect grandparent and parents of outwardly conformist beliefs and behavior. In New England, he would surely have that. Young Sylvester, for example, was well supplied with them. But Jonathan Edwards had changed everything. It was because Edwards had tried to upset this lenient and comfortable order of outward conformity and had insisted again on inward experience as a prerequisite to full participation in the church sacraments that he had been driven out of Northampton in 1750. Defeated in his life, Edwards had triumphed from the grave. The Half-Way Covenant was not accepted in Westhampton? and the pressures on a man to be saved, if not for his own then for his children's sake, were unrelenting.

In 1813, when the future author of *Margaret* was born, Judd the father could look back on a youth that had been somewhat wild. The squire had found frequent applications of the rod necessary. The Judds were always an independent set, and the remedy seemed only to inflame the disease: the squire's teenage son had run away to Boston for six months. There he "hurried into the vortex of sin and wickedness" and picked up from the "men of learning" and "professed debauchees" who were his companions some of the elegant vices of the city: an acquaintance with Unitarianism and deism, a growing thirst for knowledge, and Chesterfieldian urbanity.[3]

Back home, he shed his "vicious, illiterate companions" and began to educate himself in earnest. Chesterfield was to him what Addison had been to Franklin. With nobody to urge or assist him, he quickly developed an incisive prose style and other attainments astonishing for one of his age and circumstances. The dissipation of novel-reading was left behind. Since he could not get from books anything about events since 1783, he dug the facts out by systematically going through bound volumes of old newspapers and making copious notes. Thus he began a habit of historical research that would continue through life. This period of American history, from 1780 to 1800, would always be of particular interest to him; and his son would use it for the setting of his novel *Margaret*.

In 1810 Squire Judd set up his son, Sylvester II, in the business of running a general store, across the street from the church. William Hooker, the doctor's son, became Judd's partner and closest friend. The store was an expansive undertaking, but doomed to eventual collapse, a lesson to all of the vanity of worldly ambitions. The squire had a handy knack of making money that he seemed unable to pass on to his son. Perhaps the storekeeper's habit of reading Latin and Greek while tending the store did not contribute to his success.

Another companion of the squire's son, in 1810, was Apphia Hall. Her father was Aaron Hall, a leading man in Norwich, a town just west of the Hamptons. Apphia, his oldest child, was blue-eyed and light haired, but her five younger half-sisters and two half-brothers were dark—all except sister Arethusa, younger by sixteen years. The two blue-eyed sisters were considered quite beautiful, especially Apphia. Apphia was the one who would marry Sylvester Judd II and give birth, in 1813, to Sylvester Judd III.

The fair-haired Judd was exceedingly eligible and even handsome, and his visits in 1810 were matters of some consequence at the Hall household. Their form was rigidly prescribed by custom. Their memory was still vivid to Arethusa fifty years later.[4] The young man, perhaps unannounced, would knock of an evening and enter to the family circle around the kitchen fire, requesting of the daughter the pleasure of her company. After perhaps some silence and embarrassment, punctuated by titters from the younger girls and desultory attempts at conversation, Apphia would rise and take a shovelful of coals from the hearth to light the fire carefully prepared in the parlor. If, in her embarrassment, she knocked the tongs down, or spilled some coals in the passageway, a great and general bustle would ensue, followed by further awkward silence, delays, and passing back and forth to inspect the fire. All this took place under the gaze of two or three heads that kept popping up above the end of the trundle bed. When all was in readiness, came the finale for which Arethusa and the other little ones had been waiting: "Will you walk into the other room, sir?" announced the young lady. In those halcyon days and in that place "it was hardly etiquette" to have the interview terminate before the small hours, long after the others were in bed. Custom demanded that the hour of departure be a strict secret.

On January 16, 1811, just a few months after coming of age and becoming a full partner in the storekeeping business, Judd married Apphia Hall. The next years were busy ones, and journal writing ceased until 1821.

The long cradle was crowded during those years. Young Sylvester, in 1813, shared it with James Walker Judd, aged twenty months. The foot that rocked them was not Apphia

Judd's, however. Her sister, Arethusa, at age nine somewhat superfluous in a family of seven children and a dying mother, had in 1811 joined the Judd household. She was a second mother to the boys. At night Arethusa would sit by the cradle, an edifying book open in her lap, a stocking or baby's cap growing perceptibly under the moving needles. Before and after school hours, during the sporadic summer and winter sessions, and full time at other seasons, she would be busy with the washing, milking, mending, and baby tending. It was her special job to mind the children, pulling them around in the little wagon, taking one or both to bed with her during the crying spells that attended weaning. The two mothers were not indulgent. They left the children to amuse themselves as much as possible, seeking to inculcate the habit of self-reliance from the cradle. When, in 1837, young Sylvester found himself responding to the stirring notes of Emerson, he would find that self-reliance was already part of his family inheritance. Bedtime, for the child of three months as for the older one, came at dark; and they quickly learned that crying would not earn them a respite. The evenings were for the pursuit of knowledge, and no prattle would be allowed to interfere; Arethusa, like her "demi-père," as she called father Judd, read far into the night. He guided her studies and started her early upon French. After the "Token for Children" and "The Shepherd of Salisbury Plain" age, she was ready for perhaps Milton, Cowper, or Thomson. Apphia Judd, though amiable and kind as well as handsome, was never very strong and did not follow Arethusa in studying or providing her husband intellectual companionship. To Arethusa, her demi-père was "an imposing presence in the household" and, as she grew under his tutelage, she "came to feel for him the affection of the child, the reverence of the teacher, the respect of the man of knowledge, and almost the admiration of the lover."[5]

Arethusa's ability to read and knit while rocking the cradle with her foot was an example of the skill required of a woman in those days. Servants were unheard of in Westhampton, and all the work from spinning yarn to making the finished clothing fell upon the two girls. But compared with their status at the farm in Norwich, here they were ladies of leisure and a modest competence. It was probably not necessary, as it had been in Norwich, for Arethusa and Apphia to get furs for their muffs by hanging their kittens from the end of the well sweep. The farming was no more than a garden, chickens, and one cow; the girls were not required, as was one almost legendary pair of women in Westhampton, to do all the washing, cooking, and mending for twelve laborers and at the same time to take care of the milk of thirty cows.[6] By early rising and sheer efficiency, the sisters settled things into place "without hurlyburly or noise" and by late afternoon could sit down to quieter occupations, dressed to receive any visitors, objects of admiration to their less fortunate or efficient neighbors.

For father Judd the store across the green from the church and his house did not provide a perfect refuge from children and women. Though his studies continued in odd moments, advancing from Latin to Spanish and eventually to Greek, he could not escape the monotony of storekeeping. Business became drudgery after a few years of "exchanging pins, tape, and snuff, for a few eggs and paperrags; of measuring off calico and ribbons for their value in butter and cheese; or drawing molasses, rum, or brandy, for waiting customers."[7] The gossip of neighbors across the counter must have become a bore, even though it was later to furnish his son Sylvester with some amusing pages of satire.

In 1813, however, times were exciting in politics and provided some diversion. From his vantage point in the circle around the stove, Judd argued self-confidently with

his customers and partners on all the issues of the day. Politics was the consuming topic of interest. Northampton's
Caleb Strong, brother-in-law of Dr. Hooker, was Governor
of Massachusetts. Squire Judd was in the legislature, sagely
nodding to the governor's speeches. Together they resisted
the folly of "Mr. Madison's war."[8] Young Sylvester was
surrounded, even in the cradle it seemed, by influences
that would lead him, like his father, to an obdurate Yankee
prejudice against war.

And as young Sylvester grew up to eavesdrop upon the
elders in council around the stove of his father's store, he
caught the rhythms of their speech and the words that kept
recurring. Later, with a little research and imagination, he
was able to reconstruct, for his novel *Margaret,* a vivid picture of the debates his father and grandfather had engaged
in. Although the scene was set in the 1790's, the voices of
the people in council and their topics of discussion did not
change so much in twenty years or thirty that Sylvester
Judd could not recapture them.

> *Deacon Hadlock.* "Dark times, indeed, Brother Penrose; we
> have contempt in the Church, as well as abuse in the State. Things
> are getting worse and worse every day. We are all at loose ends.
> Judgment follows judgment. The Christian religion itself is just
> tottering to fall."
> . . . .
> *Captain Tuck.* "Raggedness and ruin! what do gentlemen mean?
> Have we not had a glorious War! Are we not independent! Isn't
> this a great country? Was there ever an era like the present, and
> will there ever be another such a one? Isn't America the envy of
> all worlds, ... Our children will sigh and pine for the golden
> period in which we now live."

The battle in the American mind between the prophets of
disaster and the boosters was already joined. Now Judd
played variations on his theme, orchestrating his score, first
with the mellifluous voice of the practiced orator, then with
the twang of the cracker-barrel Yankee.

Esq. Bowker. "I think, if I may take the liberty to express my thought, that I partially agree with our friend Captain Tuck. We discern indisputable signs of improvement. There is an amelioration in the order of events; there is a softening of the crude and undigested matter with which the breast of the ages has been so long gorged; Influence has a vigorous but better regulated pulse, gladness and love are on its countenance; History is emerging from its corruptions and appears in a regenerated form. . . ."

. . . .

Deacon Hadlock. "No, Adolphus, worse than that; worse than Throat Distemper, or Putrid Fever, or anything else. The Jacobins, the Jacobins are in amongst us; all the bloodhounds of the French kennel are let loose upon us, Freethinkers, Illuminatists, Free-Masons, Papists."

As Judd added still more characters, each spoke with a sharply individualized voice: pewter fips and jawbones twanged the air.

Mr. Whiston. "I agree with the Deacon exactly; he has put the case right on its own legs. For one, I am near about done for. I havn't hardly a hair left to my hide, or a pewter fip in my pocket. Taxes, taxes are eating us all up; taxes upon your whole estate, then on the parts of it, horses, carts, tools; taxes on all you eat and drink; taxes paid by taxes, taxes breeding taxes; and when all is gone, then tax the body and lug it off to Jail."

. . . .

Deacon Hadlock. "Hasn't Tom Jefferson threatened he would burn up all the Bibles in the land, if he comes in President? Isn't he the jaw-bone of Jacobinism in this country . . . . What is all this but playing into that whale's hands, Buonaparte, and he means to swallow us all up?"

Captain Hoag. "These things are jest so. We heard in our part of the town last week, that he had taken the city of London, and was burning over all England; that he had made the Pope God of the whole airth, and that they were both coming to America, were going to put us all into the Inquisition, and then set fire to't." [9]

It would seem that the frenzy into which Dorus Clarke worked himself in 1878, over the spectacle of communists, assassins, and ghouls taking over America, was one which he might well have learned in the Golden Westhampton of his childhood. And all of this Judd the novelist caught and reconstructed on paper, though he was not alive in the days when Jefferson was "the jaw-bone of Jacobinism." Dorus Clarke would have squirmed had Judd impaled him on his needle as an exhibit of the "aspect of eternity" that Westhampton wore, with its jeremiads of "degenerating times" that were as old as New England.

It was little wonder if father Judd eventually began to tire of the Westhampton quiet life, with its limited stock of ideas and intellectual challenges. Ralph Waldo Emerson would phrase it thus: "From 1790 to 1820 there was not a book, a speech, a conversation, or a thought" in Massachusetts. In 1813, however, still in the pride of life, father Judd's disputatious fever raged.

Of his worldliness, father Judd was acutely aware, and not a little proud, at the same time that he recognized that he was perhaps neglecting a proper attention to his more eternal concerns. With a growing family came growing responsibilities. As if by some premonition that a future minister had entered his household, he resolved, a few weeks after the birth of young Sylvester, to reform. Perhaps his religious conversion would result, giving his two sons the right to be baptized. But father Judd's reformation was modeled on Benjamin Franklin rather than Jonathan Edwards. Like Franklin, he thought it good practice to adopt an air of "*being instructed*, rather than of attempting to teach others." He read religious books, but admitted frankly to himself that he was more interested in the disputes about speculative doctrines than in the essential piety underneath. His mind was moralistic rather than pious, prosaic rather than poetic. And in the economic boom of the war period, in which the young shopkeeper rode high, it was difficult to be sourfaced and worried about the morrow.

In short, his state was typical of large numbers of those even in pious Westhampton. Though a more theocratic society could scarcely have been found in the United States, only 265 from a population of over 900 were actually members of the church. Even so, under the Puritan system, which barred from membership those who, despite exemplary and pious lives, were not *sure* that they had received a special sign of their election by God, it was quite an accomplishment for parson Hale to have so large a proportion visibly elected. His membership "was twelfth in size of 134 churches reporting to the General Association of Massachusetts and fourth in its number of male members."[10]

The Puritans had always placed such hurdles in the way of church membership that few could pass. Only members could come to the communion table, and to qualify they had to testify to a special experience of God's grace. No mere conformity, no mere assent to speculative doctrines would do. The Holy Spirit must descend from the heavens with an inward flash of lightning and roll of thunder. A special inquisition by the church elders or the minister was designed to bar the sheepfold to wolves or to assist the conscience of the honestly uncertain. To hang back with false modesty from the life-giving Elements was bad, but to drink them unworthily was more damnable still. On this rack of doubt and torment, every New England soul was tried.

The great problem of the New England church, around which the ecclesiastical battles of two centuries had been fought, and which Sylvester Judd III would struggle with all his life, had always been how to keep the church alive when such obstacles were placed in the way of the potential convert. Birthright membership, the solution of Episcopalians, Catholics, and Quakers, was out of the question. Half-Way Covenants had been tried and dropped. Naked and unaided by such human expedients, the church must watch and pray for the divine, unpredictable rain. The problem of Sylvester Judd, unbaptized and unhouseled there in his cradle, was not merely a problem then for Judds, Hales, and Hookers to ponder. It was the problem of all New England.

The rains came to Westhampton. But the divine mercy for some was attended by the lightning of wrath for store-keeper Judd. His baptism was one of fire. The hopes of 1813 for acquiring virtue, knowledge, and some worldly success, though modest, were far in excess of what the barren soil of Westhampton could actually supply to him. Blow after blow crashed down, until in 1822 he was forced from town by economic disaster. His vigorous health and bright hopes gone, he was at thirty-two already hoary-headed and deaf in one ear. He felt his mind "broken with troubles and losses, its energy . . . gone, with no resolution to go forward, and no patience to remain as I am."

In 1816 the first revival since 1806 came to Westhampton. The rumbling had been heard up the Connecticut Valley for some months past. The Valley, still swayed by Jonathan Edwards, had a social and economic unity perhaps more real than the political bands that tied Northampton and Boston together. When in one town the first signs of grace appeared, ministers began coming in from neighboring churches to assist in the harvest, to man the machinery of anxious meetings, prayer meetings, and extra preachings that enlivened life's usual routine. As the converts increased, they became carriers of the good news: by letters and visits to neighboring towns they spread the revival up the line.[11]

One might almost propose, with tongue in cheek, a theory of economic determinism about this particular revival, if not of the revival in general. The waves of religious emotion seemed to coincide with economic depressions, in 1815, 1819, and 1857 at least, as if the breaking of worldly bubbles induced men to take refuge in heavenly ones. The causes of the revival can be analyzed by looking at each town, indeed each individual, in isolation. At the same time, the revivals tended to travel in waves, as if a chain of powder kegs, all built up in individual communities over a period of years, should be ignited by the travelling of the same spark. Certainly, we can trace the life cycle of the bubble in the case of both father Judd and his sister-in-law, Arethusa Hall.

Arethusa's bubble was out of phase with the rest of the town: her troubles were not economic, but a matter of the affections. Young Nason Erhook (the anagram resolves easily into Hooker), whose movements she followed eagerly from her bedroom and kitchen windows, had won her highly susceptible heart. The evidences of his many little gallantries—leaping over fences to carry things for her, offering his arm—were not backed up by any declaration of love, but that was supplied via Arethusa's best girl friend, who was Hooker's relative and confidante. When Arethusa had "become entirely permeated by his image," the rug was yanked from under her. Her friend, the confidante, had been playing a cruel joke upon her. Arethusa felt the blow "with almost annihilating force"; insomnia and a "morbidly sensitive" nervous system were the long-term results.[12] One can only speculate about the effects of all this upon the young boys in her charge. Certainly young Sylvester acquired somehow the same high-strung, nervous temperament. One immediate result was Arethusa's anxious concern for religion. The sought-for release from tension and sorrow came after much earnest searching in prayer meetings of elderly neighbors. Her sense of joy was short-lived: her religious bubble burst too.

Father Judd was tempted into overextending himself by the deceiving appearances of wartime prosperity. Withdrawing from the partnership with Hooker, he built a house on the corner between the church and the store and then decided to go it alone in the storekeeping business. Confident of success, he bought goods extensively in the spring of 1815 on his trips to New York, Hartford, and Boston. By fall goods started pouring in from abroad and prices fell disastrously.

Judd's ego had been further inflated by the important part he played in town affairs in 1815. He pushed hard to get a vote in town meeting for a new church building. Then he took on the job of overseeing the construction, neglecting his own affairs entirely for the year 1816. His New England conscience was working overtime, and nothing but vexation of spirit resulted. The contractor did a shoddy job, money was scarce that year, the contractor could not be paid in full, and everyone was thoroughly miserable. Judd berated himself for years as headstrong, vain, and presumptuous, and refused to tax the town a cent for his year's labor. The citizens rewarded him the next year by electing him to the legislature, but he took little interest in the session he attended and "was disgusted with this, as with all other public business." He "became misanthropic" and refused all further solicitations to accept public office, though they came repeatedly for many years.

Before the unhappy issue of his labors for the church had become fully apparent and before the reaction had deepened into misanthropy, Judd was caught up in the wave of revival interest. His reading and writing centered on religious topics, and he felt a "remarkable excitement" respecting his future welfare. It began to appear that he would soon join the roll of converts. But Enoch Hale counseled patience and careful examination in all things; his caution was rewarded when Judd slipped back, his impressions transient and insubstantial. The backsliding of the convert, experienced by Arethusa and her brother-in-law, and still later to be lived through with agony by young

Sylvester, was a familiar phenomenon. The line between true and false conversion was exceedingly important, although so fine as to be scarcely distinguishable to the most honest and careful observer. If, misled by transient impressions, the false convert should push his way to the communion table, he would "drink damnation" to himself by his presumption. Such were the subtle engines of torture for every New England soul, including Arethusa, father and mother Judd, and all their children.

Fortunately for the Judd children, now increased to three by the birth of Chauncey Parkman Judd in 1815, Apphia Judd's nature was less complicated than her husband's, and the warm emotions of the revival were not counteracted by intellectualizations. She had not read Locke on the Human Understanding, as her husband had been doing, and she felt free to announce her conversion as accomplished.

The baptism to which the three boys—J.W., Sylvester, and Chauncey Parkman—now became eligible took place with all deliberate speed. The mass immersion of converts' children took place on January 5, 1817.[13] The meeting house was unheated, of course, and the inauguration into the Christian life was a chilly one. If the children complained, at least they had the luxury of the new meeting house, just completed, to symbolize the newness of all things at the beginning of the year.

Enoch Hale was at this winter season out in the cold, testing the lesson that one should not rely upon worldly things. On October 25, 1816, his house had burned to the ground. Two men trapped inside had leaped from a window. The Judd boys ran down the road to watch the blaze. People who came to help as Enoch Hale dragged out books, desk drawers, clothing, beds, stood by and took virtually nothing from the house. One brave woman dashed in and saved a pair of window curtains. Most of the important papers were destroyed.[14] Father Judd had the oversight of building the new parsonage and brought it to a speedy conclusion. This was one building project in which he could take satisfaction, since this time his altruism had results which pleased all.

Back in the storekeeping business with his friend William Hooker in 1817 and 1818, Judd found prices continuing to slide. He began now to enlarge and improve his new farm, taking up farming more in earnest, but found himself balked at even this new turn. The soil of Westhampton was as hard and unyielding as the impersonal economic forces that were slowly rolling him under. To make matters worse, the children started coming at an even faster rate: Hall and Hophni were born in 1817 and 1818. In desperation Judd tried operating again on his own, and in 1819 went into the tanning business. In one grand effort he bought up hides in large quantity and more than doubled his debts, to the amount of about $8,000. But in this year, the postwar depression hit with its full force, and Judd found himself long on groceries, debts, and shoe leather, but very short on cash.

Vexed, restless, almost frantic, he did not know where to turn as he contemplated bankruptcy and the loss of reputation. He longed to get away. In vain were all the exhortations from the pulpits of the Valley about the sin of a restless spirit that longed for change and movement. The plain fact was that the Valley was full of restless spirits, and the revolt from the village was not exclusively a twentieth-century phenomenon. We can infer as much from the fact that there was so much preaching against restlessness. Golden Westhampton was the one place Judd wanted to escape. He wrote to Enoch Hale's son, Nathan Hale, in Boston, but Hale had no position for him on the *Daily Advertiser*. Hale's letter counseled him to stay in Westhampton rather than undertake the "anxieties and vexations" of business elsewhere.[15] To Nathan Hale, Westhampton was a remembered garden, a place of repose. The American myth was already being formed.

In the fall of 1819 Judd made a temporary escape from women, children, dullness, and disaster by scouting out the Western Reserve and Genesee regions as possible places of retreat. The frontier was perhaps less a place for idealistic pioneers to advance the American destiny than a place for retreat from personal failure. On the frontier Judd found fertile land that made the hills of Westhampton look barren indeed. But the frontier was as rich in vices as in soil; good men coming from the East quickly sank down to the general level; cheating, stealing, sexual license, drunkenness, swearing prevailed to a degree that shocked Judd. Nevertheless, on returning to Westhampton, he cast looks back over his shoulder at the fleshpots of the Western soil; in New England he was astonished at the dismal countryside: no wheatfields, no elms, lofty maples, or black soil in level fields. Only "dreary hemlock," dwarfish timber, brown grass, old houses, and barren soil greeted him. "I would gladly have exchanged the view for the newest farms of the west, where stumps & trees checker the fields & a loghouse is the only dwelling." "As I passed by farms along back I wondered they did not all leave this barren country & go to the west."[16]

Back home, responsibility and family ties caught up with father Judd again, and he resolutely set the idea of going west out of his mind. For another two years he dragged along in Westhampton, paring his losses and settling debts, turning once again, in the absence of real employment, to his books. Even here, he found his early hopes unrealized. He had read many books, too many for his worldly advantage, but found himself at the end a man of many smatterings but no thorough, systematic knowledge of anything. All things spoke to him with one voice: *vanitas vanitatum.*

> The gilded hopes of youth, the projects of ambition, the impa-
> tience of disappointment, the allurements of future life, *these,*
> *these* things have left me. Poverty and obscurity have lost half
> their terrors. Indeed, they sometimes appear pleasing. Instead of
> being *great* in the world, I am willing to be *small.* [17]

With submission to the God who "reigns in Heaven, and
governs all events" came the peace of numbness, the melancholy and worldly wisdom of Ecclesiastes.

To those who did not have to live there—the Nathan
Hales, the Dorus Clarkes, the Chauncey Parkman Judds—
the return to Westhampton on holiday occasions and centennial celebrations or in the misty nostalgia of memory
could be a visit to eternal boyhood and innocence, uncorrupted by time's changes.[18]

For father Judd, who had to live there, the return to
Westhampton, down the Mohawk and over the Berkshires,
was a Return into Time, a resumption of the battle with
the hard, implacable Fact. It pursues a man wherever he
goes.

3

The Village as Utopia:
Timothy Dwight and Sylvester Judd

In 1817, the year of storekeeper Judd's discomfiture and of his sons' baptism into Christian life, the Standing Order of the Connecticut Valley lost its greatest and most influential intellectual leader, Timothy Dwight. The age of post-revolutionary consolidation, symbolized by the glacial calm of Enoch Hale, was ending. Henceforward, the mighty oaks of conservatism would topple one by one—Governor Caleb Strong and the Reverend Solomon Williams of Northampton, the Reverend Enoch Hale and Squire Sylvester Judd of Westhampton: together with John Adams of Quincy, all would soon exit. Timothy Dwight was of their generation, having been born in 1752, the same year as Squire Judd.

The grandson of Jonathan Edwards, Dwight had been raised in Northampton and had a tradition to uphold. He had been president of Yale College since 1795 and, as the Valley's chief defender of political and religious orthodoxy, had led a slashing counterattack against the incursions of French infidelity and Jeffersonianism. The revival was his weapon. With it he drove back the creeping Unitarianism which had threatened to spread from Harvard to Yale. The Connecticut Valley was kept relatively free of the virus, and in New Haven, Unitarianism was dead. For Dwight, the revival of 1816 and 1817, that resulted in the baptism of the Judd children, was another victory, a climax. He had been determined to show that the sophistications of the metropolis could not subvert the solid piety of the town. At the high water mark of the struggle, success apparently assured, he died, unaware that the future belonged to the city and to change.

In 1794 Dwight had published *Greenfield Hill,* a utopian rhapsody in heroic couplets, declaring that the future belonged to the village, the New England village of "the modest competence," where virtue and piety flourished. The New Jerusalem, the City on a Hill for all the world to emulate, was not Boston after all, but Northampton or Westhampton or New Haven. Such talk may have rung hollow to storekeeper Judd after 1817, but the archetypal image of the town as utopia was nevertheless an important part of the intellectual heritage of his son Sylvester. Into the idealized image, the author of *Margaret* would etch the acid irony of his realism, and then, with a spirt of the acid, the golden ring at the end of the book would emerge: the vision of the perfected village, freed from all taint of Calvinism.

If to many of his contemporaries Dwight seemed to be looking backwards, to be a Calvinist reactionary, to many others he seemed progressive. He supported the American revolutionary ideals of freedom and equality. With his fellow Connecticut Wits he labored to raise America's literary prestige by writing the Great American Epic that would effect our literary independence. Dwight's *The Conquest of Canaan* made it plain to its audience of 1785 that America was indeed the promised land, Washington its Joshua. The self-conscious, adolescent nation had forsaken the past and could justify its rebellion only by pointing to the glorious present and future. Dwight's works were a prime example of the increasingly secularized millennialist writings that were suggesting that the millennium would begin in America. Like Cotton Mather and Jonathan Edwards, Dwight looked expectantly from his pulpit, hoping that the millennium might begin right there, on God's chosen soil.

Sylvester Judd, though decidedly not parochial or chauvinistic, would depict, in both *Margaret* and his long poem *Philo,* a millennium which began in a New England town. America as the Garden, preserved from the beginning of time, America as promised land, America as refuge from the corruptions of Europe: this configuration of images had always been with America, was popular in Dwight's day, was central to Sylvester Judd's books, and would remain a permanent element in America's self-conscious explanations of its nature and destiny.[1]

In this bright vision the village played an important role. The idealization in *Greenfield Hill* was imitative of the fashionable poets of England and owed perhaps as much to Goldsmith's "The Deserted Village" as to the New England countryside. But the point was that the country, which in England was being left deserted by the rush to the city, was in America green and vital with abundant life. Goldsmith had written a nostalgic lament for a vanishing virtue, just as Dorus Clarke would find himself doing in 1878, at a similar stage in American history. For Timothy Dwight, flourishing rural life was not a relic of the past but a fact of the present and a guarantee of America's future. Infidelity might corrupt her cities, but America, at least in New England, was still a land of small towns where Enoch Hales and Squire Judds could exert to the full their beneficent influence. Here no wealth could corrupt, no lasciviousness entice, no French infidelity overwhelm the Garden with weeds. Close to the soil, the honest townsman and farmer would find "a modest Competence" and learn the virtues of frugality combined with healthful cheer. From the tightly knit, familial society of the town would flow personal security and social stability. A man would know who he was.

In Dwight's millennial vision, therefore, progress was defined as stability, the retention and spread, throughout the nation, of the blessings of modest competence and orthodoxy. This was a good, solid, "businesslike" concept of progress. A converted nation, which would simply be the rural Connecticut Valley writ large on the face of America, would in its turn serve as a model for the world to emulate, as the Puritans had envisaged when they first came to America. The millennium was related to expansionism and to the later concept of the American Century.

New England men were divided within, however, in their attitude toward the frontier. Like father Judd, returning from the Western Reserve in 1819, they looked with both longing and apprehension at the rank growth springing up in the rich soil of the western garden. To ensure that things would not get out of hand in the West and explode into something quite different from Dwight's comforting vision, New England men began, under the leadership of such men as Westhampton's own Justin Edwards, D.D., to support frontier missionaries and to build in the Western Reserve model towns patterned as closely as possible after those in the Connecticut Valley.

This focus on the frontier did not mean a romanticized vision of virtue coming from the forest symbolized by Natty Bumppo, Judd's Margaret, or Andrew Jackson. It meant restraining and guiding of the frontier. To restrain frontier expansionist forces, New England men would oppose the War of 1812, would support measures like the Foote Resolution of 1830 to slow down the sale of Western lands, and would drag their heels during the Mexican War. For Dwight, as for the earlier Puritans, the forest was dismal and savage, and the frontiersman was one of the unwashed.[2]

Sylvester Judd's *Margaret* likewise reveals an ambivalent attitude toward the wilderness. On the one hand, Margaret is the child of nature, growing up wild in the woods outside of town, cut off from the civilizing influences of Calvinism as dispensed by school and church. Wildness is her salvation: she grows up uncorrupted, a prize exhibit of the Rousseauistic thesis that man is naturally good.

On the other hand, the woods are populated with characters even more unsavory than those in town. Margaret's foster father, Pluck Hart, is a shiftless drunkard with attacks of delirium tremens. His son Hash has all of Pluck's failings plus meanness; for example, Hash kicks over a fence that his eight-year-old sister has made around a dandelion. Sylvester Judd's portraits of rustic depravity are realistic. Also, Judd fails to portray the village in tones of unredeemed black to contrast with forest purity. The village contains the seeds of redemption, needing only the touch of Margaret's purity to make it blossom. The transfigured village then becomes a model for other towns, and in a utopian fantasy—a wild, rhapsodic coda at the end— the millennial day is ready to dawn. The village, for Judd as well as for Dwight, was a source of hope. For Judd, the village was potentially, though not yet actually, the scene of a happy compromise between the values associated with nature and those associated with civilization.

Because the village, then, served a vital function in the embodiment of the American dream, in establishing America's sense of identity and purpose, its defenders were doing much more than entering into the debate in England between Oliver Goldsmith and George Crabbe over the merits of the village. They were defending America's unique gift to civilization. Timothy Dwight was saying that America's gift to the future was not restless change for the sake of change, not mere revolution, but the possibility of stabilizing the ideal present, universalizing it in time and space. Here the village would not decline, the victim of enclosure movements and the industrial revolution, but would show its virility by dividing and multiplying, like the amoeba, in the limitless expanse of North America.

It would remain for people like Sylvester Judd, in the 1840's, to deal with the acute anxieties about America's mission and future, anxieties that came when industrialism and the city cast their cloud over America and it became increasingly apparent that progress would become identified with the city, not with the town. In *Richard Edney and the Governor's Family* (1850) Judd faced the problem of the city and industrialism. He proposed to meet the evils of the city—class-consciousness and snobbery, slums and saloons—by efforts to restore the social unity characteristic of the village. Upper-class people of good will should go slumming, become amateur social workers, and try to break down social barriers. But Timothy Dwight, parson Hale, and father Judd lived in a more unified, simpler world. For them, America and progress were Westhampton, or Northampton, or Yale; here was the scene of the cosmic drama, and every man could find significance in playing his part.

We can hardly wonder that storekeeper Judd, the failure, in 1819 felt vaguely uneasy at the thought of deserting his post, as if his attempts to get away were somehow subversive of a way of life and of the American dream. The voice of tradition simultaneously told him to submit to his fate as a judgment of heaven and exhorted him to struggle against it manfully. Tradition told him to stay put in the ideal environment of the village and yet to try to rise in the world.

Yankee minds, like many others, were full of such contradictions. The apostles of unity were the exemplars of paradox. Loyalty to the past, the conservative principle, conflicted with the lure of the future, the principle of change, adventure, romantic excitement. This generalization is a key to understanding the romantic revolution with all its various manifestations and internal contradictions.

The city, with its opportunities for wealth and the possibility of moral decay, represented both the corrupt past of London and Rome and Paris, rejected by America, and also was a painted lady of the future, beckoning alluringly from Boston or New York. The city represented authority and repression, and it also represented change—which could be both "progress" and "evil." The village, which antedated the city, represented the faith of the fathers and patriarchal simplicity of living. For both Timothy Dwight and novelist Judd, the village, as a model of the future, beckoned to a return in time to the womb of time where time and its contradictions ceased and eternal light flowed limitless.

Thus were drawn up the opposing poles, seemingly simplistic but in reality radiating complexity, ambiguity, tension—the opposing poles in the conflict of nature vs. civilization, primitivism vs. progress. In this paradoxical world a conservative could be a progressive. New England men, typically, straddled the issue: true to the Puritan heritage they knew how to have the best of both worlds. Sylvester Judd, the novelist, would prove to be no exception. In his novels he tried to have it both ways, to make his hero and heroine equally at home in the woods or the drawing room.

Timothy Dwight, the conservative high priest, though idealizing the village as the pattern for the future, at the same time envisioned something like the imperial America of the American Century: in *Greenfield Hill* he declared that the American flag would fly from Atlantic to Pacific and would "court Korean gales." "Appian Ways" would crisscross the continent and canals would join the two oceans. "Startled China" would wake from "the long torpor," and America would be copied everywhere. This was in 1794.

Only   minds that throve on paradox could survive the tension of simultaneous commitment to such opposites. Timothy Dwight and Samuel Sewall, like Polonius, ordered coats that were rich but not gaudy. Dorus Clarke, Nathan Hale, and Chauncey Parkman Judd extolled the virtues of simple village life but found their livelihoods in railroads and publishing ventures. Storekeeper Judd, who lived the simple life, choked on his surplus shoe leather. Even Thoreau, who knew better than to lay up cowhides where moths and the worm do corrupt, would feel the fascination of the railroad's power. Emerson would grudgingly admire the industrial magnate who manipulated mighty forces.

Sylvester Judd, in his novels, would find himself torn between nature and culture, uncertain whether he was writing an attack on the Calvinistic village of his boyhood or a nostalgic reminiscence. Certainly he could not escape it. His imagination would bring the New England village to life as no other novelist prior to 1850 would do. Some readers would protest that his realism distorted the truth, but James Russell Lowell would say that "Deacon Ramsdill is the first real Yankee I have seen in print,"[3] and in that same year, 1846, he would bring out his own tribute to the New England homespun philosopher, *The Biglow Papers.* Judd's book, like Lowell's poem, was full of bite and satire, but nonetheless Judd's dominant impression of Westhampton and his boyhood there would be of "a pleasing dream." And as his father, around 1820, contemplated the prospect of leaving the house that he had built, "with its flourishing young shade trees, shrubs, and flowers, and the promise of fruit from the orchard, which he had taken pains to plant, and the ground around, that had received the footprints of one of his little boys that had passed away from sight," it was not without feelings of painful conflict.[4]

It was, after all, a good life in many respects. The period from 1800 to 1820 was exactly the time that later nostalgia would hark back to as the golden day, the period when America was most American, not yet corrupted by the foreigner and the city. The pulpits of the established order resounded, in the years from 1800 to 1820, with the praise of things as they were. Religion was solid and established, supported still by the civil government, making a comeback after years of aggressive deism. Catholicism and Anglicanism were static or declining; and America, for all the cries of "Jacobinism," was more insulated from immigration and foreign influences than ever before or since. An isolated America, having little contact with Europe and not yet visited by Mrs. Trollope, was scarcely aware of its own boorishness. Plainly, if Dorus Clarke was to find a halcyon day, this was it.

The tensions leading to the Revolution were resolved, and Tories had conformed or had left. The political conflicts over attempts to establish an American aristocracy were short-lived, though still the subject of much frothing at the mouth in the rabidly partisan press. Despite such noisy political division, even Timothy Dwight would join Thomas Jefferson, that "jawbone of Jacobinism," in preferring the relative equality of the "modest competence," found in the country and small town, to aristocracy and the city, with their extremes of wealth and poverty. Dwight and others had expressed their bright hopes for the future in such massive poems as *The Conquest of Canaan* and *The Columbiad*. Slavery seemed to many a dying institution which Americans North and South might unite in condemning. Louisiana dropped like a ripe plum, and rich land seemed limitless. The tree and the vine were fruitful, and the temperance reform had not yet reared its long, blue nose. Timothy Dwight thought the cause of women's losing their bloom at an early date was their excessive "abstemiousness." Material prosperity during much of this period helped the cheerful cup on its merry rounds. Historians were to characterize the latter part of the period as "the era of good feeling," by which they presumably meant the period's sobriety and stability. If, amid the general felicity, storekeeper Judd was less than happy, he had no cause to complain. As James Mill was even then explaining to his son in England, it is the statistical average of happiness that counts in the calculation.

In Westhampton the three Sylvester Judds—son, father, and grandfather—belonged. They went back to the beginning. That which men labor to achieve and buy—status—was young Sylvester's by right of birth. A society founded on tradition, upon authority, gave to each of its members a place in the substantial structure. Each person belonged. Not that the society was hierarchical: it was relatively democratic as societies went in those days. Compared with the European village, Westhampton society was more open, more fluid, more egalitarian. But the Judds were more equal than most.

The symbol of Westhampton life was not the pyramid of aristocracy but the unbroken circle, the perfect sphere. There could be no gaps in the unified vision of life which placed the church on a white eminence at the town's center. Just a little below and to the east of the hub was father Judd's house and store, and around the hub the spokes and rim of the unbroken circle revolved. It was a question whether equality or uniformity would be the better word to describe the society. Effective dissent in this idyllic community was not easy. Everybody read the same Bible, attended the same church, voted the same political ticket,* read the same newspaper, chewed over the same time-worn gossip, and celebrated the same holidays. Disparities of income and standard of living were not large. The Squire was

---

*In the election of 1801 Caleb Strong of Northampton, the Federalist candidate for governor, received all the votes in Westhampton, Northampton, and thirty other towns.

comfortable, not wealthy. Most families had come to West-hampton at about the same time, and it was not easy for an outsider to become an insider. A Westhampton woman, interviewed in 1960, commented, "Oh, we're outsiders here. We've only been in Westhampton some thirty years."

Things moved slowly in Westhampton. But a circle, symbol of unity and timeless perfection, can become a wheel, symbol of time and change. Young Sylvester Judd would discover that fact to his sorrow.

4

*"Let Us Spend One Day
as Deliberately as Nature"*

There were wheels within wheels. The family circle, sober and solid, was the foundation of all good order. And Sunday was the day for the clan to assert its solidarity. The central location of father Judd's house made it a natural place of resort between services on Sunday. That day it was filled with as many relatives and friends as its ample white walls would hold. Westhampton's chief ritual, with which Judd's *Margaret* was so concerned, was repeated with unvarying monotony.

Young Sylvester Judd, aged six in 1819-1820, might have sat on the settle by the huge kitchen fireplace somewhat restively those Sunday mornings, glancing furtively from his catechism toward the southeast window. Along the road would shortly come an old-fashioned chaise, one of the few luxury vehicles in frugal Westhampton, bearing Squire Judd and Grandmother Judd. Even in winter, when the chaise would be exchanged for a sleigh, their arrival would be as predictable as Parson Hale's chronometer, prevented by nothing short of a four-foot blizzard. The family breakfast, consisting of the usual bread and milk, had been finished, though at the leisurely pace appropriate to a day in which work and play were equally forbidden.

After that came family prayers and Bible reading. A single prayer in Westhampton could often last as long as an hour, and small boys were "tired out and out again" before the last regiment of stereotyped phrases had droned into silence. It was no wonder that Dorus Clarke's brother Tertius spoke of "the veteran christians of those bygone days."[1] Military metaphor came naturally to the lips in speaking of Westhampton religion. As Dorus Clarke himself put it, it was "the heroic age of New England," and "there was 'no discharge in that war.'" But we can doubt if father Judd was so athletic as this in his Christianity. He probably left such public displays of endurance for others to perform on special occasions, and there was enough time left after prayers for the boys to look at their Sunday lessons.

The Westminster Shorter Catechism was the children's staple diet on both Sundays and weekdays. Young Sylvester would not be called to strict and public account for the entire catechism until he was eight, but his older brother, J.W., was, at age nine, a veteran of the public recitations in the church. Sylvester, who showed signs of inheriting his father's bookish inclinations, could already recite a good deal of it in a singsong voice. Arethusa Hall or her sister, Mrs. Judd, would give out the questions: "What is God?.... What is sin?....What are the decrees of God?....Did all mankind fall in Adam's first transgression?" And the answers came rolling back:

> God is a Spirit, infinite, eternal and unchangeable in His being, wisdom, power, holiness, justice, goodness, and truth. . . . Sin is any want of conformity unto, or transgression of, the law of God. . . . The decrees of God are His eternal purpose, according to the counsel of His own will, whereby, for His glory, He hath foreordained whatsoever comes to pass. . . . The covenant being made with Adam, not only for himself, but for his posterity, all mankind, descending from him by ordinary generation, sinned in him, and fell with him in his first transgression.

"Against this rock of truth," asserted Dorus Clarke, "the waves of criticism have dashed for more than two centuries, and have made no impression." The Westminster Assembly of divines had sat for more than five years and had held 1163 sessions to hammer out those words of gold. The Judd boys could certainly sit still for a Sunday morning to learn them.

The great fireplace in the kitchen, which on winter weekdays warmed the room and boiled the pot, was cold on warmer Sabbaths. No work, not even cooking, was permitted from Saturday at sundown until after sundown Sunday. Bread and milk, nutcakes and cheese would suffice for the Christian. And Arethusa Hall was preoccupied with keeping her pack of boys quiet.

In 1820 Apphia and Arethusa had five Judd children to care for, and another was due to arrive in October. Though Apphia's parents had defied the laws of probability by having five girls in a row, the Judds had set about to restore the balance of nature and demonstrate the love of symmetry of nature's God, who had provided the Judds with five boys and no girls. Thus, Arethusa had no prospect of additional help in washing, mending, and child care. She hardly needed her secret sorrow, the disappointment over the Hooker boy, to explain her emotional state. Now eighteen years of age, she thought about getting away from Westhampton to see something of the world.

The Judd children at this time began with nine-year-old Jacob Walker ("J.W."), who later insisted on changing his name to James, and ended with little Hophni (Hop), aged one. In between, spaced at two-year intervals with a methodical regularity of which Enoch Hale would have approved, were Sylvester ("Ves"), the second oldest; Chauncey Parkman ("Park"); and Hall. Eventually, the Judds would produce six boys and two girls to match Grandfather Hall's family of six girls and two boys.

The Judd boys were lively, imbued with their father's doctrine of independence, and on weekdays "their usual uproar," as their father called it, did not contribute greatly to the calming of frayed nerves. Mother Judd commented that the boys were "as wild as ever." Although Mrs. Judd had somewhat wilted and was often sick, Father and Arethusa were a match for their spirited family. Judd may indeed have been "highly genial," as Arethusa said, but his own judgment was that his temperament was not notably "placid" or "amiable."[2] He was no weakling. The rod was not spared in Westhampton, and we can guess that all was properly quiet in the Judd household on Sundays at least. Sunday was not a day for children.

This freezing up of the normal outlets of surplus energy began early: at sundown Saturday night. Then children had to stop their chasing of butterflies in the fields, their gathering of wildflowers in the woods, their hunting of beehives, their fishing and swimming in the creek. Games of hide-and-seek around the meetinghouse, mimicry of militia training day or sham fights in the barns with dry mullein stalks for guns[3] —all had to cease. If it was winter, the Judd boys might come down the hillside on their sleds, flashing past the meetinghouse steps to a halt at their own front door, the last cries trailing off as the gloom gathered. In the shadow of the great hill, sundown came early.

On those Sunday mornings there were no late coffee and oranges. As the elders discoursed of things eternal and terrestrial, rehearsing the ancient sacrifice, the boys, glancing earnestly toward the window, struggled toward a similar decorum.

Then the awaited event occurred: up the road and over the hill from the east came Grandfather and Grandmother Judd. Sixty-eight years old in 1820, a white-haired patriarch whose years rested upon him gracefully, Grandfather Judd clambered down with a solemn twinkle. J.W., Ves,

Park, and Hall rallied around with the solicitude that small boys have for grandfathers who are not seen every day and who have been known to dispense a peppermint on the sly into a small fist. Not that any such event was likely to occur on this particular day, however. New England was New England. Squire Judd may have been somewhat red-faced, but he was no Saint Nicholas. He had the look of *grandeur* about him. If these boys had ever heard of Santa Claus or Christmas, it was only because someone had been speaking in disapproving tones about Europe's heathen superstitions.

Close behind the Squire's chaise came a wagon, carrying the Squire's widowed daughter, Hannah Lyman, and her three children. "Aunt Lyman," sharp of face and eye, had inherited her father's businesslike habits and forcefulness of character. It is hard to say whether she had also inherited from her mother, Hannah Burt Judd, those peculiarities that were such a matter of public record. Arethusa Hall, a model of Victorian tactfulness, did not hesitate to mention in her biography of Sylvester Judd the oddity of his grandmother and to remark that young Sylvester had inherited some of it.[4] According to the family tradition, Grandmother Judd's oddities were a matter of "being ahead of her times."[5] At the reunion of Westhampton natives in 1866, Chauncey Parkman Judd recalled Aunt Lyman as a force to be reckoned with: she had even received some votes for the town office of selectman, years before the agitation for women's rights had begun; "and they could not have voted for a better *man*." She "would have made the folks toe the mark, and no mistake." She too was ahead of her times. In conservative Westhampton the Judds seemed to have a potential for restive liberalism.

George Lyman, her son, was the cousin young Sylvester especially looked for. Somewhat younger than Sylvester, he was also destined to become a minister, though he would walk the straight and narrow of Amherst College, not the primrose path of Harvard. After the stiff bows to the elders, the cousins could turn their attention to each other, their faces set with solemnity.

This was a day of reaching for the proffered, elusive Grace, for reflection upon the awesome journey between life and death. For those who still hesitated on the brink, unable to reach across the chasm and grasp the outstretched Hand, unable to "secure a hope," it was perhaps a time of solemn meditation, of trying to whip up sluggish spirits. Fear and trembling were the necessary prelude to peace.

When the Judd boys went back into the house, there was doubtless an unaccustomed gingerliness in their gait. The floors were bare and unpainted, strewn with a layer of sand that took on sinuous designs, and the boys had been careful since the night before to leave no signs of scuffling. In Westhampton a man's care for the temporal amenities could be judged by the freshness of his sand, and Sunday gossips were quick to make comments of the type that Sylvester Judd later recorded in *Margaret*:

> "I remember," said the elder Mistress Whiston, "when old Parson Bristead down in Raleigh, used to sprinkle thirty bushels of sand on his floors every year, and I don't believe Parson Welles uses five."
>
> "Yes, yes," said her daughter-in-law, "great changes, and nobody can tell where it will end." (111)

Young Sylvester had his ears open. He had an auditory memory and a great curiosity about words and people's ways of talking.

Father Judd did not care much about what the gossips said. He paid little attention to appearances and prided himself on his frugality. Furnishings were simple in Westhampton. Tobacco chewing was common: sand, in the absence of cuspidors, made the most sensible carpeting. Father Judd himself indulged; in his quest for virtue he had recently taken up chewing in place of smoking.[6] Even such a personage as Yale's great theologian Nathaniel W. Taylor chewed tobacco.[7]

When the elders had exchanged a few pleasantries inside the house and had praised or reproved the children for their performance on the catechism lesson for the day, it was time for meeting. The breath of fresh air would be brief, for the walk was less than fifty yards. From the outlying areas of Westhampton, the townspeople had already begun to converge on the church. Sylvester Judd described the scene in *Margaret:* "Many are on horses, more on foot, and a very few in wagons. The horses' heads are garnished with branches of spruce and birch, to keep off the flies" (103). Carriages were uncommon; their advent within a few years would be but one more sign of the multiplicity of contrivances that would mark the new age. A usual sight in this day just before the transition was to see husband and wife mounted on the same horse, with a pillion attached to the saddle for the woman. The woman held her infant in her arms, and the next-older child was mounted in front of his father. The other children, marching in a solemn file behind the horse, were barefoot in the summer, carrying their shoes in their hands until the procession came near the church. Then they reversed the process "of olden time, when sandals were put off on entering holy ground."[8] As these caravans reached the church, the parents dismounted with the aid of the horse blocks and steps and took the horses to the sheds behind the church.

Crossing the street to the throng on the meetinghouse steps, the Judds busied themselves with greeting friends. Deacon Edwards, one of the politest men in town, returned the bows of the children with courtly grace. The rest of the tableau can be reconstructed only by turning to the pages of *Margaret:*

> Mistress Ravel, in common with many other of the women, carries on her arm a large reddish calico bag filled with nutcakes and

cheese. You will also see coming down the West Street Mr. Adolphus Hadlock, nephew of the Deacon's, with his wife and six children, and Mr. Adolphus will contrive in some way or other to give you the names of all his children without your asking, even before he reaches the steps of the Meeting-house; Triandaphilda Ada, Cecilia Rebecca, Purintha Cappadocia, Aristophanes, Ethelbert, and a little boy he carries in his arms, Socrates; and you will hear the young men and boys that are lolloping on the steps repeat these names as the several parties to whom they belong arrive. Philip Davis the sexton, who has himself been watching the people, now strikes the second bell, and those who live immediately on the Green begin to turn out, and when he commences tolling, it is a sign Parson Welles has issued from his house....The Parson and his wife reverently, sedately ascend the steps, the crowd of men and boys who have been modestly waiting about the Porch, opens to let them pass, then all fall in behind, and enter the Church; the bell ceases tolling, and the Green is still as the grave. (104-05)

Inside the door the Judd family divided. The smaller children went with their parents and grandparents down the broad center aisle, through the remembered, creaking gate into their first world, where the familiar pew, high-walled, dry and brown-edged, filled with children out of sunlight, noisily. In the formal pattern of the Westhampton church, each family moved on a fixed course, each Sunday to the same destination. The Judd pew, bought and owned like any piece of real estate, was doubtless near the front, as befit the Judds' social station.

The older children, and this included J.W. and possibly Sylvester, clattered up the stairs to the gallery. There the children divided again, girls on one side, boys on the other, just as in the school. Here they could get a good view of parson Hale as he punctually ascended the stairs to the high pulpit. By now the hush of worship had descended, and the last latecomer had cautiously lowered his hinged seat. There was no music. Tithingmen stalked the galleries to insure decorum. Then, from the triangular sounding board over parson Hale's head, rolled out the awesome, expected words, "Say to the south, Give up, and to the north, Keep not back; bring thy sons from far, and thy daughters from the ends of the earth." The mere sound of these words, as Arethusa Hall later recorded in her autobiography, was enough to induce solemnity. For the children in the front pews below, the awesomeness of the voice was heightened by their inability to see its source: the minister's head was invisible behind the high pulpit.[9]

Few today would accuse the Westhampton church of yielding to worldliness. Paint, gilt lettering, stained glass, carpets, seat cushions, organ, flowers, even stoves were items easily dispensed with by those whose minds were caught up in the drama of salvation. The spirit was rich in proportion to what the body could do without. Even Governor Strong of Northampton had not adopted the Boston practice of putting carpets and cushions in the pew.[10] Yet, some people in the Westhampton of 1820 noted with uneasiness or open disapproval signs of creeping corruption. Parson Hale was occasionally more willing to accept innovations than some of his parishioners.[11] When the people rose to sing, they no longer waited before each line for the deacon to "deacon out the line." Hymn books, musical instruments, and organized choirs had but recently been introduced in Westhampton and the other towns nearby. Organs were of course banned, but a bass viol, a flute, or a violin might be used to keep the singing to some semblance of tune and tempo. A few decades earlier even the introduction of a pitch pipe had been opposed by some. Now the young people were welcoming the "singing schools" on weekday evenings that gave them an excuse for social gatherings.[12] Accordingly, when the Judds rose for the hymns, they participated in something different from the disorganized, agonizingly slow, and tuneless notes that formerly had passed for worship. Among the hymns sung in Westhampton, "O God, Our Help in Ages Past," "When I Survey the Wondrous Cross," and "Joy to the World" (which was *not* sung in celebration of Christmas) would still be recognized by a modern ear. Methodical parson Hale insisted that the hymns be "read straight through in course," whatever their relevance or lack of relevance to the sermon subject.[13] The singing did not always cease on schedule. Babies were subjected to the divinely appointed means of grace as soon as they could be safely carried abroad, and their crying throughout the service was taken for granted.[14]

A main event of the service was the long prayer, which resounded with stereotyped phrases such as the plea that their "children and their children's children, down to the latest generation, may be converted to Christ," and that "their souls with ours may be bound up in the sure bundle of eternal life." Small boys in the gallery did not always understand the phrases they heard. Sylvester Judd's cousin, George Lyman, for example, was fascinated by Squire Judd's regular reference in family prayers to our Father, "whom to know aright is life eternal." George kept wondering for years who was this mysterious "Noah Wright," whose claim to heaven seemed secured.[15]

It was small wonder then that George, Ves, J.W., and Park waited anxiously for parson Hale's great watch to tick off the precise moment for the prayer's end. That moment was reserved by tradition for the boys' one great contribution to the service. The hinged seats, which had been raised for the prayer, were now given a soul-satisfying slam, and the racket was regarded by at least one New England boy as scarcely less harmonious than the "noise of wind and catgut in the gallery." James Russell Lowell, who remembered the old *"slam-seat* meeting-houses" with fond aversion, was in tune with the spirit of Judd's *Margaret* when he commented that the seat-slamming was "a free motion of the spirit and a genuine enjoyment" and that it was therefore to be considered "real worship."[16]

The tithingmen in the galleries, though helpless to do anything about this customary commotion, were always on the lookout for individual offenders. One of the tithingmen was notable for the peculiar way in which he himself punctuated the Sunday devotions. The noise of his periodic holy exhalations resounded through the church. The large bandanna to which he had frequent recourse had, a few years earlier, contributed to a disturbance not sanctioned by tradition. Dorus Clarke's younger brother Tertius had special cause to remember the occasion, as did Squire Judd and his family. It seems that a boy smuggled a pint of beans into the church and disposed of the evidence by pouring it into the tithingman's pocket. The explosive charge was most skillfully laid: the handkerchief, one end of which dangled outside, was suddenly pulled out by the tithingman; the beans were propelled in all directions, and the church was thrown into an uproar. The culprit "maintained the most impertur[b]able gravity" but Tertius "burst out into a shout of laughter." The red-faced tithingman descended and took Tertius in hand for the eventual confrontation with Squire Judd's magisterial brow. Tertius was "in a state of awful fear and trembling. Most unexpectedly his life was spared, and he was let off with a reprimand never to do so again. He promised he would not, provided *the boys did not bring any more beans.*"[17]

At the climax of the Sunday service parson Hale placed, with no noticeable thwack, a little hand-sewn sermon, four-by-six inches, on the lectern. In former years it would have contained exactly twenty-four closely-written pages, but times were changing, and Hale could adapt. Pitch pipes, catgut and horsehair, singing schools and choirs, missionary societies, Sunday schools; and now the sixteen-page sermon. Progress, said some; degeneration, said others. Where would it all end? But Hale knew how to keep innovation within safe limits. Sixteen was exactly two-thirds of twenty-four, and there was satisfaction in mathematical neatness. The writing always carried thriftily to the bottom of the last page, with never a blank one left over. The bolts of cloth from which Hale took his sermons were few and plain: the material could easily be cut to size. The relative brevity of a Hale sermon may help to explain his popularity and his reputation as a judicious man who said the right thing, always.

Young Sylvester had no visions of spiders or sinners barbecuing on spits to excite his young imagination. Though Hale certainly mentioned God's righteous wrath often enough, he was not a hellfire-and-damnation preacher. Young Sylvester doubtless did not listen very closely to preaching that typically consisted of verbal jugglery like the following:

> The bible represents God as acting in three relations, distinguished by the names the Father, the Son, and the Spirit, or the Holy Ghost, and in each relation sustaining a personal character. The Father is a person, the Son is a person, and the Spirit or Holy Ghost is a person. For this reason it is common to say, God exists in three persons; or, there are three persons in the Godhead. At the same time it is allowed, that the word persons applied to God as three in one, is not used with exact propriety as when applied to men. For in whatever manner God is three persons, he is one being. There is only one God, though the Father is God, the Son is God, and the Spirit is God.[18]

This was one of the *published* sermons. Calm, that was the word for such preaching.

Sylvester Judd had to go elsewhere to find the earthy language and vivid metaphors that salted the pages of *Margaret*. Though Hale occasionally got around, especially on Fast Days, to the standard New England jeremiad on the theme of degenerating times, his shafts lacked barb. He never got very specific about the real world. Even in 1804, when Thomas Jefferson was to be fought, Hale, in a sermon, could only refer vaguely to "the spread of infidelity and atheism" which must be resisted with "all the power of the gospel."[19]

In Westhampton sin was apparently merely an abstraction, a theoretical necessity in the balancing of theological equations. If we are to believe a reminiscing native of 1866, even profanity was practically unheard of in early Westhampton. Westhampton was a new Eden in the wilderness, a city set upon a hill that all the world might copy. Sin was necessary, but even good healthy sin must be kept within proper limits. To father Judd, Westhampton was Problem. To Enoch Hale, Westhampton was Promise, and his harvest of souls from 1816 to 1820 was perhaps a hint that something important in God's plan of history was in the wind. Hale had said in his sermon of 1804 that the very "spread of infidelity and atheism with the reduced condition of antichrist indicate the approach of this blessed millennium." Hale took the hopeful view. Novelist Judd's interest in the millennium, which was so prominent a feature of all his books, was but standard New England doctrine that had been taught to him from the beginning.

According to Hale, atheism and sin were cause for hope. On the other hand, the smiting of antichrist was also cause for hope. New England, by its very existence and obvious prospering, was cause for hope; and above all Westhampton, as the microcosm of all that was best in New England, was cause for hope. This rocky land of challenge would separate sheep from goats. In Boston and Westhampton man lived by the sweat of his brow, but in Heaven on his unearned income.

Thus far, father Judd, there in his pew, could find comfort. But on the other hand, misfortune was cause for alarm, as it indicated God's displeasure and was probably the result of sin. Father Judd squirmed. When parson Hale surveyed one year the epidemic sickness that prevailed, the excessive snows of winter, and the drought of the previous summer, he reached the only possible conclusion: these were "indications of God's righteous displeasure." Laying it home, Enoch Hale thundered his answer to Satan:

> We are called upon to examine ourselves, and search out the evil, that we may put it away. Christians, does the sin lie at your door? or O impenitent sinners is it with you?[20]

When the minister rose to such eloquence, perhaps his auditors, even young Sylvester, were briefly roused to a delicious shudder. Of such stuff was a revival made. The possibility that one might personally be responsible for an epidemic or a drought was certainly frightening enough to a small boy, though sufficiently remote to a man like father Judd to keep him from the roll of converts.

The corollary of such preaching as Hale's was one that ministers hesitated to draw explicitly, but that parishioners might draw for themselves: if misfortune was often the result of sin, might not material success be at least a tentative sign of the individual's state of grace? As father Judd had put it, "a conformity with the divine precepts of the Gospel is necessary, not only to our own future salvation, but also for our happiness and well-being in this world."[21]

This preaching, then, which seemed to offer such hope and which claimed to have all difficulties resolved by neat formulas, was full of unresolved tensions that would in a few years drive young Sylvester from his childhood Eden. This world was a vale of tears and to be spurned; this world was a foreshadowing of Paradise and was to be turned into a garden. Both images pulled at the Puritan mind. As Leo Marx puts it in his discussion of the American image in Shakespeare's day, "America was *both* Eden and a howling desert; the actual conditions of life in the new world lent plausibility to both images."[22] Man's life in the world and his life in the soul were both full of paradox. Everyone's chief business on earth was to get to heaven, but no human efforts could get him there. When worldly adversity was overcome, by God's grace, what then? On the one hand, the material success of New England was a sign of God's favor; on the other, that very success was producing evil effects: as land values in Boston, New Haven, and Northampton went up, recognizable piety went noticeably down.[23] God was always picking unlikely spots like Kentucky for his revivals and passing Boston by. The rich merchants were the ones who turned to Unitarianism and Episcopalianism. The New England mind was split down the middle. Only intellects that throve on paradox—young Sylvester Judd would one day call it muddle-headedness—could survive the tension. Small boys, who did not listen, also did very well.

The sermon over and the benediction answered by a solemn slamming of seats, the boys could take a deep breath in the noon sun in preparation for the next part of the Sunday ritual. They watched a cluster of elderly people make their way at a leisurely pace, past the horse sheds and the flies, towards the Noon House to share cold nutcakes, cheese, and a prayer. Others went for a visit with relatives and friends in homes near the church. There the cheese and nutcakes accompanied the snuffing of snuff, the smoking of pipes, the talk of health, sickness, and the weather. On the Sabbath they would avoid such topics as the coming presidential election, the recession, the omnipresence of taxes. Talk of births, deaths, marriages, sin, and redemption was in order. Arethusa Hall recorded later:

> At these sabbath-noon gatherings, every face wore a serious aspect; and if, as often happened, the muscles of the elders were relaxed by the outbreaking wit, or rather drollery, of an old aunt, and her antagonist a gentleman of about the same age, it would be accompanied by "a half-deprecating, half-laughing" expression, which seemed to say, "She is so droll, that a body must laugh, though it be sabbath-day."[24]

The familiar topic of progress and change was one that young Sylvester remembered well, and his report, many years later, of those Sabbath conversations had the authentic ring:

"Sing!" rejoined Paulina Whiston. "I wish we could have some decent singing. I was up to Brandon last Sunday, and their music is enough sight better than ours; they have introduced the new way almost everywhere but here. We must drag on forty years behind the whole world."

"For my part," said Mistress Orff, "I don't want any change, our fathers got along in the good old way, and went to Heaven. The Quakers use notes and the Papists have their la sol mee's, and Deacon Hadlock says it's a contrivance to bring all those pests into the land . . . . It's only your young upstarts, lewd and irregular people, and the like of that, that wants the new way."

"If our hearts was only right," said Mistress Tuck, "we shouldn't want any books; and the next thing we shall know, they will have unconverted people singing."

Deeply ingrained in the New England mind was the theme of "degenerating times."

"If we once begin to let in new things, there is no knowing where they will stop," replied Mistress Orff.

"It is just so," said the Widow Tuck. "They begun with wagons and shays, and the horses wan't used to the noise, and got frightened and run away; and our Eliashib came nigh spraining his ankle."

. . . .

"Yes, yes," said her daughter-in-law, "great changes, and nobody can tell where it will end."

"When I was a gal," continued the senior lady, "they didn't think of washing but once a month—"

"And now washing days come round every Monday," added Paulina. "If you will let us have some respectable singing, I will agree to go back to the old plan of washing, Grandma, ha ha!"

"It's holy time, child," said her mother.

"I remember," said the Widow Brent, who was a little deaf, "milking a cow a whole winter for a half a yard of ribbin."

"I remember," said Mistress Ravel, "the Great Hog up in Dunwich, that hefted nigh twenty score." (110-11)

Looking backwards had been a habit of the New England mind since the days of Cotton Mather. Judd's *Margaret,* concerned with the double pull from both the past and the future upon the present, reflected the New England practice of looking both backwards and forwards. The millennium, which potentially was near, was a spur to man's efforts. The jeremiad, which compared the corrupt present with an idealized past, was also a spur to man's efforts. Thus Sylvester Judd could write a utopian novel, *Margaret,* which looked to the past for its setting and paradoxically mixed nostalgia and rebellion, though its nostalgia was less evident than its rejection of the past.

Judd's attitude in *Margaret* is essentially realistic in many scenes. The desire simply to create a world triumphs over the ostensibly didactic purposes behind the book. In the following passage he catches something of the traditional litany of remembrance, the mournful strain, mixed with the crabbed vigor of Yankees whose hands have felt the spinning wheel and the soil.

> "Mournful times these!" added Mistress Joy.
> "It is most as bad as the Throat Distemper that was round when I was a gal," said one of the ladies. . . .
> "What is that to the Camp Fever, we had in the War!" echoed the Captain.
> . . . .
> "That was nothing to the Great Earthquake when I was a gal, and lived to the Bay," said Mistress Joy. "The spindle and vane on Funnel Hall was blown down, chimblys were cracked, brick and tile choked up the streets. It sounded as if God Almighty's chariot was trundling over the pavements in Old Marlboro."

Disaster is somehow vaguely suggestive of the promised Coming of the Almighty. The litany continues:

> "That was the same year one of the niggers in Kidderminster cut his master and mistresses' throat, as I have heard Ma'am tell," said Sibyl Radney.
> . . . .

"The Indians and Negroes never did us much good," said Mistress Whiston; "and I am glad there are going to be no more slaves."

"I kalkilate as much," said the Widow, "if you had seen the niggers burnt alive down teu York, nigh fifty of um, for bringing in the Papists. My Granther was on the spot and saw it all, and said it did his heart good teu see the fat fry out of the sarcy dogs."

"I remember," said the Widow Brent, who was a little deaf, "milking a cow a whole winter for a half a yard of ribbin."

"I remember," said Mistress Ravel, "the Great Hog, up in Dunwich, that hefted nigh twenty score." (277-78)

Sylvester Judd wrote this without moralizing comments.

As the crowd in the Judd house concluded their snuffing of snuff, their talk of past and present, their smoking of pipes, with perhaps an occasional story by Grandma Judd for the children, the Judd boys braced for another period of confinement. Ahead was the prospect of still another singing, preaching, and praying. The Sabbath would not be complete without at least two opportunities to brisk up the soul.

Young Sylvester, though of somewhat restive, nervous temperament, was probably as docile and attentive a six-year-old as could be found at those afternoon church services. He was of the studious rather than the athletic type. Although he joined in outdoor sports, he was always distanced by J.W. and even by his younger brother Park. Ves was extremely quick to learn, had a great interest in vocabulary and language, and was distinguished for conscientiousness, amiableness, and "a tendency for getting into sympathy with others." On such an impressionable boy Enoch Hale's ministrations were not completely wasted; for, although Aunt Arethusa said Ves had never been known to utter an untruth, Ves himself later remembered of his boyhood that "I supposed myself totally depraved." He added again, "I had from my earliest days thought much of God, and very often did I retire to pour out my soul in secret to him."[25] This serious cast of mind distinguished young Ves from his brothers, especially Park, who had the more pragmatic temperament necessary for his later worldly success.[26]

The close of the afternoon church service by no means meant that the Judd boys could relax. If they understood anything that parson Hale said, they understood that they were miserable sinners and that even an entire Sunday was little enough time for the pursuit of one's salvation. But in the summer the sun was slow in going down, and the Sabbath spell hung on and on. The summer Sunday school, a modern concession to the weakness of the flesh and a harbinger of the Reverend Sylvester Judd's child-centered church, had been adopted in 1818,[27] perhaps to take up the slack of those long summer afternoons. To be sure, some shook their heads and predicted this sort of thing would lead to just what the Reverend Sylvester Judd came to represent, what Dorus Clarke sourly called a "lavender religion."

Certainly we get no hint of softness in Dorus Clarke's description of Enoch Hale at the catechism recitations. Like a general marshaling his troops the stiff-backed old parson shook the galleries on a certain afternoon each summer with a call to duty. The time was close at hand for the three annual catechizings. To Clarke, the dignity of the occasion called for a military metaphor, nothing less than a Homeric figure:

> When the time arrived for commencing the exercise, the excitement was tremendous. As the great battle of Trafalgar was about to begin between the immense armadas of England and France, Lord Nelson displayed at the masthead of his flag-ship, "The Victory," the exciting proclamation, streaming in the wind, "ENGLAND EXPECTS EVERY MAN TO DO HIS DUTY!" That proclamation woke all the national enthusiasm of his officers and men, and strung every nerve for the awful conflict. Scarcely less imperative and exciting was the annual announcement by Father Hale: *"Sabbath after next, the first division of the catechism will*

be recited here." It sent a thrill through the town.

There was "no discharge in that war."

Though children, even of the Dorus Clarke type, had rebellious feelings, there was no discharge indeed. The Judds had a status to maintain, a reputation for scholarship.

At the close of the afternoon service on the appointed days, the children marched downstairs and ranged themselves in two lines, girls on one side and boys on the other, from the "deacon's seat" beneath the pulpit, up the "broad aisle," around the back, and down the side. The mothers, "tremblingly anxious," according to Dorus Clarke,

> bent over that scene with solemn interest, handkerchief in hand, the tears of joy ready to fall if their children should succeed, and tears of sorrow if they should happen to fail. It was a spectacle worthy of a painter.
>
> Father Hale, standing in the pulpit, put out the questions to the children in order; and each one, when the question came to him, was expected to wheel out of the line, *a la militaire,* into the broad aisle, and face the minister, and make his very best obeisance, and answer the question put to him without the slightest mistake . . . . many were the "knees which smote one against another;" and many are the persons who recollect, and will long recollect, the palpitating heart, the tremulous voice, the quivering frame, with which for several years they went through that terrible ordeal. But, if the nervous effects of that exercise were appalling, the moral influence was most salutary.

Young Sylvester Judd did not thrive, in the long run, on dogma and military drills. He remembered the flowers, birds, and people of Westhampton and was not stirred by its parades, *a la militaire.* Here is his version of Dorus Clarke's splendid, heel-clicking spectacle:

> "How many persons are there in the Godhead?"
> "There are four persons in the Godhead"—replied a little boy in the same tone of confidence that characterized his predecessor. But before he could give the entire answer, there was a cry all about, "'Tan't right, 'tan't right." . . . "'Tis right," said he in a whisper loud enough to be heard over the house, at the same time

> counting on his fingers, "Marm said 'twas just like her and Daddy and me that made three in one family, and now Grandad has come to live with us it makes four."

Instead of machinelike precision, we get another sample of a "rapid, disjointed answer" to a question that went "stumbling" from one child to another. After that, nature-child Margaret, who is visiting church for the first time, lets her attention wander, "and the whole Catechism, Effectual Calling, Justification, Adoption, and Sanctification, were disposed of, without further attention on her part," or on Judd's (112-13).

The mechanical quality of such exercises and abstractions oppressed Judd the man as much as it had Margaret the girl. As Judd looked back on the scene in the West-hampton church, he saw words recited lifelessly, religion spewed out in yard lots, form without meaning. Judd's pacifism was closely related to his romantic rebellion against Calvinism and all its works. He saw the catechism drills as all of a piece with the compulsory military training days for the town militia and with the compulsive bowing to elders. It was all drill: drill a man down to a mechanism, a thing, an abstraction; round off the rough edges of individuality, pour him into the mold, whip him until the blood ran if he didn't fit,[28] turn him into an interchangeable part for the machine of abstraction. Judd provided a phrase for the process: he called it "the science of puppetry."

But the young Judd of 1820, who had not yet learned rebellion, waited like a proper puppet for the older boys and girls to drone the catechism finally into silence. Then came the shuffling of feet, the patch of sky overhead, the flies buzzing thick around the horses, the round of good-byes, and once again the doors softly closing behind. Through the windows the boys could see the long, silent afternoon. "The sky was blue and tender; the clouds in white veils like nuns, worshipped in the sun-beams." Or perhaps they watched, instead of nuns, the "squads of dogs that trolloped to and fro on the green."[29]

What the Judd boys actually thought in 1820 about the Puritan Sabbath, we have to guess. They were doubtless assisted in their earnest striving toward decorum by the indispensible birch rod. Arethusa Hall, from the vantage point of 1875, could write nostalgically,

> The Sabbath seemed a hallowed day, with its stillness and cessation of business . . . . I recollect how solemnly the sound of the cock-crowings coming through the still air from "meeting-house hill" fell upon my ear of an early Sabbath morning. There was a sort of awe in it as a call to worship such as no bell ever had to me.[30]

For Sylvester Judd, writing in 1844, there was little nostalgia:

> "It was a despit pinched up sort of a time," said Mrs. Whiston to me awhile since, "as if God was asleep and we had to go tip-toe all day, and couldn't speak above our breath for fear of waking him." (417)

Margaret, once a nature-child, now almost a woman, commenting upon her few contacts with the Puritan Sabbath, says,

> "There seems to be something *above* the people in the village, something over their heads, what they talk to, and seem to be visited by occasionally, particularly Sundays, making them solemn and stiff like a cold wind." (230)

This reaction against Sabbath stiffness is so central an element in Judd's *Margaret* that it is worth pausing further over the point. In it is summed up Judd's whole case against Puritanism. Puritanism and flowers did not mix, and Judd loved flowers to a degree that was difficult for others to understand. Little Margaret, making her first visit to church, was stopped from giving flowers to the prisoners as she walked by the jail; and, when she got to the church, the sexton asked her to leave her flowers outside: "'These

flowers are a dreadful wicked thing on the Lord's day,'"
he said (109).

To Judd, the orthodoxy of his youth was *unnatural*. It
went against the grain of nature. It assumed that natural
impulse was from the devil, that holiness was quite different from happiness, at least from natural happiness. Therefore, discipline and severity were the key words in the raising of children, the treatment of criminals, and in international relations. Impulses to evil had to be checked by stern
measures. Sin was everywhere, sin was natural, sin must be
fought. Nature versus God: against this dichotomy Judd
rose in rebellion. It ran counter to his deepest feelings,
denied the testimony of his consciousness to the oneness
of God, man, and nature. Judd rejected Puritanism and
called it monster. It was not, to use Emerson's phrase, "one
with the blowing clover and the falling rain."[31]

Judd's ability to project the issue not only in metaphor
but also in dramatic scenes like the following, rather than
in mere abstractions, was in itself a triumph of liberation
from the influence of his Puritan upbringing. Margaret, at
eight years of age having wandered into church for the first
time in her life, engages Calvinist Miss Amy in theological
discussion:

> "Would you like to come down to Meeting again?" said Miss
> Amy.
> "I don't know as I like the Meeting. It don't seem so good as
> the Turkey Shoot and Ball. Zenas Joy didn't hurt my arm there,
> and Beulah Ann Orff and Grace Joy talked with me at the Ball.
> To-day they only made faces at me, and the man at the door told
> me to throw away my flowers."
> "How deceitful is the human heart, and desperately wicked!"
> "Who is wicked?"
> "We are all wicked."
> "Are you wicked? then you do not love me, and I don't want
> you to go with me any farther. . . . I guess I shan't come to Meet-
> ing any more. You and the Minister, and all the people here are so
> wicked. Chilion is good, and I will stay at home with him."

"The Minister is a holy man, a good man I mean, he is converted, he repents of his sins. I mean he is very sorry he is so wicked."

"Don't he keep a being wicked? You said he was wicked."

"Why, yes, he is wicked. We are all totally depraved. You do not understand. . . . It's wicked for children to see one another Sundays."

"I did see him at Meeting."

"I mean to meet and play and show picture-books, and that little boy is very apt to play; he catches grasshoppers, and goes down by the side of the brook, before sundown;–that is very bad."

"Are his eyes sore, like Obed's, sometimes, so that the light hurts him?"

"It is God's day, and he won't let children play."

"He lets the grasshoppers play."

"But he will punish children."

"Won't he punish the grasshoppers too?"

"No."

"Well, I guess, I an't afraid of God." (115-17)

Miss Amy gives up.

A summer afternoon must come to an end, even for a six-year-old. There must have been some feelings of warmth towards the beneficent hill that cut the day short. When the shimmer of sun had died at last from the hilltop and from the eyes turned towards it, the spell was broken. "Sun's down! Sun's down!" rang out in every family, an unrestrained and jubilant shout, echoed from door to door. "The tether was cut, doors and gates flew open, and out the children broke into the streets." Hands and feet stretched, wiggled, danced; lungs took the luxurious air in great gulps and expelled it in shouts.

> An avalanche of exuberant life seemed to have fallen from the glacier summits of the Sabbath, and scattered itself over the Green. The boys leaped and whooped towards the Meeting-house, flung their hats into the air, chased one another in a sort of stampede.

Short-lived games of ball, tag, hide-and-seek were begun. A six-year-old of more solitary habits might go down to the barn and sail chips in the horse tank,[32] or might have time for a walk to the top of the hill in pursuit of the departed sun. There he could see the brilliant pageant of the distant clouds, "some in flocky rosettes, others in broad, many-folded collops." As Margaret saw the scene,

> There were clouds, to her eye, like fishes, the horned-pout, with its pearly iridine breast, and iron-brown back; floating after it was a shiner with its bright golden armory; she saw the blood-red fins of the yellow-perch, the long snout of the pickerel with its glancing black eye, and the gaudy tail of the trout.*

Then, while the sun "weltered in ruddiness" and sank for a second time,

> the fishes swam away with the sun, and plunged down the cataract of light that falls over the other side of the earth; and the broad massive clouds grew darker and grimmer, and extended themselves, like huge-breasted lions couchant which the Master had told her about, to watch all night near the gate of the sun.

The sun that presided over Sunday was gone. Deep in the woods a woodpecker "rapped and rattled over among the Chesnuts." "A black-cap k' d' chanked, k' d' chanked over her head, and a wood-thrush whoot whoot whooted, ting a ring tinged in earnest unison. 'We are going to have a meeting here to-day. . .won't you stop?'" (119-20, 106).

For the Judd boys the few minutes of evening exhilaration were soon over. As the sheep bells tinkled from the pasture, unwilling bare feet dragged inside for the last time. There a quick meal of bread and milk with perhaps an Indian pudding awaited them. Bedtime came early.

No one kissed them goodnight. No one kissed children. So far as could be publicly ascertained, there was no kissing in Westhampton.[33]

---

*cf. Emerson, "Nature," *Works*, I, 17: "The long slender bars of cloud float like fishes in the sea of crimson light. From the earth, as a shore, I look out into that silent sea."

Part II

East of Eden

5

Northampton in the 1820's

For the Judd family, as for the rest of the nation and the world, the years around 1820 were a time of endings and new beginnings.

The year 1820 was perhaps of particular significance for young Sylvester Judd because it brought the reality of change home to him in a personal way. Parson Hale had often spoken of death and of heaven,—indeed, the fact of death seemed more central to orthodox religion than the possibility of love—but Sylvester did not really know about death. In 1818, at age four, he had lost an uncle, his father's brother Hophni, a Williams College graduate. But Hophni had been away in Northampton, where he had set up as law partner of a future U.S. Senator, Isaac C. Bates, and as proprietor of the influential *Hampshire Gazette;* and young Sylvester rarely saw him. Shortly after the uncle's death, Sylvester acquired a new brother, also named Hophni, as a symbol of the turning of the wheel of life.

In the presence of little Hophni's babble and antics, it was difficult to restrain a smile even on the Sabbath. He and his father were close. Hophni had the treat of being fed by his father at the table and followed him wherever he could, in the house or around the store. Hop and six-year-old Ves were of a kind. Both had flaxen hair, blue eyes, a quick intelligence, and "feelings easily excited to joy, grief or anger." Ves, watching the unfolding body and mind of his little brother, found the winter and spring of 1820 interesting. Before long, Hop could "say *pa* and *ma*, and could imitate the sounds of many animals, sing and read in imitation of others, but could not articulate words."[1] With his bright ways, Sabbaths in the Judd household lost some of their mournful aspect.

The Judds knew how to laugh, and young Ves acquired his father's sense of humor in double measure, as his novels reveal. Once, perhaps about the time that Hop and Sylvester were following their father around the store, a stranger came into the Judd store in Westhampton, claiming he could locate gold with a witch hazel wand. While the diviner was out getting a sprig of witch hazel, father Judd changed the money drawer from its accustomed place. With a crowd of men, women, and children watching, the diviner moved gravely round and round the room with his crotched stick, stopping frequently, balancing the stick delicately. Finally, he came to rest in front of the spot where the money drawer had been, teetering back and forth, his rod pulsating. "There," he cried out, "there is the money, see how the rod moves." Loud laughter poured out as Judd produced the money from its new spot across the store. Young Sylvester took note, and later included in *Margaret* a search with a divining rod for buried treasure.[2]

But the year 1820 had other mysteries to reveal besides buried gold. Shortly after Sylvester's seventh birthday, Hop was taken ill. The disease was swift, and in a few days Hophni was dead. The date was August 18, 1820; the boy was twenty months old. Sylvester watched. If it could happen to Hophni, it could happen to anyone, even to himself. Grandmother Judd, at sixty-six, was visibly declining. On January 27, 1821, she died. Of her eleven children, Grandmother Judd had buried all but four, and Sylvester II had been the only son left. Death was common. But it seemed so particular with young Ves because there is a first time, and a second. Who would be next?

Henceforward, death would be near to the imagination. The ancient litany of bright hopes blasted—the grass withered, the flower faded—had rung from the pulpit; now it echoed in the ears. It was necessary always to be prepared for death, lest it catch one unawares. To the Christian, holiness was almost synonymous with a consciousness of death's imminence. The more zealous he was, the more likely to incline toward morbidity. Hence, there was a fascination with lengthy death scenes in the novels and poems of the day, in Arethusa Hall's biography of Sylvester Judd III, in one or two of father Judd's journal entries, and in the fiction of his son.

In 1837, on his twenty-fourth birthday, young Sylvester, who in another month would hear the bracing tonic of Emerson's "American Scholar" address, recorded in his journal, "Twenty four. Shall I live to record Twenty five. Hope I may." Ten months later, ill but braced, he entered in his journal: "This may be my last record here. I fear not death,—can cheerfully commend my soul to God. World,—I can bid it farewell." In one of his early sermons he let fall that "I sometimes ask myself the question, If I were to die today, should I, too, be forgotten to-morrow?" And in 1852, confronted by Ralph Waldo Emerson in Augusta, Maine, with the question "Who are your companions?" Judd answered, "Sunsets"; then, pressed for an answer less oracular and Emersonian, he said, "I am a priest and converse with the sick and dying." Emerson, who knew something about death too but whose heaven had a great deal of earth in it, told him, "Yes, very well, if people were sick and died to any purpose; but as far as I had observed, they were quite as frivolous as the rest, and ... a man peremptorily needed now and then a reasonable word or two."[3]

The powers of regeneration had a way of reasserting themselves. "Though the grass withereth and the flower fadeth, the word of the Lord endureth forever." Or, as Sylvester Judd wrote in *Margaret*, "There is more in churning than most people think of. Time is regenerative, and new births occur every hour. The gritty Earth, alumen and silex spring up in dream-like beauty" (234). On October 27, 1820, Apphia Judd, who was tougher than she seemed, survived the terrors of another childbirth in the big white house and presented the Judd boys with their first sister, also named Apphia. Perhaps the combination of circumstances produced in Ves a special solicitude for his sister. She was the one who was nearest to him in his later years, who followed him to Augusta and married his wife's brother.

The events of death and childbirth in 1820 combined to have a salutary effect on Ves's father: "These events tended to soften my feelings, to mitigate uneasiness on account of losses, to place little dependence on anything beneath the sun, and to wean me from earthly pleasures." Through the winter he turned to reading theology in Greek, Latin, and English, but without obtaining a "saving hope" of election. Then in the spring the depleted ranks of the Judd household enlarged again. Squire Judd moved into the town center with his son's family.[4]

The wheel had come full circle. But it did not stop. The great age of change lay just in the offing. The smashing of father Judd's hopes that was driving him outward into the world seemed symbolic of that fact. His life in Westhampton, from 1789 to 1822, was lived during the age of consolidation that followed the Revolution. Now the forces of change, always present, would speed up to the tempo that gave the nineteenth century its distinctive character as an age of transition.

The ending of the so-called "era of good feeling" and the rise of the Jacksonian democratic turbulence coincided almost exactly with the passing of the town elders in Northampton and Westhampton. The Judds fled from Westhampton, and young Sylvester's secure and unified childhood world was broken. Religious dissension tore Northampton and Westhampton into contending factions.

Sylvester would learn that he had a choice of what religion to believe. Hitherto religion had been deterministic, an inheritance, a matter for official sanction by family, society, and even state. In the religious sphere and in the economic, monopolistic grants of power by the government had been taken for granted. Some people could scarcely conceive of any other way. Now religion was to become disestablished, an individual matter. Free will and free choice would reign, and the open marketplace of ideas would match the open marketplace of economic life. The American pattern of competing churches would replace the inherited European pattern of religious monopoly.

At the same time, the great economic-political issue of the day was the fight against monopoly; the monopoly of power by the property holders was broken up and the vote given to the multitude; corporation charters were given out freely to anyone who wanted them and thus ceased to be monopoly grants; Andrew Jackson fought bank monopoly. Whole new industries appeared: textiles, railroads, canals. A canal was built from New Haven to Northampton, and enthusiasts talked of putting a canal across the Berkshires to connect with the Erie Canal, or even a canal to the St. Lawrence.[5] The democratic yeast fermented.

Some called it progress; some called it chaos. Nearly all would have mixed emotions as familiar ways broke apart and new paths opened. The revival, hailed by the conservatives as the instrument for regenerating and preserving old ways, fell into the hands of strange and uncouth enthusiasts, in Westhampton as well as in the towns ignited by the Finneyite flame from New York state, and the revival itself became a sword that divided families and towns into competing factions. It had happened before, in the days of Jonathan Edwards, George Whitefield, and the Tennents.

In later life, the Rev. Sylvester Judd would himself not quite know what to make of it all. A man who had been swept along not once but several times, in revival experiences, he would reject the revival as an institution. A man who had rebelled against the inheritance of his family's religion, who had rejected predestination and embraced the principle of free will, he would in later life talk about the need for religious unity in the family and of "training up children" so they would not leave the family religious heritage. A maverick and almost an outcast, in a tiny and despised sect, a practitioner of "the dissidence of dissent," he would talk about the need for religious unity, of bringing all sects together.

In 1821, when grandfather Judd moved into the house opposite the church, Sylvester's world seemed unified and secure. But the first cracks in the monolithic edifice were even then appearing. The Unitarian enemy, which had been, as the orthodox put it, creeping stealthily through the land for decades past, taking over church after church without a shot fired, had been driven into the open in 1815 with the publication of Thomas Belsham's pamphlet; and in 1819 William Ellery Channing had run up the Unitarian flag openly with his famous Baltimore sermon.[6] It was a manifesto, a rallying point, and henceforth the battles would be pitched ones. The story of the battle as it was fought from 1815 to 1830 was told in a pair of polemical pamphlets published in 1830-1831[7] that Sylvester Judd III later read, marked, and had bound in leather.

The revival of 1816 had been an initial victory in the war against infidelity, a rallying of the faithful. Made confident by success, the orthodox ministers united to press their advantage. There were several efforts in Massachusetts to imitate Connecticut's crushing of the heretics by concerted action. But when the ministers attempted to unite and to increase the power of the county ministerial associations to act against Unitarians in their midst, the Unitarians rose up and cried, Tyranny! A threat to "liberty and the rights of conscience."[8] The autonomy of the local church was a principle of Congregationalism; and when whole churches went Unitarian, claiming that they were still good Congregationalists but had a right to the free exercise of their own opinions, there was little that orthodox outsiders could do about it but look on in impotent rage. Worse yet, when a church split in two, the Unitarians claimed the church building and other property whenever they outnumbered the orthodox remnant. The courts backed up the Unitarians, and the orthodox party in such a church lost the visible symbol of its claim to be the true First Church in its town.

In 1821 young Sylvester Judd probably did not know anything about Unitarianism, although liberal tendencies had penetrated as far as Northampton. There, some of the wealthiest members of the orthodox church were heretics, in a minority and politely biding their time. There were no Unitarians making trouble in Westhampton, but parson Hale knew all about the problem. In 1815 he had served as one of seven ministers on a state-wide committee to consider a plan for uniting against the Unitarians.[9] Apparently, however, he cherished a certain respect for the Congregationalist principle of local autonomy, for the committee rejected the plan; and when the Westhampton church was asked in 1818 to join in a Hampshire County plan of union, Westhampton declined.

But in 1821-1822, just as eight-year-old Sylvester Judd was joining for the first time in the annual catechism drills in the church, Westhampton joined with the rest of Hampshire County in the battle against infidelity and sin. There could be no dissent from the crowd as one boy after the other swung out of line "*a la militaire*" to discharge the verbal bullets of the Westminster Shorter Catechism. There was a war on, and henceforward no sensitive young boy could grow to manhood without being touched by it. Unitarians like Bernard Whitman and William Ellery Channing could talk of the dangers of "human creeds" and of an enforced conformity all they wanted: the creed was the divine truth, and conformity to it was the only path to salvation.

In 1821 reports of still another revival came up the Connecticut Valley from New Haven. A chief concern of the promoters of the revival was for greater discipline in the churches, more "system." By "discipline" they meant that churches should purify themselves and "cut off those offending members, who by their vices, brought scandal on the Christian name."[10]

Westhampton and the rest of Hampshire County were already responding to the call for purification. On February 6, 1821, the Hampshire Association of Congregational Churches and Ministers met at South Deerfield and voted to cut off the Rev. Winthrop Bailey from its fellowship. A committee had found his doctrines unsatisfactory.[11]

Three months later the Association struck again. When the Rev. Dan Huntington of Hadley, which was within walking distance of Northampton, refused to come to the carpet for questioning, the Association excluded him from its fellowship. Eight months later, as the Judds were preparing to leave Westhampton, the Association, with Enoch Hale playing his usual weighty part, succeeded in preventing the ordination at Phillipston of a new minister whose doctrines were unsatisfactory.[12]

These events were still at some distance from young Sylvester Judd in 1821, but other issues were fought out on Westhampton and Northampton soil within earshot of his bedroom. Before 1821 the church had met twice a year with routine placidity to settle the arrangements for the summer Sabbath schools. Now the church began considering the matter of church discipline, of censuring offending members—whether their vices be rum, fornication, or rebellion against established doctrine and authority. This same battle was being fought with even greater intensity in Northampton, where there was more point to measures against heresy; and when the Judds moved to Northampton in 1822 it was like stepping into a performance of the same play with a different cast.

In both towns the weapon being prepared by the orthodox against the liberals in 1821 was the creed. It was easy enough to bar the communion table to new applicants of uncertain piety, but it was hard to deal with those already admitted who had become lax in their doctrines. Another problem was what to do with applicants for membership who had letters of transfer from other churches, churches that were part of the loose confederation called Congregational but that were hazy in doctrine or even avowedly Unitarian. The solution was to administer the Confession of Faith to those transferring by letter, just as if they were new converts. Westhampton went even farther: the church voted to require every member to assent to the Confession of Faith and to the Covenant every three years. Under Enoch Hale's leadership, the Westminster Catechism was made the official "basis of union" of all the churches in the Hampshire Association.[13] If there had been any doubt before, there could be no doubt in the future.

What the Sylvester Judds were seeing was a loyalty-oath program, designed to bring hidden Unitarians into the open where they could be dealt with, a program much as is frequently adopted in times of crisis, hysteria, and eschatological conflict between God and Satan. As always, it involved a polarization of forces, a sharpening of blurred lines, a changing of flesh-pink into red or white. People pulled apart from each other in a general scramble to prove their innocence by dissociation. The pressures to conform intensified. It was a bit like the 1920's, or 1950's, those other postwar periods of commercial expansion and ideological contraction. In Westhampton, in 1822, big brothers were appointed to give "benevolent care" to the town. By "benevolent care" the Westhampton Church meant that the brethren should "watch over each other and admonish one another as there is occasion in the Lord."[14] (At age thirteen, Ves Judd would himself catch the fever and would admonish his playmates and younger brothers to seek diligently after salvation.)

Excessive drunkenness—hitherto not regarded as particularly sinful—Sabbath-breaking, and heresy were to be cleansed from the land. The result was a series of accusations, trials, excommunications, and secessions. In 1822 Squire Judd assisted in bringing a young man to justice for "gross lewdness" with a member of his household. The church fathers began meeting, not every six months but every week. The dry church records still crackle with the charged atmosphere. The trial was ecclesiastical rather than civil, a matter for the whole church to vote on, not to be discreetly hushed up. The culprit was convicted by a divided vote. Then drunkards and Sabbath-breakers were called to account. The thing that was new was not sin, but that something was being done about it. Also new was the rebelliousness of the sinners. Three of them refused to repent, despite repeated admonishings, and finally were excommunicated.[15]

As the Judds moved to Northampton in 1822, they found the same drama being enacted there with an even larger cast of drunkards, adulterers, and Sabbath-breakers. One Kentfield, who might well have served as a model for profane and jolly Pluck Hart in *Margaret,* was labored with repeatedly for his profaneness and Sabbath-breaking. He was asked "if he could not trust the never failing Bank of faith." He "replied (in a light manner) that Bank would not furnish Rye for his family—but his days work would produce him 2 Bushels."[16]

Sylvester Judd later commented on such incidents in *Margaret* and poured his scorn upon attempts to force people to be good. He wrote, "'The sense of right becomes the author of innumerable wrong'" (249). Pluck Hart, Margaret's foster father, is put in the stocks for hunting a cow on the Sabbath and as a result becomes confirmed in his anti-religious ways. Judd wrote a perceptive diagnosis of the disease that had destroyed the peace of Westhampton and Northampton: "'Dissonance and disorder are themselves sympathetic and reciprocal. Aversion reproduces aversion, and selfishness is answered by selfishness.'" "'It is ever Nature *versus* the Unnatural. The institutions and organizations of men, founded upon the new basis, partake of the general corruption, and only foster evils it is their design to prevent'" (249).

The incidents of *Margaret* illustrate this point at every turn. For example, the secondary heroine is a fallen lady named Rose. Judd delighted in making her the daughter of an orthodox minister. Having been seduced by an elegant stranger from New York, she is condemned to wear a scarlet letter. The result is disastrous. Her father is driven from his pulpit and into a grave. Friends and even her sister desert her and doors slam shut. Distracted, rebellious, atheistic, she flees the town. She wallows in self-loathing and hatred for others, believing herself damned, as indeed her father's doctrine has taught. Only the ministrations of natural-hearted Margaret and of a Unitarian minister are able to recall her to her true self.

Judd also commented on heresy hunts. Margaret loses her job as schoolmistress because she will not teach the

children the Calvinist creed. Judd had himself lost a job as
schoolteacher for similar reasons. The church, as Judd saw
it, had fallen from its primitive simplicity into a tangle of
man-made creeds and systems. This was the Fall: not that
man was depraved by nature, but that he was corrupted by
the System. "'And they have carried this matter [of creeds]
so far, as to condemn a man to everlasting perdition if he
depart from these Gospel-substitutes. You may examine
them and canvass their qualities, you will find no more
Christianity in any one of them than apple-juice in that
stone'" (251).

Judd's words were written from personal knowledge
and experience. The systematic censoriousness of 1822
only introduced in Westhampton a spirit of backbiting and
dissension that tore apart Enoch Hale's Eden. The frantic
effort to hold on to the past only accelerated the movement toward change. Unity, peace, and the triumph of
God's kingdom had never seemed closer than in 1820
when the fruits of the revival were being reaped. In a few
years Northampton would be torn apart by one religious
explosion after another, and in Westhampton Enoch Hale
would, in his old age, see the edifice he had built come
crumbling about his knees.

On March 29, 1822, father Judd made the long-expected
break with Westhampton. His wife and children followed
him to Northampton in May. His sister-in-law, Arethusa,
who had been away for six months visiting relatives, joined
them. Squire Judd remained behind in the house by the
church, and his daughter, Hannah Lyman, and her children
came to live with him. Storekeeper Judd had wound up
his business less disastrously than he had feared; he had
pared his $8,000 debt, paid off most of his creditors; the
Squire had absorbed his son's loss of $2,457.[17] Judd thus
stepped from the wreckage with his reputation and his
credit intact.

In Northampton, a town of 2,854 population in 1820, he acquired a business of some consequence. His brother Hophni had left a quarter interest in the *Hampshire Gazette*. With the Squire's help, Judd bought the other three-quarters and became editor and sole proprietor of the most influential newspaper in Western Massachusetts. Under Judd's able editorship, the paper became a force of enlightenment, characterized by a lofty detachment from political and religious squabbles. Judd was conservative enough to win the confidence of his readers, progressive enough to lead them in such matters as temperence reform, astute enough to have occasional tidbits like statistics on crime and prostitution in London for his readers to cluck their tongues over. Under Judd the circulation doubled, and the *Gazette* became the second "most widely circulated paper in the state." Probably this claim did not include the big Boston dailies. There was a saying in Northampton that to amount to anything socially a man had to own a plot of meadow land, have a pew in the orthodox church, and subscribe to the *Gazette*.[18] Eagerly awaited each week, the *Gazette* was read aloud in the kitchen, where children crept up around the chair to hear.

Father Judd's new occupation enabled him to turn his love of reading to some account. A newspaper in those days was a scissors-and-paste job composed of extracts from books, magazines, and other newspapers with only incidental attention to local news. For years, father Judd had been gathering miscellaneous knowledge from books, newspapers, old records; had been compiling a kind of encyclopedia for his own use. Now he could collect extracts in the *Gazette* and be paid for doing what he most enjoyed. He was already beginning his antiquarian researches into Northampton history, interviewing elderly townspeople and copying old documents. The result was a legacy to future historians of about seventy-five manuscript volumes. Some of his lore he published in the paper.

His novel-writing son shared some of his interest and later got from his father a great many of the facts about costumes and customs that freighted the pages of *Margaret* with a weight of detail almost too great to be borne. Father Judd had little use for fiction. The only novels in his house were *Eliza Wharton* and *Clarissa Harlowe*.[19] Facts were what he wanted. A bit prosaic and literal minded, he was later to record as his one comment on *The House of the Seven Gables* that it was a "base attempt of Hathorne to cover with disgrace and infamy the old and respectable family of Pynchons of Springfield."[20] He was not ignorant of the literary world. One of his first issues printed on the front page an article about Sir Walter Scott. He reprinted acute reviews of such novels as *The Pilot* by Cooper. But Judd also printed the comment,

> There is in works of fiction, as in gaming, a kind of fascination which, where nothing comes in to break the charm, lures on the victim till his mind has become so stupified and deadened by dissipation, that he can find no enjoyment but in this morbid and feverish excitement.[21]

But such fulminations as these from press and pulpit could not stop the spread of the morbid fever and excitement. In Northampton was a band of sophisticates led by Mrs. Joseph Lyman, who read modern poetry and novels such as those by Scott and Cooper. Mrs. Lyman had been raised near Boston and was a Unitarian.[22] Her husband was bank president and judge. The Lymans were the leaders of the group of liberals whose wealth, culture, and charm put them at the pinnacle of Northampton society and who were still members in the old church, biding their time. The infection of novel reading later would spread even to Judd's own family, especially to his son Sylvester, who, when he was sixteen years old and away from home, voraciously read novels of which his father would scarcely have approved.

Editor Judd mixed in among the news from abroad—about famine, pestilence, war, and prostitution in wicked Europe—items that revealed his crotchets, convictions, and hobbies. Popery, strong drink, atheism, war, Mormonism, and Fanny Wright's feminism came in for attacks. But Judd was fair-minded and often printed both sides of a question, even such a one as Mormonism.[23] He put truth above party.

> He [editor Judd] was so good a man—clean in character, pure in thought, moderate in opinion, exact in statement,—that the people came to place the most implicit confidence in him and his paper. They believed every word he said; and their confidence was not misplaced.

> He published no stories and no gossip. . . . While his paper supported with moderation the Federal and Whig cause, it yet treated all parties with candor and fairness.[24]

In an original article, Judd attacked frippery and fashion, calling for simple living as the answer to hard times. Judd disliked popular excitements and had a special scorn for Independence-Day celebrations, parades, and kowtowing to famous visitors. "Shams and shows" in education, church, and state were one of Judd's pet topics of conversation. In his private diary and letters father Judd became savage on the subject of Fourth-of-July whoopee, heathen Christmas celebrations, and Episcopalians. He reported that he would not stir out of doors to see any man living. When the Marquis de Lafayette came to Northampton in 1825 and was met by a parade that Northampton still talked about fifty years later, Judd dutifully reported the events; but later when Henry Clay came to Northampton, Judd did not bother to go see him, as he noted with evident self-satisfaction.[25] Editor Judd was stern, rock-ribbed Yankee, independent to the core.

Judd's son Sylvester would grow up to share some of his father's attitudes, such as his feelings on war, intemperance, shams and shows, fashion, militia training and the Fourth of July, the vice of cities; but on other issues, particularly feminism, novels, Episcopalianism, and Christmas, he was at odds with his father.

To one raised in frugal Westhampton, it would appear that there were plenty of shams and shows in Northampton, a multiplicity of things to widen the eyes of a boy from the country like Ves Judd, and some of them were advertised in the pages of the *Gazette*. On March 20, 1822, it was announced that a dancing school would open in the ballroom of Oliver Warner's hotel, literally under the shadow of the white church steeple. On April 24 the front page advertised the great annual cattle show for the following October. Before 1818 there had been no cattle shows. The pens for hogs, cattle, sheep, turkeys, and hens were erected on the green in the town center, right by the *Gazette* office. Perhaps young Sylvester heard such pitchmen as the vendor of patent medicines; a professor selling magic soap that would make greasy coat collars better than new and charm the elves into laying up a stone wall overnight; hawkers of yellow gingerbread, cheese, and whips; or the oyster man who chanted in front of his tent: "Walk up, roll up, tumble up, any way to get up! Up here you have your fine, hot oysters."[26]

Theatrical entertainments were very rare and usually had to masquerade as edification. In 1818 a travelling magician had billed his show as "Philosophical Experiments." The public was ill-equipped to draw the line between science and magic; a scientific demonstration such as that of "exhilarating gas" seemed no less wonderful than magic, especially since it seemed to duplicate many of the effects of the revival going on at that time. There were the advertisements for patent medicines: aromatic snuff, "an infallible remedy for recent catarrh.... an almost certain specific against contagion." For purposes of show there were silks for rustling dresses, millinery for Sabbath display. There was even a painter of portraits who set up shop in 1822-1823. Northampton, with not quite 3,000 population, kept up its outward appearances by maintaining dry goods stores and tailors, three hatters, a furrier, jewelers and goldsmiths, and a barber shop redolent of mysterious powders and toilet waters, a place that later figured in Judd's *Margaret* as part of the contrast of the natural with the artificial. For the inner man there were a bookstore and two drugstores.[27]

Northampton blended the natural and the artificial in a pleasing way that made it one of the showplaces of New England. The open green square lined with elms and stores, the roofs of which were covered with moss and slanted quaintly toward the street, was dominated by the white church, which served the largest congregation in New England. It was one of Asher Benjamin's classic patterns. Eight Doric columns on the portico supported a bell tower with a three-sided clock. Every evening at nine the bell rang, and guests in homes got up to go. On the new courthouse and on the mansion houses which jutted from the verdure of Round Hill, to the west, were other Greek columns, white painted and brilliant in the morning sun.[28]

Tourists enjoyed rambles on the hill, from which they could look east to the Connecticut Valley, to Mount Holyoke, whence they saw spread out the famous Oxbow panorama made memorable by Thomas Cole's painting of 1836. George Bancroft, fresh from the grand tour of Europe, who moved to Northampton in 1823 to begin his notable career as educator, historian, and politician, wrote to President Kirkland of Harvard: "But I believe, were I always to have a meadow like this of Northampton before me, and such graceful mountains, I should forget that Aetna has its volcanoes and Lydia it' sands."[29] It was no wonder that tourists sometimes came back to Northampton to retire; that Northampton became the seat of fashionable private schools, a water cure establishment, and a college; and that Jenny Lind, when she had the world in her hand in 1852, chose Northampton for her extended honeymoon.

The beautiful exterior of Northampton, though flawed occasionally in the winter by horse dung thrown from stables into the streets and left there until spring,[30] was matched by elegant interiors.

Young Sylvester Judd, used to an unheated church, was doubtless pleased by the innovation of stoves, installed in 1820. The choir numbered 125 voices, had a conductor, and an accompaniment on flute and violin. Conservatives like Solomon Williams, the church's elderly minister, had opposed such worldly shows. Overruled, he was not silent on Sunday: "The choir will fiddle and sing the Eighteenth Psalm," he announced from the pulpit.[31]

There was also music and elegance in private homes. Judge Lyman's wife was not only beautiful, intellectual, and gracious; she played one of Northampton's two pianos, and the music was not always religious. Every night before putting the children to bed she played the "Copenhagen Waltz" and the "Battle of Prague" with variations.[32] Homes such as hers were carpeted and filled with works of art, tastefully chosen, and made a pleasant contrast to the sand-strewn, barren homes of Westhampton; but, to strict Puritans, art, music, and literature were worldly entice-ments. Carpets were virtually unheard of in the frugal towns of backwoods New England. Lyman Beecher, father of Harriet Beecher Stowe, told this story on himself. As a preacher in a small Long Island parish in the early 1800's, he installed a carpet in the parsonage. The first parishioner to call at the door eyed the carpet apprehensively. "Come in, come in," boomed Beecher. "Can't, 'thout stepping on't," came the response.[33]

Sylvester Judd as a boy was much like his later heroine Margaret and his hero Richard Edney: a lad from the country, good-hearted, earnest, intelligent, and well-read, but nonetheless a naif, on the outside looking in. Thus began an important tension in Judd's life. On the one hand Judd followed his father in a rejection of frippery, fashion, gossip, and the big city. But on the other hand his destiny was to acquire a genteel spouse and enter the world of pianos, French wallpaper, cut glass, and carpets.

Father Judd wanted none of it. Although his family, his accomplishments, and his position entitled him to an entree in the best circles, he could not be bothered with mere society. His wife was an imperfectly educated,[34] often tired homebody, not at ease in drawing rooms, and the house her husband provided her did nothing to increase her worldly self-confidence or that of her children. "Very poor looking floors remained bare of carpets, and furniture, very ordinary at first, now old and defaced . . . not a picture adorned the walls, nor was there a single ornament by which the eye could be refreshed." Since her husband had no sanctum he could call his own at the *Gazette,* his books and exchange newspapers cluttered the front room at the house and flowed in disarray across the desk there. He liked to work among his family: before the fire in the front room while his wife knitted and the children made candy in the other room "with their usual uproar," or before the big hearth in the kitchen where his wife cooked corn beef hash or knuckle of veal and dumplings. This practice of writing with the family in the same room was also followed by his son Sylvester in later years.[35]

Though father Judd mingled with men of the world in the course of his business, his wife and her sister Arethusa gave up society after the first few formal calls. Unlike the self-reliant editor who "rather gloried in setting at naught the common conventionalities of society"[36] and who was so little a disciple of Benjamin Franklin that he stated his convictions even more strongly when contradicted, the women were sensitive about their outward appearances. Arethusa thirsted for some of the shams and shows which were denied her. There were dances, singing schools, and Fourth-of-July tea parties in elegant gardens, another innovation begun in 1820. At Judge Lyman's house in 1826, the fashionable liberals thronged to a daring dramatic performance of Scott's *Lady of the Lake*, in which the lovely Mrs. Lyman and other village belles together with the finest young men from Judge Samuel Howe's law school took leading roles. No one recorded whether Edward Dickinson, one of the non-Unitarian young men at the law school and later to become Emily's father, attended the production. We do know that Judge Lyman and Judge Howe pronounced the acting better than that on any stage in New York or Boston, and that the neighbors talked about it for years.[37]

Mrs. Judd, her sister Arethusa, and the Judd children had been plunged from a position at the pinnacle of Westhampton society to the status of self-conscious indigents, and they felt cruelly left out of things. Since, as Arethusa reported, she was too proud to associate with those of lower social rank and culture, "she felt lonely, desolate, . . . irritable and most unhappy."[38] That young Sylvester was also sensitive to the changed social position of the family, that he felt keenly his new role as an outsider pressing his nose against the glass can be surmised from a later statement he made:

> All my youth centres in Westhampton. Northampton is nothing to me. I seem never to have *lived* there. In Westhampton I did live. I could die there. Its hills, its meagreness, its people, all have an interest for me.[39]

For those denied the pleasures of fashionable interiors, there were places outside to lure a person from the center of the wheel, where God and the self were at one, to its circumference. Presumably none of the Judd women or children was well acquainted with Northampton's thirteen barrooms, and Father Judd had given up strong drink in 1820,[40] but the veranda of Oliver Warner's hotel was a news-and-gossip mill, a crossroads of two stagecoach routes. Every evening at about sunset the stagecoach from Boston would sound its bugle horn as it crossed the Connecticut River bridge in the distance. To a stagecoach enthusiast like Judge Joseph Lyman, who lived nearby, it "was like martial music to a war-horse." Out he ran to find what new visitors were in town and to get the news from Boston. "With a shining countenance, he would return and tell of the fine people who had arrived; how he had offered his carriage and horses to Mr. A., or Mrs. B. and her daughters, to go up the mountain next day." Extroverted Judge Lyman frequently brought home one of them as his guest, and Oliver Warner complained that he could not make a profit as long as Judge Lyman ran a free hotel. The stagecoach driver was entrusted with important errands to fetch items in Boston and was a personage of intense interest to young boys. He never made lists of his errands and his memory was infallible, except for the one time when he forgot and left his wife behind in Boston.[41] In his novel *Richard Edney,* Sylvester Judd followed Dickens' *Pickwick Papers* in a portrayal of the winking, jolly, nearly omniscient stagecoach driver, named Winkle, who carried billet-doux and "ran express between Hearts." He bowed to everybody as his stagecoach passed, to children, young ladies, old men; and everybody bowed back, smiling. "In addition, and notwithstanding Mr. St. John, he gave little gratuitous rides; he let the boys hang on behind."

Then he carried the mail, which is itself a small universe in a leather bag;—here sweet spring to some bleak and ice-bound soul,—at the next turn a black thunder-storm on some tranquil household; —now singing at one corner of its mouth, as if it was full of Jenny Linds,—anon tromboning out its melancholy intelligence; and, like a Leyden jar on wheels, giving everybody a shock as it passes, making some laugh and others scream.[42]

In Winkle was epitomized a world, the world of Irving's *Sketch Book,* of the leisurely but bustling small town.

Northampton was the county seat, and the courthouse was another scene of excitement. The old one burned down in November, 1822, and all the boys ran to see the "Damper" and the "Whale" pumped by the competing groups of volunteers. In 1823 the project of building both a new courthouse and a town hall were occasions of considerable interest. When completed, the courthouse continued to attract hangers-on. Lawyers and law students from Northampton's Unitarian-tinged law school, established 1823, mingled with those who had a thirst for drama. Trials were a chief form of entertainment. In 1806 a famous murder trial and execution had attracted 15,000 spectators. Editor Judd, who thought a newspaper had other functions than sensationalism, stayed away from the courthouse for several years, although he served twice on the grand jury and went as a spectator to a trial for murder and one for rape. Then as his interest in Northampton history increased, he spent many hours among the courthouse records discussing current affairs with others of the "Court House party"—including some of the eminent Unitarians, one of whom, Samuel F. Lyman, was destined to help young Sylvester Judd on his way into the Unitarian ministry.[43]

Young Judd apparently knew something of trials, jails, gossip, and executions. Two of the scenes in *Margaret* take place at a jail similar to the one in Northampton, and chief events in the plot of the novel include the trial and execution of Margaret's foster brother Chilion. One of the most vivid chapters dramatizes the bloodthirsty gossip and disputations of the courthouse crowd just before the trial. Judd the preacher would devote some of his reforming zeal to penology, sensing the folly of mere punishment.

Other shows in Northampton included the training days, colorful, drunken occasions. In the fall the companies mustered on Gallows Plain for a sham fight. Father Judd commented, "a contemptible affair. A company dressed and painted like Indians, acted their part tolerably well." On May Day there was artillery practice. Boys later dug the balls from the hillside for playthings or found ones in the distance that had gone over the top of the hill.[44]

Young Sylvester Judd saw these scenes and learned from them to associate soldiering with drunkenness. In *Margaret* the training day was one of debauchery, sanctioned by prayer to Jehovah. Judd etched the scene with the realism of a Hogarth. Children bought gingerbread, pitched pennies, and mimicked their elders. Later, while men got drunk, "boys crept under the legs of the soldiers, and lifting up the pails, tugged at the slops; little children on their bellies lapped the gutters, and sucked the grass, where the liquor fell." In the evening "lights blinked and glowed from booth to booth. The black shadows of men showed unearthly, like demons in a pit. Boys yelled their excitement, Indian-like, across the Green. Horses breaking loose, plunged madly through the crowd." Old toper Pluck Hart pressed the liquor mug to eight-year-old Margaret's lips: "'won't you drink a little, now do drink a little. See how it creams; don't be snuffy, Molly, none of your mulligrubs'" (99). Pluck ended the day with an attack of delirium tremens. This passage, like others, proved too much for Judd's more queasy readers, and in the second edition it was toned down by judicious omissions. It would be impossible to know whether Judd's self-censorship was motivated by respect for propriety or respect for truth. Still, it might be noted that Northampton's 3,000 people supported thirteen taverns in addition to the kegs of rum in grocery and drug stores, where about every third charge went for liquor,[45] a fact which came in for some notice in *Margaret.*

It was apparent that young Sylvester Judd saw more with his wide eyes than Arethusa Hall in her genteel biography wanted to admit. To Arethusa, Sylvester was her golden-haired boy, half son and half brother: "There was an originality, a quickness of perception, a facility of acquisition, and an indication of reserved power, which, added to a loveliness of nature, especially attracted me to him." In 1824 they both left home and together attended school at Westfield Academy, near Springfield. Judd competed in Latin, composition, and elocution with boys much older than himself who were preparing for college. His first composition was submitted for Arethusa's inspection. It was good but very short. Asked why he did not write more, "he very naively replied, 'because he was afraid he should not have anything left to say in the next one.'"[46]

Both Arethusa and Sylvester won distinction for their scholarship and their charm. The boys voted Arethusa the second most beautiful girl in her class. Sylvester was awarded parts to speak in the public exhibition, and the kindly minister who headed the school remarked that it was a pleasure to teach Sylvester because he never made the same mistake twice. Sylvester learned the savor of feminine approval too. Arethusa recorded:

> He was at that time a bright, pleasant-looking boy, gentle in his manners, and very obliging in his disposition. He became quite a *pet* with the young ladies of the school, much older than himself, who used to gather around, and make him the subject of their caresses.

It was an innocent age in which people did not know what fire they played with. Judd's temperament was volatile and ardent, and his parents were not demonstrative in their affection. Arethusa wrote that "with him almost every emotion was a passion," "his susceptibilities were quick and tender," his face at times was "radiant with a refined and spiritual beauty," and his more nervous states of mind were "as purely physical and beyond control as the electric shock consequent upon seizing the poles of a voltaic battery."[47] In this period at Westfield Academy when he was the center of the circle Judd was continuing the transition between childhood Eden and adult awareness.

Judd's earlier schools had not been such idyllic places as Westfield. In the Westhampton school, spelling was the subject emphasized. Arethusa commented "reading was mere jabbering, writing was sufficiently rude, and arithmetic of no value." At the grammar school in Northampton where Sylvester had gone in 1822-23 only the bare rudiments were to be learned. The broken windows and loose clapboards rattled in the winter wind, and the master's switch beat on the scholar's hand and back. Truancy and school-hating replaced study. "For philosophical experiments, the combined skill of the school was employed in constructing a fire of green logs, and keeping it active during the day."[48]

Another survivor of the town school, which was appropriately located near the old jail, supplied further details:

> The prevailing crime of the scholars was whispering, varied by playing 'fox and geese' on rudely constructed lines on the seats, boxing up flies, emptying ink stands upon the smaller boys who sat in front and below the larger boys, throwing paper balls at one another, and, in the winter, clandestinely eating molasses candy.

The teacher, Captain Hutchins, a veteran of the War of 1812, was described as follows:

> No man could now beat his horse as I have seen boys whipped, without being brought before a magistrate to answer for it. For some not very aggravated offence, I have seen a boy severely rawhided, and then placed with his back on the floor, held there

by the master's feet upon his outstretched arms, and a pailful of wet snow thrown slowly by handfuls in his face, till he was well nigh strangled. The terror with which I witnessed this punishment, though then very young, I shall never forget. Another favorite diversion of our master was to take the lobe of the ear between the nails of his thumb and fore-finger and press it till the blood ran, all the while hearing a class recite!

Coughing, an "unpardonable sin," was controlled by tincture of asafoetida, a "nauseous mixture"

administered in the barrel of a huge quill, the head of the unfortunate urchin held back, mouth wide open, and the nose held tightly to compel him to swallow it. The disgusting odor filled the room completely, and would have cured the hysterics of all the women in Hampshire county.

Under such tutelage,

the older scholars grew hardened and brutal, and the younger ones were in constant fear of their violence. . . . Many attempts were made by some of the most desperate boys to fire the building, but it seemed as fire-proof as the rum sold now-a-days.[49]

Young Ves Judd, who was not athletic or robust,[50] could not imitate the rough-and-ready example of his elders, but he could observe. Here he learned the impotence of negative thinking, the inability of force to produce harmony and develop the mind. At Westfield he saw what kindness could do to stimulate a love for knowledge. Westhampton and Northampton, even then engaged in a cold war with the enemy, might have profited by the lesson. The parable of the north wind, the sun, and the traveler's cloak was being enacted in Judd's life, and as he thought about his experience more and more, he decided that he was on the side of the sun.

In 1824 a notable educational experiment in Northampton, a private boarding school, one of the first of the romantic efforts to replace corporal punishment entirely with kindness and persuasion, was just a year old. The Round Hill School was an imaginative adaptation of the

German gymnasium. Joseph Cogswell, Episcopalian, and George Bancroft, Unitarian, were brilliant enough to get away with their medley of unorthodox ideas. Bancroft, not yet become America's first great historian, was shortly to begin the romantic and Jacksonian *History of the United States*; but he so far succeeded in overcoming Northampton's prejudices that he received an invitation to be the principal orator at the great Fourth-of-July celebration of 1826, won a seat in the state legislature in 1830,[51] (despite his leadership of the Jacksonian Democrats), and most important for our purposes acquired a considerable influence over his fellow-historian and friend, Sylvester Judd of the *Hampshire Gazette.*[52] Bancroft and Cogswell were the first to bring a really cosmopolitan culture to parochial Northampton. They were in the first wave of scholars bringing new ideas back from German universities, ideas that were the foundation of the romantic movement in literature, religion, philosophy, and history. Through Bancroft, Northampton was exposed to these ideas at a time when only a handful of people in America knew how to read German books. Within a dozen years, young Sylvester would become one of those who could and did.

Through the small group of Unitarians Northampton was receiving a steady influx of ideas from outside. Bancroft was a frequent visitor at Judge Lyman's house. Catharine Sedgwick, who had just completed the first Unitarian novel of New England life, *A New England Tale* (1822), also made visits there. Later, in September, 1827, Ralph Waldo Emerson spent two weeks with the Lymans and preached in the Unitarian Church.[53] Still later, about the time young Judd turned Unitarian, Lydia Maria Child, who with Sylvester Judd completed New England's trio of romantic Unitarian novelists, set up shop in Northampton. The home of Jonathan Edwards, the bastion of conservatism, was buzzing with liberal heresies.

When Arethusa and Sylvester reluctantly came back from Westfield in 1824, they found Northampton aflame with excitement. The Unitarian party in the old church, which thought it had just won a notable victory for free thought, had instead been handed a humiliating defeat. Worst of all, they believed they had been tricked. Old parson Williams, a beloved but quaintly conservative man with old-fashioned knee breeches and legs like sticks, a man noted for his gifts of new-minted pennies to children,[54] had held the factions together for years. Judge Lyman in particular was attached to him because of the help Williams had given him in his early education. But now Solomon Williams was too old to preach regularly and a "colleague pastor" had to be found to take over the pulpit. All were delighted when young, dashing Mark Tucker came along. The orthodox thought him safely conservative and a zealous orator who could be counted on to whip up the necessary revivals; the Unitarian party thought they detected some liberalism about him and believed they had an understanding with him to let liberal preachers occasionally be heard in the pulpit. At a heated town meeting of February 24, 1824, Tucker received the call to the pulpit with the express proviso, adopted unanimously, "that pious Clergymen of any denomination of Christians might be invited into the desk." The word "might" later became the crux of the issue. The liberals were very pleased with this happy solution which gave them all they could hope for. Judge Lyman proposed a toast he later regretted: "Mark, the perfect man." Pleasure turned to slow anger when months went on and Tucker found convenient excuses for not exchanging pulpits with liberal clergymen. Judge Lyman wrote letters to Tucker which grew more heated as Tucker grew more evasive; then Tucker stopped replying. The liberals were, as one put it, "Tuckered out." The Unitarians published the correspondence, thus arousing further antagonism.[55] Failing in their efforts to have Tucker dismissed, the Unitarians decided to secede. Doors previously open slammed shut. The issue was becoming dramatized in terms that young Sylvester could understand.

As all this was going on, the bell in the steeple, which had for sixty-four years tolled at every funeral in Northampton and on every Sabbath, suddenly cracked. A new one was ordered and first used August 1, 1824; but that one did not suit the people as had the old one, and then it cracked too.[56]

The circle was broken.

Nor was that all. The Baptists, a despised sect of low-caste enthusiasts, had begun sending a missionary to Northampton in 1822, and in April, 1824, they organized a parish. The first immersions in the river were the sort of show that boys would flock to, and a crowd of one thousand witnessed them. Then came the Episcopalians, who organized in August, 1826,[57] led by Joseph Cogswell and supported by many of the wealthy Southern students from Round Hill School. Father Judd could stomach almost anything else; he could get along with Unitarian Bancroft, but at the religion of England and the slaveholding aristocracy he drew the line. When, in 1826, Arethusa Hall went to teach a school in Portsmouth, New Hampshire, and was influenced by the Episcopalian family she boarded with, editor Judd turned on her. "Fully imbued with the old Puritan spirit, and deeply impressed with a sense of the wrongs and oppressions which had driven our fathers to this country, he regarded with almost hate those who adopted the views of the old established Church."[58] The serious differences led for a while to a partial estrangement from her "demi-père" for whom she had an almost romantic attachment. For years afterward he made angry jottings in his diary at Christmas time about the heathen goings-on at the Episcopal Church.

Young Sylvester was at this time in no danger of being drawn away from the orthodox faith. He was an earnest boy, anxious to be good and much inclined to seek salvation in the prescribed orthodox manner. As he wrote later about his boyhood, "I earnestly longed for the 'one thing needful.'" But his "irrepressible desire" for the necessary "extraneous and special operation" of the holy spirit was paralyzed. "The influences of my creed came over my spirit like an autumnal frost, and sealed up the fountains of emotion. . . . I supposed myself totally depraved." The natural sympathy of his heart for nature was perverted by his creed's insistence "that my own nature was cursed, and that the earth had been cursed." A revealing statement follows, central to our understanding of Judd and the romantic movement:

> I used to repine almost, that I had not lived with Adam in Paradise, when the earth was *really* beautiful, and man's nature could properly sympathize with its charms. I used to hope that I might live to see the millennium, when this double curse would be removed, and men would be restored to the true enjoyment of nature.[59]

The quest into the future of the utopian was a search for a lost Eden.

Finally Sylvester's subconscious mind responded to the conscious will in the prescribed orthodox manner. He "obtained a hope" of salvation at age thirteen. The revival which swept the town and the valley and which was the answer of the orthodox to the Unitarian upheaval had a special fervor about it. Nothing like it had been seen since the Great Awakening of Jonathan Edwards. Mark Tucker in three years converted 222 persons. Jonathan Edwards in twenty-three years had converted 495.[60] Father Judd, rather suspicious of it all, wrote: "To tell the truth the revival has been quite a *Methodist* one, and Mr. Tucker has, on some occasions, discovered a want of prudence." Meetings were held in all parts of town and "at almost all hours of the day." Father also took a dour view of Sylvester's pious emotions: "We feel encouraged with respect to him, but are not without fears that his religion will prove like that of many other children—transient and ineffective."[61]

Judd was quite right in commenting on the more emotional tone of this revival. With Mark Tucker a new era had begun. The sermons of parson Williams, though well received, had had a certain sameness about them: "He would begin with 'firstly' and continue on to 'tenthly,' then say 'once more and I am done,' and wind up with 'finally.'"[62] The sermons of Mark Tucker, in contrast, were more loose in structure and glowed with an ardor and exaltation to which young Sylvester could respond. Though the doctrines were old, Tucker spoke a new language, the kind of poetic language which Sylvester Judd would use in his sermons. Words much used by Tucker included "light," "ardor," "desire," "luminous," "glory," "affection," and "kindling." His words caressed the ear sensuously: "The sweet singer of Israel sang doubly sweet as he poured out his plaints on the banks of Chebar, among the fastnesses of Palestine, and along the valleys of Baca."[63] Religion would be music to the Rev. Sylvester Judd also: "Have you not reflected that Christ was a singer? . . . In many of Christ's words are harmony and softness, mellifluence and music. The Gospels seem to me truth melodized." "The world may wholly leave us; but the thrush sings sweetest in the loneliest woods, and we will keep up our song in solitude" (447-48, 460).

It is evident why Sylvester Judd responded to the Orphean music of Mark Tucker and why Mark Tucker had a special affection for Sylvester and "regarded him as his spiritual child."[64] Tucker for the first time made religion beautiful. That was important. Parson Williams had inveighed against pleasure and the growing profanation of the Sabbath by persons who were "riding out of town or strolling in the fields, seeming to defy all instructions, rebukes, worthy examples and prosecutions and punishments." The rising generation instead of asking "How shall we avoid the damnation of hell" were "mirthful, reading useless or hurtful books, mingling in the jovial circle." He exhorted them:

> perishing sinners! accountable creatures! immortal beings! yet easy in your pleasures, sins, and danger!. . . .cry to God for mercy for them and for ourselves, lest some are soon sealed down to judicial blindness and incurable hardness of heart.[65]

In this contrast of the new rhetoric with the old we can see in microcosm the mutation, the generation leap which was taking place in the 1820's in New England. The new God was beautiful; the world and the Sabbath were made for man. As Sylvester Judd later wrote, "God is Beautiful, and Christ has always seemed to me the Beautiful One, beyond all created description or compare." "Innocent gladness is one of the most beautiful things under the sun; it is the roses and pansies of humanity" (448-49). Sylvester Judd longed for beauty. In the Judd home in Northampton the walls were bare, the floor uncarpeted, and there was no piano.

Young Sylvester threw himself with enthusiasm into anything he did, and he entered zealously into the revival. He not only attended meetings, he organized them.

> He, with others, often held meetings in a barn, where, mounted on a barrel's head, he would put forth earnest appeals to his playmates to forsake sin, and enter the pathway of eternal life. There was in his prayers an unction which moved the hearts of those even of maturer age.[66]

Sylvester inevitably absorbed the atmosphere of controversy which surrounded the revival. George Bancroft wrote, with obvious irony:

In the church we thrive superbly: we have had a religious awakening, great beyond all telling: President Humphreys of Amherst University preaching in our school-houses and anxious meetings, and meetings of the church, and meetings of those under conviction, and meetings of those that have a hope; Cogswell has cleared out of the old church, and set up an Episcopalian establishment; the baptists have been organized, and the methodists are stirring; so that I belong no longer to a new society. We are the second of five.[67]

Unitarians had little use for revivals. One of them had written:

In Hadley the fanaticism of the people is astonishing—They neglect the common avocations of life to attend to daily and nightly conferences—Three Clergymen are kept under pay besides Clodhopper Zealots gratis—Doctr Pomeroy of Warwick told us the other day that he stopped at a House in Hadley to purchase some Corn Brooms, the man was from home and his wife told him that her husband could not make any more now as he spent all his time in attending conferences.[68]

Young Sylvester, preaching on a barrel, was one of the "Clodhopper Zealots." People were choosing up sides, and Sylvester's preaching was a declaration of which side he was on. Father Judd wrote that there was "much jealousy and suspicion, and many hard speeches, on all sides. The revival has excited the zeal of the orthodox, and the opposition and hatred of the Unitarians."[69]

Even the great Fourth-of-July celebration of 1826 had overtones of religious controversy. On July 3, in a letter reporting young Sylvester's religious awakening, father Judd wrote, "It is the intention of many to make a high day tomorrow—a great celebration; but such is the state of religious feeling that it will go hard. The Unitarians endeavor to be more merry than usual since the excitement began." The next day amid the annual tea parties, dancing, carousing, and interminable strings of toasts from which Judd pointedly averted his editorial gaze, George Bancroft, as chief orator of the day, announced for the first time his devotion to the principles of Jeffersonian democracy.[70] We do not know whether young Sylvester heard the oration or whether he was himself exhorting in a barn. That same day John Adams, last of the Federalist presidents, spoke his last words: "Thomas Jefferson still survives." But Thomas Jefferson also died that day just fifty years after July 4, 1776. The younger generation was left to refashion the fragments of the world that was breaking up.

The exhilaration of 1826 dissolved; the revival ended. The morning-after was not pleasant. In the poisoned atmosphere, Mark Tucker, no longer regarded even by the orthodox as "the perfect man," felt uncomfortable. He pleaded illness, grabbed at an offer from Troy, New York, and got out. Northampton was unable to find a suitable replacement for Tucker. A pastor from a small town in Vermont actually declined the offer of this, the largest church in New England.[71]

Young Sylvester Judd matched Northampton in instability. After a year or more of being "changed in many respects" and of being "a pretty good boy to his mother,"[72] his "saving hope" began to evaporate before he could receive the final conversion experience necessary for church membership. As Mark Tucker left, with no one to replace him, Sylvester must have felt rejected by God and alone, deserted by his spiritual guide.

Among the other upheavals of 1827-1828 was the controversy over Episcopalianism between Arethusa and father Judd. After spending the winter of 1827 in Northampton, Arethusa did not come back to the Judd household to live for ten years. It was for fourteen-year-old Sylvester like losing his own mother. Then came the great disappointment, the interruption in Sylvester's schooling.

Since the return from Westfield, Sylvester had continued at private schools, not because his father was wealthy, but because there was nothing to be learned at the public school anymore. In the spring of 1827 Sylvester was tantalized by the possibility of being sent to a good private school in Haverhill, Massachusetts, where Arethusa was now in charge of "the female department." But a month later father Judd announced rather curtly: "I cannot afford to send Sylvester to Haverhill." Father Judd had been saying for years that education was another one of the "shams and shows." His election to the school committee and his visits to the schools seemed only to confirm him in his opinion that formal schooling was of questionable value. He had educated himself, and he didn't see why Sylvester could not do likewise.[73]

In 1828 it was time for fifteen-year-old Sylvester to think of making his own way as his older brother J.W. was already doing. Sylvester's schooling abruptly ceased, and his father pressed him to come into the *Gazette* office as an apprentice.[74] But Sylvester was not one to follow the model of Benjamin Franklin: he was more the type of a Jonathan Edwards. Young Judd stubbornly and persistently refused. A college education was what he wanted, and that was denied him. His mother wrote, "S. is a strange boy." He became morose, irritable, restless. There is reason to suspect that perhaps among his other frustrations was an unhappy love affair. He talked a great deal about going to sea.[75] Instead, he returned to Westhampton. When he could not go forward, he went back. It was a classic case of regression as a response to frustration, and it was not the last time that Judd would enact in his life what Mircea Eliade calls the "myth of the eternal return." Timeless Westhampton was a source of strength.

But Westhampton had changed, just as Northampton. The five or six months Sylvester spent there after September, 1828, were the climax of the most shattering event in all Westhampton history. Enoch Hale's church, like the one in Northampton, was splitting in two, very audibly indeed. The issue was not Unitarianism. Enoch Hale did not breed Unitarians in his parish, and city folk did not come in to create trouble. The problem was not lack of revival enthusiasm but an excess of it. The difficulty stemmed from the minister who had been assisting parson Hale part time since January, 1828.[76] As it seemed later that year, he was one of those who, as Milton put it in "Lycidas,"

> for their bellies sake,
> Creep and intrude, and climb into the fold.

The Reverend John Truair, who had been helping to organize a mission for sailors in New York City,[77] was so much in need of a job that he was glad to get even part-time work in Westhampton. Though almost in the backwoods, it looked like a good place, quiet, eminently respectable, with good prospects of advancement.

As it seemed to Enoch Hale in the fall of 1828, Truair also answered to Milton's description of those whose

> lean and flashy songs
> Grate on their scrannel pipes of wretched straw,
> The hungry sheep look up, and are not fed,
> But swollen with wind, and the rank mist they draw
> Rot inwardly, and foul contagion spread.

The contagion was certainly spreading, as young Judd could see from his observation post at the town center, but what of the "lean and flashy songs"?

In May, 1827, Truair had first appeared in Westhampton with a travelling medicine show for the soul, the like of which Westhampton had never seen before. He not only preached and prayed in the evening, but he gave a lecture on "Sacred Music." He talked with authority about Handel's "Messiah" and "The Beggar's Opera" and dropped such names as Mozart, Sacchini, Pleyel, David, Purcell, Crofts. He knew about semitones, about chromatic intervals, "which are to music, what the most exquisite shade and coloring are to painting," and about "dissonants," which "in music are what the darker shades are to painting."[78] To climax this dazzling display, Truair sang—a "singing concert," as Enoch Hale commented in his diary that night. Here was a Moody who did not even need a Sankey to travel with him. Truair was an enthusiast, a revivalist, a striking contrast to judicious Enoch Hale. His experience with sailors had taught him how to put the gospel on the line in compelling, urgent terms:

> Dying sinner! Doubting soul! . . . Jesus has died for you. . . . O do not make your way, in spite of this salvation, which even now presses hard upon you; and in spite of bleeding love, and beseeching mercy! do not make your way ruinous down to blackness of darkness, and the undying-worm! Believe! unbelieving, doubting soul! Believe that *Jesus is the Christ*; and that he died, and has purchased, and given even to thee salvation! It is an urgent case! Why will you die! . . . . The door of mercy is now wide open, and a kind messenger inviting you! Be persuaded at once to arise, and go in!—The year of your jubilee is now proclaimed! believe only, and go forth the Lord's free man.[79]

Fifteen-year-old Sylvester Judd must inevitably have been attracted to this fervent, yet earthy sophisticate who could discourse to him of music, religion, and the seven seas. The only record we have of the acquaintance, however, is a sermon of Truair's that Judd later had bound, with others, in a leather-covered volume. The sermon, concerning the shocking conditions of vice and impiety prevailing in the seaports, was inscribed "A present from the author."[80] To this lonely, warm-hearted boy who wanted to run away to sea rather than face the monotony of merely making a living, Truair could present the comfortable Calvinist doctrines and yet make religion seem thrillingly forbidden. Judd must have shivered when he heard Truair proclaim the alternatives: "the blackness of darkness" or "the Lord's free man." But he did not accept the invitation.

Truair was certainly stamped "forbidden" after November 10, 1828, when it became evident that his contract as part-time assistant was not about to be renewed. Truair made himself at home anyway. A small minority of Westhamptonites were so attached to Truair that they persuaded him to stay, and they "polled off" to form a second Congregational society for his support. From Truair's point of view, in staying he was merely accepting a call from a new but legally constituted Congregational parish. From the old church's point of view, Truair was an interloper whose "flashy songs" had seduced his followers: he had made nasty insinuations about Enoch Hale and had persuaded his followers to secede.[81] Such things simply were not done in an orderly New England town. Enoch Hale's forty-nine years of labor for the stability and unity of Westhampton were culminating in chaos. Adaptation to change was not a skill he had practiced, and at age seventy-four he was too old to begin learning it.

The secession was only the beginning of the events Sylvester Judd witnessed. His grandfather was prominent in futile efforts to get the two societies back together again. The parson and the squire were in solid agreement on the dangers of disunity and innovations. Dr. Hooker also stood firm for the status quo.[82] In February, when it seemed that a peace treaty had been concluded, young Sylvester, just before returning to Northampton, saw the climactic event of the tragicomedy. Across the street from him, the church burned down. In the excitement wild accusations flew. Some said that Truair had burned it, or that his supporters had. Others said it was a judgment of God for permitting Truair to preach there.[83] In the murky half-light of February, 1829, the breach became final. It hardly seemed like Westhampton anymore.

In the winter of 1830-31 young Judd returned to West-hampton and saw the sequel of the story. A revival had been going on for months. But it was not Enoch Hale's church that was being revived. Not one conversion had occurred there in a year and a half. Truair had converted 130 members, had delusions of grandeur, and was branching out to take over the neighboring towns.[84] His Union Church, dedicated to religious freedom and the abolition of sectarianism, was becoming a new sect. The same thing had happened to the Unitarians. With the Truairites, however, all propriety was forgotten in an explosion of the uncontrolled emotionalism Enoch Hale had always cautioned against. Truair had been accused by the Hampshire Association of Ministers of improprieties, including "great indecorum of manners and lightness and vulgarity of conversation, particularly in his intercourse with females, altogether unbecoming a minister of the gospel," and he was in process of being defrocked by the Presbytery of New York.[85] Truair was breaking up families and charming wives away from their husbands. Even Dr. Hooker was not immune. His own wife

attended their midnight meetings & used to come home at 12, 1, or 2 o'clock in the night; the Dr. thought this very improper, & after attempting in vain to dissuade her from this course, he locked or fastened the doors of his sleeping room; this incensed her & things have gone on from bad to worse, until all domestic harmony & happiness are destroyed. [86]

With nothing more to lose, Truair had turned his church into "a camp meeting in miniature," as father Judd put it:

such an one as you would expect among ignorant Methodists in Norwich Hollow, if anywhere—meeting until 2 or 3 o'clock in the morning; women, girls, children, all praying & bawling together; some wallowing on the floor; some talking, laughing, singing;[87]

The parson, the doctor, and the squire looked on, aghast.

Young Sylvester, even if he dared not go to their meetings, could easily hear the praying and preaching from the Judd homestead. Furthermore, the Truairites paraded "through the streets shouting, singing hymns &c." Truair, intoxicated by his success, had gone beyond Calvinism to the antinomianism which always lurked in the ditch to the left: not only were good works not necessary to salvation, they were not even an evidence of salvation; emotion and faith were all that counted. Truair's meetings "abounded in visions, prophecies, and dreams,—holy kisses and ecstacies."[88] Truair preached perfectionism, a heresy that lurked beside antinomianism; he embraced millennialism—orthodox, but disreputable in Truair's version.

Later, when Sylvester Judd flirted with transcendentalism, he was in danger of laying himself open to the same charges. Transcendentalism was a nineteenth-century revival of Anne Hutchinson's seventeenth-century antinomianism, said Caroline Healy Dall, a leading transcendentalist who knew Judd.[89] Though Judd rejected millennialism he was fascinated by it, making it the subject of his long poem *Philo;* and mystical dreams played an important part in *Margaret.*

Revivalism, however, was anathema to Judd in his later life. He had been there before. At the beginning of *Margaret* he makes the brimstone burn with a camp-meeting scene (49-55). A preacher exhorts as thunder clouds roll up, darkening the woods:

> "That," said he, "is the shadow of hell. It is the smoke of torments that ascendeth up forever and ever." The thunder burst upon the camp, its hollow roar reverberated among the hills. "Behold!" he exclaimed, "God proclaims his law in fire and smoke!" It began to rain, "What!" continued he, "can you not endure a little wetting when you will so soon call for a drop of water to cool your parched tongues?"

Lightning "blazed through the trees."

"The great day of the Lord is coming," he went on, "when the elements shall melt with fervent heat; the heavens also shall pass away with a great noise, the earth also shall be burned up." There was a movement in the congregation; some shrieked out, some fell upon their faces, some flung their arms wildly in the air. "Oh my soul!" "Lord have mercy!" "Jesus save!" "Glory! glory!" rang from seat to seat.

Amid sobs, groans, spasms, foaming at the mouth, and thunder, the preacher moves with evident satisfaction. "'This beats the Great Earthquake all hollow,' exclaimed one of the congregation. 'Yes,' echoed the Preacher, 'what a rattling among the dry bones.'" A little later, in one of the tents, Margaret's friend Obed succumbs:

They had Obed down flat on his back. His mouth was open, his eyes shut; he shook spasmodically, he groaned with a deep guttural guffaw. Men and women were over and about him; some looking on, some praying, some uttering "Glory!" The Preacher came in, a bland smile on his face, rubbing his hands; "Good!" he ejaculated with a short, quick snap of the voice. "The Lord is here, Miss Palmer, " said he.

Still later, as Obed comes to, little Margaret, amid a great hubbub, tries to come between Obed and the Lord's work; her foster brother Nimrod, half drunk, thrusts himself in with his dog. " Bite um Bull, bite um," he says, making the dog yelp.

"Satan has come in great wrath," cried the Preacher.

"Yes, and I guess you know as much about him as anybody, old cackletub!" rejoined Nimrod. "You set them all a going, and then snap them up like a hawk."

"Hoora!" shouted another of the scoffers from the other side of the tent. "I hearn him comin down from a tree just now; look out or he'll be in your hair, white-top."

"I've cotched him by the tail," said another of the fry, twitching the dog, who thereupon renewed his roar.

"Pray, brethren, pray!" said the Preacher, and the people began to pray more lustily. "As with the sound of rams' horns the walls of Jericho fell down, so shall these sinners tremble before God."

The scene ends in a wild melee of trampling feet and falling tents.

In 1830, when Sylvester Judd saw scenes almost as dramatic as these, he was seventeen years old. In his few years he had already seen enough to fill the better half of *Margaret*. He had seen the timeless world of Westhampton, where woodpeckers rapped and rattled in the woods, and had seen that world changed by the wheel of time. By 1832 the life of Sylvester Judd would be half over.

6

The River and the Rainbow

The secession of the Truairites from the Westhampton church on November 10, 1828, followed by only a few days the election of Andrew Jackson to the presidency. The decade seemed to be full of coincidences. Perhaps those who believed so firmly in the doctrine of Providence should have read the portents and should have perceived a shaping hand. If they could not see what was plain, George Bancroft was ready to tell them. "Progress" was the motto of the new era. "Westward the star of empire takes its way," to be emblazoned on the cover of Bancroft's American epic, was a slogan that summarized the pattern of God's design.

The design was being worked out by an ebullient Democracy: a tramp of muddy feet in the East Room of the White House, shouts and singing at midnight in the streets of Westhampton. The common man was coming into his kingdom. Any honest, vigorous man with ideas could run a government, a business, or a church in this paradise of amateurs: he was an interchangeable part in the machine of progress. One of Truair's travelling exhorters, a "clodhopper zealot," was, in father Judd's phrase, "probably the greatest numskul that was ever raised in Westhampton."[1] While the orthodox minister who replaced Hale in the old church cautioned that "women were forbidden to speak in the church," in the new church of Truair, women and even children were encouraged to speak up.[2] The Enoch Hales, old and tiresome, would have to get out of the way. Progress implied expansion, competition, multiplicity, letting every voice be heard. Dr. Hooker could have commented that it also implied a house divided against itself.

As Sylvester Judd reached adolescence, the term "the new man" had several possible connotations. In the context of the revival it could mean, as it always had, the converted man who secured a hope and a new heart. In the context of economics and politics it could imply the self-made man, who mastered things and people and led the forces of change. In the context of ideological conflict, it could suggest the emancipated man who cast off stale ideas and dared to think for himself. In the years after 1828 when Sylvester Judd was asserting his new manhood, each one of these connotations took on meaning for him.

Editor Judd, himself a self-taught man, a dabbler in many fields of knowledge but a master of none, saw no reason in 1828 to pamper his son with a liberal education at a sacrifice to himself. After Sylvester's winter vacation in Westhampton, his father thought it time to push the fifteen-year-old boy out of the nest and let him make his own way. Accordingly, in the spring of 1829, Sylvester, who was still adrift but in a measure reconciled to the necessity of making a start in life, was sent to Greenfield, a few hours' ride up the valley. There he became, for about a year, clerk in the store of his uncle, Richardson Hall.* Judd's efforts to settle down in the trade his father had first followed bore little fruit other than some lively pages of store-counter gossip in *Margaret*. On August 3rd, mother

---

*Hall had married Enoch Hale's daughter, Sybella; their son Henry was destined to marry, in 1867, Jane, the daughter of the Rev. Sylvester Judd.

Judd reported that Sylvester was going into business for himself.

> He is soon to enter into partnership with a Mr. Smith of Gnfld in the Gunnery business and the first of Sept. is to take a load of guns and go to East Port in Main and open a shop and sell them. he is sanguine that he shall do well.

What happened to this scheme is a mystery. Sylvester's activities that August—what little we know of them—were hardly such as to inspire the confidence of Mr. Smith. Instead of tending to business, Judd began to withdraw books from a circulating library and to write reviews of his reading. This notebook is the earliest writing by Judd to survive, and it gives us an interesting look at what was going through his mind. Between August 11th and September 3rd he read nine books, a rate of one every two or three days. By October 3rd he had read nine more. Judd's interest in guns was reflected in his reading. In August, along with *The Prairie* by Cooper, he read a book of historical sketches by Scott, two war novels about a young rifleman, and a novel about the Crusades. Judd's revulsion from violence had not yet occurred, and he thirsted for something besides spending the rest of his life in a small-town store.

Judd approached the subject of love somewhat gingerly. The first book he read, apparently a novel, shows how sensationalism broke past the inner moral censor by masquerading as history and morality. He summarized an exotic tale of seduction of an Englishman by a beautiful Cashmere dancer in Hindostan. Wrote Judd: "Yet he was what we call a moral man. . . . After all he was not able to withstand so great temptations. . . . The whole object of the story seems to be that others may learn by his sad history and not give way to temptation of the world especially of the wicked and fascinating female. But place your dependance upon God and look to him in every time of need." On August 24th Judd registered his astonishment at a history of the Inquisition with its sensational stories of sin, childbirth, and abortion in Catholic nunneries. (The anti-Catholicism which formed part of the New England heritage was being whipped up again by the renewed religious fervor of the period.) On September 24th Judd squirmed as he read a book of French "Moral Tales": "a gross imposition . . . being a succession of faintings, sickness and melancholy all for love. These are your good moral tales."

As Judd read on, outright bawdiness seemed to bother him less than sentimentality. Peregrine Pickle "seduces married ladies . . . works himself into the favour of a young bride and tries repeatedly to violate her chastity and succeeds so far as to get under the bed cloathes but is prevented by some accident. . . . We have not been able to procure this whole life and cannot tell how much further he went in his licentiousness."

A rather earthy satire on revivalism, Richard Graves' *The Spiritual Quixote* (1816), got the most detailed review. It was further poison in the ear of the young enthusiast Judd, who had preached to his friends in a barn. A "Spiritual Quixote" named Wildgoose and Tugwell, his Sancho Panza, out to save the world by preaching, stopped to reprove some persons cursing in the upper story of a Birmingham house. The sinners, reported Judd, "not caring for their souls emptied a pisspot full out upon the heads of our travellers. Poor Tugwell who happened to be looking up at the moment received a good dose into his mouth and face a portion of which went down his throat. They being satisfyed proceeded on their way." As Tugwell is "constantly spitting and gagging," Wildgoose "tells him that persecution is sweet and wholesome." Soon after, when Tugwell "sets greedy eyes upon" a plum pudding, Wildgoose "tells him not to lust after the carnal pleasures of this world and the like." Tugwell replies that "he only wanted to get the *parsecution* taste out of his mouth which his worship said was so sweet and wholesome."

Judd's notes imply that he had already acquired a considerable familiarity with other novels. He was not content with reading sermons, histories, and newspapers; although much of what he read he could have shown to his parents without blushing, he had also read the luridly romantic *Lallah Rookh*. He would not be content with writing sermons, histories, and newspapers either. His imagination was aroused, and it demanded expression in ways that were dangerous and thrillingly forbidden. Revivals and romantic literature had much in common. Both aroused dangerous emotions in the name of spirituality. Enoch Hale knew that fact well and counseled sobriety in all things.

Judd's career in the gunnery business must have been very brief indeed, as the family letters make no further allusion to it. Perhaps it ended before it started. Judd continued as clerk in the Greenfield store until spring. The forty books that he reviewed in six months must have kept him busy with surreptitious glances below the store counter. Judd "had little tact or inclination" for storekeeping. A storekeeper needed to "know how to flatter his customers or persuade the ladies that he was their lovesmitten adorer," claimed a deacon in the Northampton church who had himself failed in the drug business.[3] Judd had been raised by his father to think for himself and tell the truth, even if feelings were hurt. As Arethusa Hall put it, "Not succeeding very well . . . he remained about a year, and returned home, where for some months he made himself useful to his father in keeping books and settling accounts. His spirit had in a measure resumed its natural quietness: at least, he had done much towards patiently submitting to the inevitable." Sylvester's desultory apprenticeship at the *Gazette* office was even briefer than his tenure at the Greenfield store. Two years earlier he had exhibited a form of adolescent rebellion in refusing to join the family firm;

it was apparent that a life spent under his father's thumb
was still not going to work out. It was a bit futile to suppose that this dreamy youth of seventeen would succeed as
a bill collector when his father had shown little aptitude
for putting on the requisite pressure. Sylvester had been
merely marking time.[4]

In August, 1830, Sylvester went to Hartford, Connecticut, for a fresh start. His older brother, J.W., had found a
way to combine books and business and was working there
in a bookstore. Sylvester got a job as a clerk in a dry goods
store. As he later wrote the story, in *Richard Edney,* of a
young man's coming to the capital city to seek his fortune,
it was a success story that anticipated the Horatio Alger
formula. Edney came to town, like Benjamin Franklin to
Philadelphia, got a job, saved the governor's daughter from
frightened horses, subdued the town bully, escaped the
clutches of the wicked and fascinating female, rose to
prominence in his business, organized societies for town
improvement, married the governor's daughter, and became
mayor. It was a cheerily optimistic and moral tale in the
manner of Nathaniel Parker Willis or the *Knickerbocker
Magazine,* with Pickwickian winks and nods.

As Judd himself lived out the story of his own coming-
of-age, in Greenfield and Hartford, it was a tale of disaster,
short and final. In Hartford Judd began as a store clerk,
and when the story ended seven weeks later he was not
even that. His business career was over. In an agitated letter
of October 14th to his father, he dramatized the climax in
the stiff and slightly absurd rhetoric of the 1830 novel:

> I have been doubly diligent, and fondly hoping I was pleasing to
> my employer. Monday morning last, Mr. S said to me, without
> any previous warning, "Sylvester I do not think you will answer
> our purpose." After a little explanation I asked if it were *deter-
> mined* that I should not stay. he replyed "*Yes.*" If a bolt from
> heaven had struck me to the earth, I could not have been more

startled. The reasons *why* I hardly know myself, at least I cannot now state them to you, Sir, so distinctly as I could wish. Thus, Father, am I again thrown out of employ and my dreams of future happiness, connected with Hartford and my present circumstances, blasted in a moment. But that is not the worst. An indelible stigma is fixed upon my character, at least so far as concerns my capacity of remaining a Merchant's clerk. I know not what to do. I might perhaps obtain a situation at the West or South where I am not so well known.

In the role of Ishmael in which the fates had cast him, Judd again looked to the sea as his "substitute for pistol and ball":

New York is so near that I have a good mind to go down and get aboard ship in some capacity or other, and sail for distant climes where neither the queries of *present* friends, the inquiries of *present* relations, nor the sneers of *present enemies* will trouble me more. But still I say, "New England, with all thy faults, I love thee well."

At the conclusion of the letter, Judd turned from the escapist fantasy of the sea to the subject of his own deepest ambitions:

Had I known half as much of myself years ago as I *think* I do now, instead of handling the yard stick I might now be treading my way, at least to *some* distinction in the paths of literature and science. Still, I hope it is not now to late to appeal to the heart of a Father. . . . Do I appeal in vain, when I ask, in short, that I may have a *liberal education*?

To support his case, Judd took the risk of quoting from his father's diary: "I reccollect reading not many years since, in the diary of a person, an expression to this effect, 'I ought to have been sent to College, a place by far best calculated to develop the natural propensities of my mind.'" Thus did the boy puncture the father's talk about "the sham of education" and the value of self-education.

Judd, notably, said nothing about God and Providence in this letter. He spoke instead of self-knowledge and of his own "great, unceasing, and, as I had supposed, *well-directed* exertions." He spoke not about sin and punishment but about inexplicable misfortune. His conception of education was not vocational. He did not want to go to college to become a lawyer, as his deceased Uncle Hophni had done, or to become a minister, as he knew would have delighted his mother and perhaps would have opened his father's purse strings. His ambitions were more grandiose and more vague: he spoke of "a *liberal education*," of rising "at least to *some* distinction in the paths of literature and science." We need look no farther for an answer to the question of how a minister of the gospel became a novelist. We might better ask the question, how did this boy with literary ambitions become a minister of the gospel?

At the end of his letter to his father, in a passage that, along with others, the Hall biography omitted, Judd expressed his intention "to visit N. Y. & stay a day or two. Can go down for 25 cts." In his mental turmoil, pulled both toward the sea and a New England which he still professed to love, Judd seemed ready to compromise on a weekend in New York. Whether he actually made the trip or what he expected to find in his first venture outside the safe confines of the Connecticut Valley, we have no way of telling. The only allusion to New York in Judd's early writing is contained in a poetic drama written three to five years later, while Judd was preparing for the orthodox ministry.[5] In this drama New York is the source of evil, the home of deception, unprincipled ambition, atheism, liberalism, and Sin. The concluding scenes take place in a boarding house which turns out to be a brothel, where the heroine has been lured under false pretenses by the villain and deflowered. The catastrophe, in which fallen hero unexpectedly meets fallen heroine in the brothel, leaves the stage strewn with the bodies of the entire cast and has ironic overtones of *Othello* and *Romeo and Juliet*. Judd's early writing was not characterized by optimism and Dickensian flourishes. Of course, Judd had read enough novels of seduction that he did not need to visit New York to get the suggestion for his play, and if he wanted to read shocked reports about sin in the seaports, he needed only to read the pamphlet Truair had given him or the pages of the *Hampshire Gazette.*

In his extremity, Judd once more turned to Westhampton. It was a return to happier times and associations. His father showed signs of yielding and allowed Judd to divide his time between serving as a clerk in the store formerly owned by the Judds and attending a private school taught by a Dr. Wheeler. Even the controversy over Truair did not seem to dampen the enthusiasm with which Judd returned to his studies. His attachment to Westhampton, kept alive by the Thanksgiving celebrations at his grandfather's home and by the visit there in 1828-29, was growing. Judd longed for peace. As he wrote to a cousin in this winter of 1830-31, "I always loved Westhampton, its hills and dales, its woods, fields, and gurgling brooks, yes, and its inhabitants too!"[6] Westhampton was becoming for him a symbol of the childhood Eden before separations and divisions began. In 1838 Judd would say, at the Northampton Lyceum,

> Childhood is every good man's Paradise, a perpetual Paradise, from which he shall never be driven, to the entrance of which no swords of fire shall be interposed. Manhood has its cares. Age its infirmities. Youth blooms ever. Then he was happy, then he was free.

Indeed, as Judd contemplated the image of Adam and Eve in the Garden, he almost pitied them their lack of childhood memories:

> Adam lived in Paradise. Eve, Heaven-moulded, and Heavenly-beautiful, bloomed at his side. The uncursed Earth expanded before him, with a luxuriance that regaled every sense. The sun shone out upon, in the undimmed effulgence of its new Creation. Yet Adam had no childhood. No associations of Childhood came

rushing upon his thoughts, and throwing their rapture of emotion over the beautiful world he dwelt in. With Eve, in bright-eyed girlhood, he had never revelled among those flowers, or sauntered on Pison's banks . . . Childhood is every good man's Paradise.[7]

The lecture of 1838, freighted with its Emersonian vocabulary and effulgence, reflected, however, the mood of a later, mellower Judd. He may indeed have felt a renewed "zest" in life at the resumption of his studies in 1830, as Arethusa Hall recorded, enough to write an essay satirizing the girls of Dr. Wheeler's school for chasing after one boy to the exclusion of others, but he had certainly not yet responded to George Bancroft's optimistic philosophy of Progress. The childhood Eden may have been in his mind, but he was also brooding over man's exclusion from the Garden.

The mournful strain of the New England jeremiad, the theme of "degenerating times," was the note he struck in 1831 when he rose to deliver an impassioned address to his Westhampton classmates:

Van[i]ty is stamped on all earthy things. Human grandeur what is it? The glory of renown how evanescent. The ruthless hand of time lays all things low. Kingdoms and empires rise and fall. With the sad example before their eyes others still, are dashed to atoms in the same whirlpool of desolation. . . . What is Carthage? The wild Arab and the wandering corsair walk proudly through her streets sole masters. Desolation meets the eye at noon tide. the screech of the owl, and the howling of the hyena are heard at midnight.[8]

Rome, Greece, Napoleon, the Indians of New England—all were conquered. The flag of liberty in Europe was at that moment about to be "crushed by the iron grasp of tyranny." Then Judd wavered between the two traditions he had inherited: the optimistic and the pessimistic. "Methinks I see a light proceeding from this western hemisphere. it crosses the Atlantic and rests upon the Nations of the old

World." New England at least was pure. "They follow the course it points out, the storm subsides. . . . Oh America, the land of liberty, under thy wing the oppressed finds a shelter, here every one lives under his own vine and fig tree with none to molest or make afraid." Then Judd's next words raised the same question about America's future—the question of whether America would go the way of Greece and Rome—that was expressed in such diverse forms as Thomas Cole's allegorical and perhaps pessimistic series of paintings "The Course of Empire" (1836) and William Cullen Bryant's optimistic poem "The Ages" (1821). Judd addressed America: "Art thou destined to share the fate of Nations? . . . . I see in our Western horizon a cloud arising. it is black with party spirit, intemperance, infidelity, and the mark of the beast is upon it. it increases as it rises."

It was the same cloud, with the mark of popery and foreign influences upon it, that Dorus Clarke would see full-blown in 1878 ominously rumbling with the preparations of "communists, assassins, and ghouls" to take over the country. Eighteen-year-old Judd, like Clarke, called on his audience to bestir itself: "Had I a voice of thunder, its echo should be heard from Maine to Florida—from the Atlantic to the Pacific calling upon the present rising generation to awake from their lethargy." America already extended in 1831 to the Pacific in the excited imagination of the orator. Judd's "voice of thunder" was in tune with the "manifest destiny" spirit of his father's friend George Bancroft, who stamped "Westward the star of empire" on more than book covers: later, as Acting Secretary of War, Bancroft ordered the troops to the Rio Grande and California. But Judd, in 1831, was on the side of the Enoch Hales and the Dorus Clarkes against divisive "party spirit" and "infidelity." Judd went on: "The voice of our fathers calls upon us to awake. . . . The adherents of Infidelity & Catholicism, foreign hirelings, are concentrating their powers. The question is soon to be decided, shall the priests or the people rule?" This did not sound like George Bancroft. In Northampton, Bancroft, a leading "infidel," was doing his best to promote party spirit by defending the Democrats, the group later to be identified with foreigners, rum, Romanism, and rebellion.[9]

Judd was merely imitating his elders. In Boston, Lyman Beecher, a leader of orthodoxy and a defender of the New England way against the revivalistic excesses of the New Measures men and inchoate perfectionists like John Truair and Charles Grandison Finney, was also preaching against infidelity, Unitarianism, and Catholicism. Beecher's sermons are usually blamed for helping renew the intolerant Puritan spirit and thus contributing to the anti-Catholic riot that burned down a Catholic convent in Charlestown, Massachusetts, in 1834.[10] Beecher's influence reached to the Connecticut Valley and beyond; his sermons against Catholicism of 1830 were widely reprinted and imitated. Arethusa Hall had been living in Boston and attending Beecher's church. She remembered all her life his militant Puritanism and the way he thundered and pounded away at the sin of theater-going: when the admission price was reduced, Beecher proclaimed, "Now the way to hell is cheap, you can go at half-price!"[11] Sylvester Judd, in his speech of 1831, was echoing the same parochial, Puritan spirit. America was the hope of the world and would save a fallen Europe which had been corrupted by the shams and shows of popery, infidelity, tyranny, and pleasure. But first America must save itself and win the battle against the "foreign hirelings . . . concentrating their powers" and must have a revival of the spirit to save it from inward corruption. In this insistence upon the uniqueness and destiny of America, both conservative and liberal could unite. Bancroft, Beecher, Clarke and Judd presented different aspects of a common belief.

Judd's oration of 1831 provides a base point from which
to measure his departure from the world of the Dorus
Clarkes and the Lyman Beechers. It shows the mélange of
ideas that swirled through his head, the contending moods
of optimism and pessimism, the apocalyptic assumptions
that underlay New England thought. The clichés came naturally into the mind of an adolescent putting on the oratorical tone. His oration was like a mirror, catching the
catch phrases, often contradictory, of his age. When would
the mirror become a lamp, the echo a voice?

Two tones of voice were struggling for mastery in Judd's
mind. One spoke with a tone of thunder, and the other was
like fresh wind in dry leaves. One of them, with the rhythm
and sound of Dorus Clarke, said, "The adherents of Infidelity & Catholicism, foreign hirelings, are concentrating
their powers. The question is soon to be decided, shall the
priests or the people rule?" The other said, "I always loved
Westhampton." In 1845, when Judd was thirty-two years
of age and a minister in the Unitarian Church of Augusta,
Maine, that second voice, grown less simple, would speak
through the heroine Margaret:

> In myself seems sometimes to reside an infant Universe. My soul
> is certainly pistillate, and the pollen of all things is borne to me.
> The spider builds his house from his own bowels. I have some-
> times seen a wood-spider let off a thread which the winds drew
> out for him and raised above the trees, and when it was sufficient-
> ly high and strong, he would climb up it, and sail off in the clear
> atmosphere. I think if you only begin, it will all come to you. As
> you drain off it will flow in. (245)

In this limpid yet mystifying utterance of 1845, which rep-
resents Judd at his most Emersonian mood, the soul is no
longer in a Lockeian prison, an echo of forces from outside.
It is a voice, unfolding organically by its own laws of development. It is a microcosm. The only thing left of the world
of Jonathan Edwards is the ecstasy and the image of the

wood-spider sailing in the wind. In crossing the chasm from the echo to the voice, Judd went from one world into another, from the world of clichés and conformity to one where every separate individuality was a priceless thing because in it resided "an infant universe," unique and yet somehow a microcosm of the whole.

But in 1831 Judd had a great deal to drain off before the new would flow in. When he returned to Northampton that spring after his winter at Grandfather Judd's, he was so in harmony with the voice of the fathers that he and his family were able to come to an understanding about the future. Sylvester's father was not anxious to finance vague aspirations after fame in "literature or science." The ministry was another matter. Although father Judd had still not been able to proclaim himself one of the elect, he was solid in his support of religion and had even been teaching Sunday school every year since 1823, despite a few doubts about doctrines like infant baptism. Whether young Sylvester would be converted and receive the requisite call to the ministry was still in doubt, but he had already shown promising signs. After his winter of probation in Westhampton he seemed to have settled down enough to justify a further venture of faith on his education.

Bancroft and Cogswell's Round Hill School, though possibly the best secondary school in America, was too expensive and was out of the question. Besides, Bancroft was retiring from it, shortly to begin the writing of his great history, which would leave Round Hill in the hands of the Episcopalian Cogswell. Father Judd got along well with Bancroft, who was exercising an increasing sway over his mind,* who loaned him books, and who doubtless viewed

---

*Nye, p. 91, asserts that it was well known that Bancroft could "dictate the policy of the local paper." Editor Judd's journal does not support so sweeping a statement, but reveals a tendency to move towards Bancroft's liberalism.

Judd's growing collection of transcripts from old records with an interested eye. But to turn Sylvester over to an Episcopalian who ran an expensive school with frills was another matter. The Hopkins Academy, three miles away in Hadley, would do well enough.

In June, 1831, young Sylvester Judd began taking the daily walk to the Academy, across the bridge and past the meadows. Never had the valley seemed lovelier, his life happier. It would be years before he would again find such peace. Eight years later he would recall nostalgically his daily walk: the broad street, the rows of great elms, an old weather-beaten barn, frolicking boys, the covered bridge and the old gatekeeper who drew up the tinkling gate, the dusty road amid corn and grass, an old tree where he habitually stopped to rest, and finally the shade of Hadley streets. But the two things which seemed to stimulate his imagination most were the old burying ground and the river. They were most alive, and they drew the mind outward to infinity:

> As he hurried by, these dead seemed to move. They joined in dance over the hillocks, in the dim moonlight, the black and the white, under funereal pines and elms, with tall, gaunt weeds that grew there. They danced noiselessly, as the dead must dance. They danced to no music; for they needed none, save the silent wind.[12]

Disembodied spirits and the wind moved and swirled, like music and like water. All were expressive of the desires of the spirit, which longed for communion and merging. Judd wanted love, both human and divine, and so he was drawn toward water:

> The bridge,—I looked through its windows northward. The river issues from green hills, wood-land. On it flows, and Nature retinues it with a thousand shadowy trees, and meadowbanks. It opens in the embrace of a green, shrubby island, imparts a lingering kiss, and flows on for ever. I would plunge into its stream, and be borne onward too.

Death and the most intense self-realization were somehow interfused. This self, which contained "an infant universe," ready to be bodied forth like a spider's thread into the wind, had longings not only to people an imaginative world but at times to plunge back to the source and be lost.* I will leave it to others to say whether the impulse to love, which necessarily involves surrender of the self, is ever related to a subconscious death wish. Certainly, the writings of romantics like Judd, Lydia Maria Child, Harriet Beecher Stowe, or Lydia Sigourney—those "sweet singers" of Hartford and Northampton—so full of the sentiment of love, also exhibit a fascination with death. Love, like religious conversion, perhaps intensifies the awareness of mortality in the very act of triumphing over it. Of this paradox, water has often been used as a suggestive image.

Since the quotations just given are from Judd's journal for 1839, after his contact with transcendentalism, we might ask what he had to say about nature in 1831-32. Towards the end of his year at Hopkins Academy, he wrote the first of his many tributes to New England and to nature:

> New England! I love thee well. I love thy rough hilly roads, thy purling brooks, thy forest shades, thy sunless mountain chasms, sending up the echo of clashing waterfalls, thy singing birds, and thy buzzing insects with mimic sun-beams on their wings. Yes New England thy God hath made thee well.

In other parts the essay lacked maturity of style and was rather commonplace, but it had life when it returned to the description of moving water:

> Along the bottom of the basin lay a mingled mass of heaped up rocks, and earthy mounds, forming glens of every form, dark caves, and frightful precipices. Coming from the Northern high-

---

*cf. *Moby Dick,* Chapter I: "And still deeper the meaning of that story of Narcissus, who because he could not grasp the tormenting, mild image he saw in the fountain, plunged into it and was drowned. But that same image, we ourselves see in all rivers and oceans. It is the image of the ungraspable phantom of life; and this is the key to it all."

lands a river here poured its swift current along. Being divided by
the many craggy ridges, it formed as many seperate streams, one
flowing smooth and clear as glass, another rolling on in white
crests, another leaping down in cascades and mimic waterfalls,
another pouring its ceaseless stream down a deep precipice, another now whirling in eddies, now dashing precipitous among the
rocks that would impede its course, now falling with a tumultuous roar beneath cliffs that projected over its bed, then boiling up
in the wildest commotion. All these seperate streams became one
at the Southern end of the basin, forming a placid river. The view
was charming. Here were blended in the most delightful unison
we ever witnessed, Nature's beauty, grandeur, and sublimity.

A rainbow came at the end:

> The spray rose high to meet the Sun and receive its rainbow-hue,
> and then with a graceful curve it fell back to its mother Deep.
> Jove himself could not have framed better thunder than here rolled
> its "eternal bass" among the hills.

Though still an echo rather than a voice, this was an improvement over the "voice of thunder" which a year earlier
had been eager to resound to the Pacific. The river had
been personally observed. A feeling of serenity mingled
with fright and a sense of falling. There were "frightful
precipices" and plunging cascades, water falling downward
to the river of placidity where, astonishingly, "the view
was charming."

This rude plunge from wildness to the merely genteel
and commonplace was a portent. It represented the direction of movement in Judd's life, in which the conflict between wildness and gentility was the major battle he faced
as a literary artist. Some of the critics—including Arethusa
Hall, in a letter of April 5, 1851—rejected his boldest, most
original strokes, and in the sentimentality and prettiness
which they applauded, Judd drowned. Water and fire kissed
and burned in rainbow hues, "and then with a graceful
curve . . . fell back to its mother Deep." The Freudians
would explain away for us very nicely Judd's ardor, his

religious zeal, his search for the childhood paradise, his
rainbow that arched to the sun and back to the mother
deep.

In the summer of 1831 Judd was received into the First
Church, Congregational, of Northampton. It was a rich
summer of harvest, the greatest revival in a decade of great
revivals. The frenzy had been advancing steadily in from
the west in great waves. Charles Grandison Finney, who
aroused audiences as no one in New England could do, had
burnt over New York state and then carried his "streak of
fire to Boston."[13] Lyman Beecher had tried to stop him
but failed. John Truair, whose protracted night meetings
and encouragement of camp-meeting emotionalism were
typical Finney methods, had been an advance guard of
the revival in the Northampton area. A rival newspaper to
the *Gazette,* established in 1829, had sprung to the defense
of Truair in article after article, but editor Judd, Olympian
as usual, maintained a dignified silence.[14] The revival which
spread outward from Truair was, then, no mere local phenomenon. As reports poured in from Boston, from the
West, from the Connecticut Valley and as the ministers
roved in swarms from place to place to the scene of the
harvest, it was apparent that a special work of grace was
being enacted. Perhaps even the millennium itself was at
hand. The General Assembly of the Presbyterian Church
reported the encouraging signs, and asked, "What more,
or what different then, does the church need to bring in
her millenial glory?"[15] Ninety years earlier, in Northampton, Jonathan Edwards had been noting similar encouraging signs and indulging in the same hope.

Sylvester Judd's mother was in a glow of excitement.
The year before, Arethusa Hall had been converted. Now
came the conversion, not only of young Sylvester but of
his next younger brother Chauncey Parkman. On July 2
Mrs. Judd wrote to Arethusa about the revival:

at times I say in my heart "ye saints assist me in my song" what
hath the Lord wrought that he should make of some of my family trophies of his grace sometimes I feel as though a whole eternity would be none to long to sound his love—But there is a thrill-
ing fear runs through my soul that they may be deceived then I
have no where to go but to the physician of souls and sometimes
I feel as though I could cast all my burdens and trust all my interests with him.

The letter went on for three pages like this, but the only
reference to Sylvester was brief: in the midst of a discussion of young Park's conversion, she said, "he prayes in the
conference on the plain also S. I have never heard them I
do not go to many evening meetings." Evidently Sylvester's
conversion was not news and had been anticipated; he had
long shown religious susceptibility. But with Park's conversion Mrs. Judd was thrilled. She ran in to her husband with
the news, roused him from sleep, "and begged of him that
if he had no interest in the Saviour that he would immediately seek one, he said nothing." "It does appear to me
that his case is a singular one I cannot see that any thing
moves him I say little to him." Father Judd was earnest,
moral, and attached to religion; but he could not manage
the requisite surrender of himself. He instinctively recoiled
from emotionalism, had scarcely a spark of poetry in him,
and did not talk of flowing, of burning, or of casting himself into the "mother Deep."

Young Sylvester, his efforts now augmented by Park's,
entered wholeheartedly into his calling, the preaching of
Calvinist Christianity. The boys were no longer playing
earnest games in a barn. Sylvester felt a great sense of ur-
gency. He felt, more vividly than most people, the nearness
of hell, the closeness of heaven. The sinner's foot might
slip and slide at any time; the great pit yawned and he
would be forever lost. At the gates of both hell and heaven
were vortices in which the soul was swallowed up, but the
difference was as day and night. Sylvester and a young

friend prayed and preached and labored for souls. They went on a tour of the surrounding towns to drum up meetings for exhortation. Sylvester was "burning with the desire that all might be saved, and filled with horror at the thought of the eternal misery of any soul," and he was not deterred by those who thought of him as a "clodhopper zealot, gratis." He was a new man.

His conversion, gradual though it had been, coming on in waves, advancing and receding, over a period of five years, released new power in Judd. According to the Calvinist doctrine which he now embraced with heart as well as mind, a man who was once assured of his election could not fall from grace. He would continue to sin, indeed dared not hope for perfection, but he would no longer hate God and the things of the spirit; instead he would hate his sin and thirst for the perfection he knew he could not completely have. Assured of his "justification" by the infinite atonement of Christ, he was ready for the steps in his "sanctification." There were those who went further and asserted that with the moment of grace such holiness was imparted that the elect man was released from sin's bondage forever, that the terrors of the Law henceforth had no hold, that the sinner could walk forth, in Truair's phrase, "the Lord's free man." Such men and women were the Marys of the Lord's kingdom. They regarded further evidence of good works as superfluous. In their eyes, those who drudged on in Martha-like servitude simply lacked the complete assurance that descended with the dove of fire. The Marthas were living a gospel of "works" rather than of faith and were exemplifying not Calvinism but Arminianism, not predestination and the perseverence of the saints, but free will, dangerous heresy. Or so the enthusiasts thought.

The drudges, of course, were always in a majority. They were suspicious of the hotblooded emotionalism of young zealots like Sylvester Judd, and when it took the extreme form of Truair's midnight meetings and "holy kisses" they knew it was heresy. Called antinomianism, it had been embodied in Anne Hutchinson and driven from Massachusetts in 1638. Called perfectionism, it was embodied in John Truair and was driven from the Hampshire Association in 1829 and from Truair's sponsoring Presbytery of New York in 1831.[16] The heresy was subtle and dangerous because it was so close to orthodox Calvinism, merely an exaggeration of the belief in "free grace." And in free grace, unearned and impossible to lose, lay Calvinism's secret power.

Filled with this power, Judd worked wonders. Between missionary tours of the countryside he solved with ease "the intricacies of Greek and Latin, and the knotty problems of mathematics." He was like the river that he described, torrential and boiling. The more he drained off, the more flowed in. An infant universe seemed to be in him. He gave a lengthy, fact-crammed, and inspirational lecture on astronomy at the Hadley Lyceum, was president of the Literary Society at the Hopkins Academy, and delivered the valedictory address in verse. Compositions tumbled out effortlessly: the Evils of War, a lament for the fate of Poland, a short story about a young Jonathan who deserts his Polly but pays the price, the life of Fisher Ames, discussions of morality and reform. Some were eloquent, some witty, some bombastic, such as the flower that Arethusa Hall, with her usual unerring taste, culled for the reader's approbation in the official biography: "*Charity*, heavenly messenger! thy look tells us how holy seraphs are. A garland encircles thy forehead radiant with gems more white than Ceylon's pearls, more brilliant than Brazilian diamonds."[17] *Et cetera*. Judd's access of new freedom could even be seen in his handwriting, which became steadily more rounded, artistic, flowing. Enoch Hale or Ichabod S. Spencer, Judd's new minister, might have counseled him against the tendency to clothe Charity with pearls and roundness. The lean look was safest. Some would insist on translating "Charity" as "Love."

Judd was adept at translations. The one which is preserved for us is the story of Pyramus and Thisbe, a poem which brings to mind *Romeo and Juliet*. Like the play, "The Deception," which Judd was soon to write, it is a story of separated lovers, cruelly deceived, who expire on each other's breast. The love-death scene almost demands music by Wagner. Although Judd uses heroic couplets in his translation up until the very end, the climax staggers in dissonant thirds:

> With both her hands she pressed the deadly steel,
> It cleaved her heart. She smiled the pain to feel.
> Her dying fall was on her lover's breast,
> Her dying arms her lover's limbs embraced,
> Her dying lips her lover's bosom kissed.
> Her slow breath soon all ceased, her spirit leaving,
> They lay, the lovers lay, their bosoms meeting,
> Like lambkins tired, at noon, neath oak's shade sleeping.
> Their blood commingled in a deep, red flow,
> It stained the ground, then sought new veins below.

In writing her biography of Judd, Arethusa Hall locked up any secrets of his heart that there might have been, other than religious ones. She mentioned none of his love poetry, which is Byronic and flushed, or his early plays and brief stories. She felt no compunctions about printing the letters Judd wrote from college to his younger brothers and sisters, in a few of which he plays the pompous ass, exhorting them at length to be good in Polonius-aphorisms;[18] but she almost succeeded in giving the impression that Judd's first love affair was the one which culminated in his marriage. Even today the biographer is balked and can provide no details; the letters and journals Judd wrote, with a few exceptions, have been destroyed or lost, and we have only that which Arethusa thought suitable to print, plus

Judd's mention, in 1841, of some of his former female friends. Perhaps Arethusa's reticent statement, referring to the period 1827-29, should be read as a hint: "At length, disappointment in pursuing his studies came, together with some other trials and crosses of his natural temperament."[19]

One thing is sure: of the seven works in verse that we now have in the Judd manuscript collections—all written before 1840—seven express strong feelings of frustration, and of these seven, six are concerned with frustrated love. Three of the six are dated 1832. Another can be assigned to the period 1832-33 by the handwriting. The other two were probably written after 1836 and need not concern us now.

In one poem, Judd writes in the melancholy Byronic vein about a lost love somewhere in the misty past:

> Time, time, where have the visions fled?
> Bright Dreams of gayest years how flown!
> Fond loves have like a meteor sped,
>   My heart tis lone.
>
> In hours of youthful heat long gone,
> I used to muse on what would be,
> It seemed like radiant noonday-sun,
>   All bright to me.

The poem then gets more specific about the vision fled:

> Yes, Cupid snared my heart, The boy
> I fondled well, He snapt his bow,
> Then flew away, but took the joy,
>   And left the woe.

Desolate and wrecked on a lonely island the speaker lies on the sand "and would die there," until the cheerful trumpet call of official morality *"Do Good"* recalls her to herself and to her God. In this meditation upon the noonday sun and its westward, downward course, perhaps some emotional ambivalence is revealed by the fact that the speaker is a young woman. This was not the last time that Judd would try to enter imaginatively into a female character, or that he would cover realities with a coating of innocence, sentiment, and conventional exhortations to goodness. There was always the danger that his genius would dissolve in sentimentality. In 1824 he had been the special pet of the young women at Westfield Academy; a painting of Judd, made while he was writing *Margaret*, made him still look like a pet—pink, innocent, and good.

Another poem of 1832, dated, signed, and intended for more public consumption, is a dramatic monologue called "Soliloquy of an Indian Chief. in a wood." This time the persona is that of an Indian chief, a sort of Childe Harold in deerskin, driven from his hunting grounds by the civilized white barbarian. "Ruffian arms" have dragged away his fair Yamoyden; she is dead. "The sere leaves fall." The tone is melancholy, the verse blank. The chief whips himself into a frenzy remembering the scene. Yamoyden's "long Black tresses caught 'mong bramble bush, as thou/ Wert hurried cruelly away, so weak." The climax of the poem, which rises from blank verse to rhymed anapests, is the chief's curse on the white man. All the frustrations that surged in Judd rushed past the moral censor and found an approved form of expression:

> But the loved ones we'll dash on your rough stony floor,
> Then their quiv'ring limbs toss to die in *your* gore.
> . . . .
> Your scarred forms shall molder, on your wide woody plains.
> Your bones shall be bleached, by sun, wind and rains,—
> Hark! tis wailing despair, tis life's dying cry!
> Devouring flames rise, black smoke fills the sky!

The last line anticipates a climactic scene in *Margaret* in which the old Indian who haunts the Pond, the last of his race, sets fire to the village, delivers a fiery speech to the flaming sky, and leaps hissing to his death in the Pond.

Ahab thunders at the fathering sky and, amid universal ruin, plunges into the mother element, water. By such disguises the artist reveals himself and quenches the hellfire that burns in him.

Sylvester Judd, though not completely at ease in Zion, was finding that adversity had its uses and was turning his to account. The frustration that he felt most keenly was one that he could assail publicly and in his own voice. Poverty was the enemy. In his poem poverty was an abstraction, but the word's meaning for Judd was his own failure in business, his father's meager means and bare floors, his tightfistedness and every thing about the Father that tasks and heaps the young. Calvinism taught that hatred of the Father-concept was central to an unredeemed man's nature. Judd, redeemed, thought he had a new heart. Later, become a Unitarian, he would deny that he had ever had an old heart, or that hatred of the Father-principle was the natural state of man. In May, 1832, Judd assailed Poverty thus:

> It will not cure
> My restlessness however tight
> Thou fitt'st these manacles. Thy might
> At least will profit nought when death
> Shall say let go.
> . . . .
> Again I say let go thy hold,
> Or I will be, as thou art, bold.
> Thou leer'st like a demon lost,
> By Jove, but thou shalt learn the cost.
> I yet will burst my fetters strong,
> And bind them where they best belong,
> I'll break thy iron teeth, thy Jaw
> I'll cleave with steely point, Thy maw
> Hot stones shall fill, thy appetite
> To ease, and raging hunger, quite.
> I will not taste thy carcase foul,
> But let the vultures round thee prowl.

Young Judd had a few wild impulses to sublimate in poetry. The apostle of love, he imagined breaking Poverty's teeth and pouring hot stones in its mouth. Self-deception is ever the lot of man, said the Calvinist, who did not believe in a this-worldly perfection.

To write a biography of Judd in which Judd is a hero and his liberalism always right would be omitting an important part of the truth. Besides, Arethusa Hall has already written that story and sugarcoated his memory. In her biography, for example, forgetting that on page 30 she has quoted Judd's poem to Poverty as revealing his desire to "reach Fame's temple" and "there to sow/ The seeds of influence and esteem," Arethusa goes on to claim on page 346, "Never, from his earliest student-life, had Mr. Judd that inkling, often existing in the youthful brain, of seeing himself in print."

An attractive side of Judd appears in the paper he wrote for the final examination in August, 1832. It is Judd's first drama, a pleasant little piece satirizing Progress, after the manner of *Gulliver's Travels,* part III. Called "A Peep into the 20th Century," the story concerns the battle between the old and the new, the aged and the young. "Fire-brained Invention has taken wings. Mankind have seized him by the foretop, and willing or unwilling he is dragged on till Mother Nature groans." Or at least Grandfather Old-Style groans. Young Insinuation, his grandson, has a cure for that and for everything that ails mankind. He has invented, so he says, "the Patent Union Gatherer, or Grand Thought Consolidator," very useful for ministers, schoolmasters, politicians, unrequited lovers, or anyone who wants to bend the world to his will. As Young Insinuation puts it:

> Let the Schoolmaster place the machine in his school, then catch the pertinacious tyro, deposit his form in this first aperture, and then turn the crank. This clapper called Firmness in Error, Stern Counte[n]ance, or *I* say it that's enough, which turns with the

shaft will come plump into his face, blunt his arguments, and stun all power of contradiction. Believe me, he will think like his teacher, whose ignorance finds a counterpoise in this expedient.

After "a force-pump for Politicians" comes help for ministers who are having trouble with their parishioners.

Here rods are affixed to the axle which make obstinacy yield under their smart. For the complaint Great Salaries, is the rod, Ministers must live—for the cavil[?] You say and do not, is the rod No one is perfect. For Hard Doctrines, the rod Nature even has misteries. For the threat You must be dismissed, is the rod Better Sermons and Increased Zeal.

Disdainful maidens receive the following treatment:

Nonsense! If you could have secured one stoop of her head into this next cavity, a single turn of the handle would bring the bit of mechanism Big Promises, Show of Riches, Graceful Carriage, to bear so hard upon the Cranioscopetic Organ of High Notions as to press out its life.

So far this was all rather harmless, but at the end Judd had an afterthought. The Grand Thought Consolidator would cure religious heresy:

O.S.: Ah that's well. For we tried long enough in my day to stop the wild-notioned heretics, by the threats, and opposition of our highest dignitaries, and by restraining their licences, and thus barricading our pulpits, but all in vain.

Y.I.: O Sir, you did not come to the root of the matter. The people *would hear*, the people were the blame, the fuel for heresy to light her fires in . . . . I have some cords in this aperture to tie the legs of these runners after "new lights." There is the cord The threat Excommunication and non Reception without confession. Another the Cry The old ways are going to ruin. Another Our *pure* Church must remain disinfected. Another We are the majority and will have the law to hold you. Depend upon it Sir with such an entanglement none will favor a cunning Heresy but will think the old ways are right.

This was dangerous, too close to home. It sounded as if Judd was favoring the Truairites, who had indeed had all of those weapons brought to bear upon them. Possibly he was under Truair's influence. He had studied sacred music, Truair's specialty, during his winter in Westhampton a year earlier. But Judd ran a line through his afterthought, to cross it out, perhaps. He was not on the side of Young Insinuation, who was a deceitful scoundrel, nor was he on the side of Old-Style, who was perfectly glad to have a better mechanism for curing free thought. Sylvester Judd was, after all, a bit like his father, who believed in truth at whatever cost, who kept asking uncomfortable questions, and who was suspended between two worlds, one not quite dead, and the other not yet arrived.

Young Judd was not sure just where he stood on the issue of Progress. He had the reformist temper, showed a lively sense of indignation at the wrongs done the Indian and perhaps the slave,[20] hated war, and flirted with liberalism and the Muse. He wrote an address favoring equal rights for women which mimicked perfectly the tone of the enlightened liberal oratory of the day and could have passed for an address by a Congressman. He seemed to be sincere and straightforward in his appeal, but he had the wit to undercut his own pomposity by beginning the address with a frame which attributed the words to a "Mr. Fanciful," who spoke "at a meeting of the Society for the *acceleration* of the march of the human mind." The line under "acceleration" suggests a faint irony. Judd had accepted the proverbial wisdom of his day, but he was still thinking. If he longed for the elegant, unimpoverished, Unitarian world of Judge Joseph Lyman or George Bancroft, he stifled the thought. He had received the baptisms of water and of fire and had received the gift of a tongue. That was rainbow enough.

Part III

The Lapse

of Uriel

This was the lapse of Uriel,
Which in Paradise befell.
Once, among the Pleiads walking,
Seyd overheard the young gods talking;
And the treason, too long pent,
To his ears was evident.
The young deities discussed
Laws of form, and metre just,
Orb, quintessence, and sunbeams,
What subsisteth, and what seems.
One, with low tones that decide,
And doubt and reverend use defied,
With a look that solved the sphere,
And stirred the devils everywhere,
Gave his sentiment divine
Against the being of a line.
"Line in nature is not found;
Unit and universe are round;
In vain produced, all rays return;
Evil will bless, and ice will burn."
As Uriel spoke with piercing eye,
A shudder ran around the sky;
The stern old war-gods shook their heads,
The seraphs frowned from myrtle-beds;
· ·
A sad self-knowledge, withering, fell
On the beauty of Uriel;
In heaven once eminent, the god
Withdrew, that hour, into his cloud;
· ·
Or out of the good of evil born,
Came Uriel's voice of cherub scorn,
And a blush tinged the upper sky,
And the gods shook, they knew not why.

Ralph Waldo Emerson, "Uriel"

7

Yale

The valedictorian of the class of 1832 at Hopkins Academy was flushed with success. He had lectured to the adult Lyceum of Hadley and had discoursed of the sun and stars, of the probability of life on other worlds:

> If we look up and consider for a moment how boundless is the extent of Gods dominion and view the rolling orbs, the central suns and circling spheres, the mass of living beings that cover the whole—the thought will press upon us with force, *what are we*?

What are we indeed? Judd's ostensible answer was that we are small, that humility is the great lesson the stars teach. But his actual answer was the infinite possibilities, the plenitude of the soul. He walked among the Pleiads like Uriel, the archangel of the sun:

> The disembodied spirit might go on from sphere to sphere with the speed of light forever, and yet new scenes would ever burst upon the enraptured vision. O the length, the breadth, the highth, the depth! Who can span it? He alone who fathoms eternity.

Judd was afoot with his vision. And now he was going to Yale.

The price he was to pay was explicitly understood. He was to prepare for the Congregational ministry. The money that father Judd, the Hampshire Missionary Society, Arethusa Hall, and a Mrs. Johnson invested in his future[1] was expected to yield a return in dollars and souls. There were realities as well as visions.

The first of these realities was the burial of Squire Sylvester Judd in Westhampton. The death came just as Sylvester was ready to leave for New Haven, and the funeral was the last event of his old life. It was like a door closing behind him as he left. Years later, when Judd thought of his grandfather, he thought of festivity and the ripe cider that went with it:

> Great times we used to have at Grandpa Judd's at Thanksgiving. There were good eating, and good drinking, and good feeling. There was the mug of flip too. I remember it well. Father thinks I am a little beset with a *spiritual* nature. Yet those were glorious times. They are gone. Their vision glimmers among the things that were.[2]

Four months after the funeral he wrote to his brother Hall, "And shall I never see him, or meet his welcome smile, or shake his aged hand again? This reflection starts the big tear, and I can but weep as I think of it. . . . his name and virtues will never be obliterated from our memory. . . ." For Judd, his grandfather was the embodiment of all that was stately and noble in the old tradition. Judd was not in rebellion against tradition and the patriarchs. Westhampton and his grandfather were even then enveloped with something of the golden mist of childhood. Judd's life had been, and would continue to be, a succession of doors that closed, sometimes with a slam.

For each shut door, there was a new one that opened. Judd entered Yale at a propitious time. Beginning in 1831, with the quieting of student unrest by President Jeremiah Day's judicious combination of firmness and reform, Yale entered upon a fifteen-year period of marked esprit de corps:

> The whole period . . . was a brilliant period in the history of the
> college. Never before had the students as a body manifested such
> an interest in study, such *esprit de corps*, such pride in the ability
> and reputation of their instructors, such affection for their Alma
> Mater. It was a period marked also by a great degree of literary
> activity among the students themselves. . . . The three great de-
> bating societies were maintained with great enthusiasm.[3]

A factor which no doubt contributed to this result was the
series of great revivals that swept the campus, especially the
one of 1831. A convert of this revival, Horace Bushnell,
had been one of the tutors (graduate assistants) at the college and during Judd's freshman year was studying at the
Yale Divinity School. Judd would have participated with
the influential Bushnell in the small meetings and discussions where the labor by the converted for the souls of the
unconverted was carried on. Judd's acquaintance with this
commanding personality would have been significant. Later,
Judd would develop thoughts, opposing revivalism and
supporting the idea of gradualism in the Christian nurture
of children, strikingly similar to those for which Bushnell
became famous.*

One of the tutors who conducted recitations and administered discipline was Noah Porter, future president of
Yale. He and Bushnell were among the avant-garde students
who had made Coleridge's *Aids to Reflection* their companion to the Bible.[4] This textbook of romanticized religion, though more orthodox than transcendental, was an
entering wedge for the Coleridge who was helping to intro-
duce German transcendentalism to both the orthodox and
the Unitarians in New England. The curriculum at Yale, as
is usual in colleges, was thirty years behind the times and
was based on rationalistic eighteenth-century defenders of
orthodoxy like Thomas Reid, Dugald Stewart, and William

---

*See Chapter 10 for further discussion of this.

Paley.[5] They were beef-eating Britons with common sense and useful ideas that suited Americans. The new thought stemming from Kant and company, with which George Bancroft was then as familiar as anyone in America, had to be smuggled in by little groups of students at Yale.

In at least one respect, Yale was brilliant and up-to-date. Students studied science under a pair of the finest teachers in America. Judd would have been interested. He had talked earlier of earning distinction in both literature and science. Denison Olmsted, the younger and less notable of the two teachers, taught mathematics, astronomy, and natural philosophy. Benjamin Silliman, whose lectures and genial personality made him a great favorite with students, taught whatever else was to be learned about the natural world, especially chemistry and geology. Silliman was pious and told students that geology confirmed the Mosaic account of the creation, but nonetheless the prestige that he gave to science at Yale was an influence in the direction of the naturalism and worldliness that are always subtly at work to undermine supernaturalism.

In contrast to the glamour of science was the somewhat pallid appearance of religion in the person of the college preacher, Eleazar Fitch, whose sermons were well written but poorly delivered and whose nervous afflictions rendered him almost speechless without his prepared text.[6] There were others at hand in the theological school, such as the trailblazing Nathaniel W. Taylor, to exert a more positive influence; but it was Fitch who was most publicly on display—two sermons on Sundays.

Still, religion was the pervasive force at Yale. Timothy Dwight, the fountainhead of the revival movement, was still alive in the spirit of the faculty members who taught Sylvester Judd. Dwight could be felt in the background, behind the curriculum and the textbooks, behind the theology, behind the ideas of what constituted good literature, good sense, and good style. Judd's college compositions at Yale show a tendency away from his former impassioned rhetoric toward moderation and the golden mean of the solid, sensible, rational gentleman. Religion was emotional at Yale, but it was not romantic; it was rational and relied on Common Sense and the facts of science to buttress the Bible. This was Yale's answer to the deism Dwight had routed: fight the deists with their own weapons, reason and science.

The revival of 1831 still hung over the campus. Judd was one of about thirty-three "professors" of religion in a class of one hundred, and at Yale it was almost taken for granted that a convert would go into the ministry.[7] At Yale the big question, often asked, was "Are you saved?" (At Harvard few would be so crude as to ask.) Judd was one of those who asked. A month after entering Yale he wrote to his cousin, George Lyman, "Permit me to inquire how nearly assimilated you are to the purity of heaven." Of his sister, Apphia, he inquired, "I would ask, as a far more important question, what proficiency you are making in the school of Christ?" He warned his brother Hall, then a student at Hopkins Academy, "I presume there is no danger that you will not study enough. But you may grow proud, and lose your spirituality." Religion was more than personal piety; it also led to social concerns. He asked his mother, in 1834, "Need I ask if your bosom is filled with pity, sympathy, and love for the poor black man?"

Judd was merely doing what he thought was expected of him. A minister was supposed to be zealous where souls were at stake. It was often thought that the pious should not even associate with non-professors, especially if they were not decidedly moral and respectful towards religion. Injunctions against dissolute or profane companions were given to the young as a matter of course. Nonetheless, Judd's zeal to make the world as pious as himself looked like fanaticism even to many of those around him. In the letter quoted above on page 166 is the revealing statement, significantly irrelevant to the rest of the paragraph, "Father thinks I am a little beset with a *spiritual* nature." And Judd's own classmates winced under his attacks. Fifty years later, Judd's biographical notice in the class records noted, as the one recollection of Judd's student days, "the high Calvinism, which had made him a terror to his irreligious classmates." Judd himself was bothered by his intensity. In the letter of 1834 to his mother, just quoted, he adds, "My natural temperament, you know, mother, is ardent, and subject to change. This occasions me some trouble. I fear sometimes going too far in too exclusive devotion to one object. I am sorry that there should be any decline of religious feeling in Northampton. It need not be. We can *always* feel." Indeed that was precisely the trouble. We can sometimes feel too much.

Judd and his classmates were not as solemn and single-minded as the above might suggest. There was the usual hazing of freshmen, "smoking, breaking windows, stealing keys, calling before mock-tutors, and so forth," wrote Judd to George Lyman shortly after entering Yale. He went on to describe the dining room:

> While the blessing is being asked at one table, there will be rapping, ringing bells, and hollowing for "Waiter, waiter," at another. This mixture of noise and sacred things is sometimes too great for my risibles, so that I am obliged to laugh in spite of myself.

The natural man was not dead. Sometimes the scene at commons bordered on riot, as John Mitchell later described it:

> Boiled potatoes, pieces of bread, whole loaves, balls of butter, dishes, would be flung back and forth, especially between Sophomores and Freshmen; and you were never sure, in raising a cup to your lips, that it would not be dashed out of your hands, and the contents spilt upon your clothes. . . . I remember a charge of six

hundred tumblers, thirty coffee-pots, and I know not how many other articles of table furniture, destroyed or carried off in a single term.[8]

The period described was ten years earlier than 1832, and perhaps conditions had improved somewhat since the revival, but manners were still rude:

> Huge pewter pitchers, filled with foaming beer,
> Were scattered o'er the table, there and here
> And, since no glassware could be had in town,
> By 'word of mouth' the malt was worried down.[9]

After his first three months, Judd had the good fortune to escape the corrosive diet of "slum" endured at commons. He must have been a personable and engaging young man who appealed to the sympathies of pious ladies, for a "Mrs. L., a mother in Israel" offered him, in December, free board at her house. Again, in his senior year, he boarded in town. As he reported then to his mother:

I am pleasantly situated this summer; board with Miss C., spend about two hours a day, attending to recitations. I enjoy very much the polished and literary society of New Haven. The ladies are said to be very beautiful.

Even with such help from pious sympathizers, Judd had a struggle to make ends meet. In his junior year he spent the winter term teaching in Middletown, Connecticut, keeping up with his college studies at the same time. He also taught in New Haven. At times he "kept bachelor's hall, and boarded himself; and made his journeys, in vacation, on foot." During the third quarter of the freshman year, Judd obtained President Day's permission to study at home. Even so, it was often only by stringent economies and thin fare in dormitory rooms that Judd managed his way through college at all. He tried not to be too embarrassed about his coarse clothing.[10] His room was doubtless not warm, for students provided their own fuel.[11]

Judd's father had come into something of an inheritance at Squire Judd's death, but it was only a few thousand dollars and not liquid. Father Judd had three sons and two daughters younger than Sylvester to educate. Besides, in the middle of Sylvester's junior year, editor Judd retired from the newspaper at the age of forty-six, followed George Bancroft's example of devoting his time to historical research, and had to scrape along for the rest of his life on the income from an estate of less than $5000. Constitutionally frugal, he preferred leisure for his historical researches and other studies to money and comforts, and he expected Sylvester to economize. This was a matter of conflict between father and son. Father Judd, who was usually reticent about recording personal family matters in his journal, noted on October 3, 1835:

> Sylvester started for New Haven on Tuesday last, rather downhearted. Some things have been said in regard to his notions about expenses; some censure has been passed upon him by me and J.W. which seems not to have been very pleasant. Hope he will conduct wisely.[12]

Sylvester was conducting himself oddly that vacation. He was fitful in temperament and had his times of depression. Even some of those with whom he felt most at ease, his mother and Elizabeth—wife of J.W., his older brother— thought he was acting strangely, and Sylvester himself used the word "odd" in describing the way his actions appeared to others.[13] He had a secret, and he would disclose the trouble to no one.

These periods of depression were the more notable because he had been so ebullient at the start of his college career. He had been able to relax from seriousness and had revealed in his letters home an engaging side of his character. He could be playful, especially when he thought of his sister Peninnah ("Pin"), born in 1826; his brother Hophni ("Hop"), born in 1823; or Apphia ("Ap"), born 1820. The younger the child, the more he could relax and forget the rhetoric expected of a young gentleman. His thoughts turned automatically to children when he was warmed by the Thanksgiving box sent to replace the festivities at home:

> . . . mother may suppose, then, of course, that it is very pleasant to resort to a little *buttery*, as indeed it is. . . . Have they forgotten me? I looked the papers all over carefully twice, but could find no "From P——n," "From H——i," and was quite disappointed. Was H——i off playing with the boys, or P——n with the girls? I do not understand what it means, and would like to have the matter explained. . . . Has P——n forgotten that she promised to write me "certain, true"?

All his life, Judd felt most at ease with children. His most intense efforts as a pastor would be devoted to bringing the children to a full sense of belonging in the church, and his happiest artistic strokes were the scenes about children in his novels. Even in his freshman year at Yale his concern for bringing children into the church revealed itself. The following letter to Elizabeth that winter makes us wonder whether Horace Bushnell and Judd had just been talking about Christian nurture, the subject Bushnell later developed in his book of 1847:

> I am sorry you have so little faith in children's conversions. . . . Just . . . bring down eternal things to their understanding and feelings, let a *child* know that a few short years set us afloat on the ocean of eternity, and all things earthly will pass away,—I say, let them know and feel these things, let parents, teachers, and guardians constantly teach, and live themselves, in view of these things, and I think there is but little danger of children's "taking in the bewitching world" as they grow older. . . .

This comment was a development of Judd's own thought and experience and need not necessarily be connected with Bushnell. When only twelve or thirteen years of age, Judd had written a school essay called "The Advantages of Early Piety," and he later said that he had known religious emotions from a very early age. This feeling that he had known some degree of holiness in his childhood proved to be a crucial point in his own developing thinking. It was the nub of his agonizing secret doubt.

In December of 1832, as he opened a box from home and emptied out "mother's care in the form of curtains, carpet, cake, and so forth," then Hophni's bag of popcorn and butternuts, Sylvester came finally to Pin's apple. He put it to his lips, and thought, "Pin shall have a kiss, and kissed the apple in place of her rosy lips." The gesture represented Judd at his most playful, but somehow the gesture was symbolic. The apple suggested innocence to him, but according to his theology it should have suggested guilt. The tempting image of childhood innocence was the apple of knowledge that would bar him from paradise as he had conceived it up to that time. Nineteenth-century sentimentality about children, particularly little girls, was about to change Judd's entire life. As was evidenced by the fact of the carpet and the kiss, unheard-of things ten years earlier, time—whether called progress or degeneration— could not be evaded.

The point was that childhood was not supposed to be innocent. According to his creed, Sylvester was supposed to believe little Pin and Appy hopelessly depraved and in need of grace. No sooner had he mentioned them playfully in a letter of 1833 to his mother, than he added ominously:

> Neither death nor severe sickness has come nigh us. But can we always live? Who shall be taken first? Is it a brother or a sister, or one of our dear parents? Is it I?

What if Pin or Appy should die? They had not known conversion and they would be damned forever. Judd's horror of hell was intense. He wrote to a college friend that year:

> Who would pronounce a man a fanatic for being all excited to pull a sleepy neighbor from a burning house? And who will sneer at and denounce those who manifest a *little* zeal at most, in saving poor blinded mortals from the fires of an interminable hell?

Judd could not relax as long as there was a hell. Then, on January 28, 1833, Judd asked the fateful question. Speaking of the conversion of children, he asked Elizabeth:

> But, when they are not able to *understand the nature* of it, how can they *experience* conversion? And on what principle of the Bible or common sense will they be damned?

How could a loving and just God damn six-year-old Pin, who had sent Sylvester a letter with a "hundred kisses"? Judd might have turned on God and asked, "Did you ever have a sister?"

Judd's heart would not let him believe in that kind of a God for long. Neither would it let him believe in no God at all. But belief could not be founded on mere feeling. It had to be based on the creed. The catechism that Judd had memorized was all that stood between him and hell. Let that go and his foot would slide. According to the creed, if his conversion was genuine, then he should be through with doubts.

The Yale theologians gave Judd some help in his difficulties. Led by Nathaniel W. Taylor of the Divinity School, they had worked out, in the 1820's, an ingenious compromise between Calvinism and liberalism, at the same time claiming that they were still faithful to every article of the orthodox creed. As Judd's question of January 28, 1833, suggests, the hardest thing for the Calvinist to explain was how a just and loving God could cast infants into hell. In the seventeenth century Michael Wigglesworth's "Day of Doom" had met this question head on, but by 1820 it was no longer enough to say that infants would get "the easiest room in Hell." Under pressure from the Unitarian challenge, the New School theologians at Yale conceded that infants were not automatically damned and that nobody was damned until by an act of free moral agency he committed sin. But the concession made with the left hand was taken back with the right. Though all had free will, all inevitably *did* sin: that was an observed fact. All would therefore merit damnation unless God's grace intervened. Moreover, admitted Taylor in private discussion once, an infant beyond the age of six months might be a free moral agent and therefore in need of grace.[14] Judd's sisters were still in mortal danger.

Judd was not satisfied and kept on asking questions. A lesser man would have glossed over his doubts, but Judd was intense. At Yale he was encouraged to speculate, to explore every metaphysical point to the fullest. Yale wanted no untried, cloistered piety. Yale believed in reason. Taylor, who believed firmly that reason and revelation could not disagree, was even willing to see the Bible "tried at the bar of human reason," whose decisions "are to be relied upon as infallible judgments."[15] Sylvester Judd could not be satisfied with blind faith. Though it was dangerous to know too much, the apple of knowledge had to be tasted.

The sun of the previous July, which had been warm with boundless possibilities, was far away that January of 1833 when Judd asked his sister-in-law, "And on what principle of the Bible or common sense will they be damned?" As months went on and doubts multiplied, they came at him in a rush and left him in terror. Fire came to have a new meaning to him: "Under the elm-trees and deep midnight of New Haven, I struggled and questioned, and doubts beat upon me like a storm of fire. All men seemed to leave me then."[16]

The doubt was the more frightening because of the height of exaltation from which he had been thrown. He had dared much, had confidently proclaimed his election. Had he committed the sin of spiritual pride which threw even Lucifer, angel of light, out of heaven? Congregationalism said that anyone who drank from the communion cup unworthily was doubly damned. Just a few months after entering Yale, Judd had drawn up a Consecration, a legal contract binding himself to God forever. It began soberly enough, with formal, measured phrases; but at the end it became breathless:

> . . . and I consecrate my all—help, Lord—can I do it? Have I counted the cost? Will my after-life bear witness to a consecration entire, and never disregarded or broken? How weak I am! Help me, dear Saviour . . . yes, I do it—I make a dedication of my ALL. Henceforth, fare thee well, vain world! Welcome, Cross! I'll take thee up, and bear thee through strifes, through sneers, though death be my portion. Come, Spirit of heaven!. . . . Thou Holy Dove! come, and rest on me.

From this did he descend to mere rationalism, philosophy, and disastrous speculation, all within a few months.

He warned his younger brothers against the temptations of worldly learning. "Let me tell you, dear brother, from experience, advancement in learning of itself does not make me happy," he wrote to his brother Hall. A year later, when he had temporarily overcome his doubts, he wrote to Chauncey Parkman—who was, as befit a future lawyer and railroad director, enamored of Benjamin Franklin,—"I regard Franklin as one of the greatest men of his times. . . . But. . . . Take care that you do not wrap yourself in your subtle abstractions about the nature of things, without making a proper use of things as they are. It may prove the winding-sheet of your soul."

In June, 1833, Judd wrote a letter to Arethusa Hall which revealed him in a more worldly mood than he had been in six months earlier. The reader learns with relief that Judd could write an entire letter to his most intimate confidante, who was both sister and mother to him, and almost sweetheart, without once mentioning religion or morality.

> I take my situation daily by the north chamber window. Here I sit and muse in my own solitude, annoyed by no bell, no tutor's call, or fear of the black mark. Here I become wrapt in the story of Helen and Priam, laugh at the fun of Horace or am half enticed

> by his sensuality, or plunge into the depths of Euclid. Love! how strange a thing it is! . . . . Yes, little naked Cupid, with his bow and arrow, effects a mightier conquest than all the crested myriads of ancient times. . . . I speak, of course, as one who stands upon an eminence, and gazes upon the busy world below; wonders, remarks, but keeps himself aloof. . . . But you and I, so wise, so experienced, look on in cold indifference. If I don't get me engaged first, I want you to select for me the most suitable of your heaven-born pupils. The wife makes the man. If you make the wife, you may make me. So don't despair yet.

This was an improvement, a more relaxed, urbane Judd. But within a week he was stricken, in a way that must have seemed to him like one of the disciplinary providences of God that Calvinists talked so much about. Sylvester was poisoned, the doctor said. Judd's face swelled up; he could scarcely study or pray. Perhaps the ailment was merely physical, caused by poison; but we should note that Judd's difficulty, described by his father as an "ague in the face," returned to plague him at least four more times in the next four years.[17] One can only wonder about the nature of the "oddities" and nervous afflictions Judd manifested from time to time after 1833 and their relationship, if any, to the facial swelling that humbled this exceedingly handsome young man, with his ruddy complexion, blue eyes, and blond hair. It is certain that within a month after his "little naked Cupid" letter to Arethusa and his poisoning, Judd was back to his old, otherworldly voice, made a bit more masculine by adversity. To a friend at Yale, he wrote:

> If,—and you see I but repeat what I have often said,—if, I say, the things which are commonly believed by Christians with reference to heaven and hell are *true, immutable truths,* what exertion can be too great, what self-denial too severe, what agony too intense. . . . Let Christians be reasonable men. Let them tear their creed to tatters, scatter their Bible to the four winds, call hell a delusion, and heaven a lie, or else act up to their belief. What! exchange the

everlasting crown of glory for fame's fading laurels, and the felic-
ities of eternity for the fleeting joys of time! Oh, is it not mad-
ness? Who will do it? Will you? Will I? Or will we see others do it,
and be as indifferent as when we see a woman peddle her eggs for
snuff?

But, with the big emphasis on the *if* at the beginning, the
oratory rang back at the advocate with a hollow note as he
stopped for applause.

That winter, Judd was heartened by a renewal of his old
religious feelings. He had just won the prize in Latin composition and was meeting with success in his other studies.
(In both sophomore and junior years he would win prizes
in English composition.) During the winter vacation he
visited J.W. and Elizabeth in Hartford and was caught up
in the revival of religion there. The pious Elizabeth, to
whom Judd confided more easily than to anyone else except Arethusa Hall and with whom he also made jokes
about Cupid, might have influenced him. Judd was always
more swayed by the heart than by the head.

If Sylvester Judd had not already come in contact with
Goethe's *Sorrows of Young Werther,* one of the seminal
books of the romantic movement that was belatedly finding its way into New England, he had a chance to read it
this vacation in Hartford. His brother J.W. was now a partner in the publishing firm of Silas Andrus, a firm that
brought out four editions of *Werther* between 1824 and
1839.[18] One can easily imagine that Judd would have spent
some time at the bookstore, thumbing through novels and
books that Yale would not let into its library, catching at
points with quick glances. It was not his habit to read a
book straight through; he preferred to dart through, pausing over points that suited his purpose and perhaps jotting
them down on the little folded sheets of paper that he always carried, a habit he had formed at an early age.[19] A

reader who could dash through a novel in a day, Judd would hardly have overlooked the piles of the best-selling *Werther* at Andrus and Judd's.

Before the school year was out, Sylvester's religious troubles returned, and he had reason to sympathize with the mood of Werther, a young man whose feelings were dammed up inside him, who lived a lie in the pursuit of truth, who longed for an impossible love and found only the escapism of pistol and ball. Judd could not turn to anyone for relief. He could not admit his religious doubts to his family, who were sacrificing for the education of an orthodox minister; he could not admit his doubts to his classmates who had been the victims of his inquisitions; he could scarcely admit them to himself. He was in a maze and was full of deception. He deceived himself to such an extent that to cover up his feelings of being a hypocrite he became more officious than ever, trying to lose his doubts in actions consistent with what he thought the Calvinistic belief in hell demanded. This made him unpopular, and Judd, whose nature was social and who needed the "sympathy" of others to maintain his own sense of balance, was shut up in himself. "I was made indeed for society. But there are few, I think, who can make more agreeable companionship with solitude than myself." The statement had a brave, Thoreauvian ring, but Judd was no Thoreau. "I am no monk, no ascetic, no solitaire," he said to his wife in 1852; "my being thrives and grows in the atmosphere of a most sympathetic love." But Judd seemed unable to establish a strong, lasting relationship with his acquaintances at college.[20] With his father and his brothers he corresponded in the slightly "official" tone. With Arethusa, Elizabeth, his mother, and his sisters he could talk more at ease. Always, Judd seemed most responsive to the feminine character. Then came the period when he could not confide even in them; the letters became infrequent and reserved.

The theme of deception was on his mind. At some time between 1834 and 1836, probably the earlier date, he began to write his unpublished drama, "The Deception," about a pair of deceivers. Geoffrey, the villain, lures Crawford away from orthodoxy, simplicity, New England, and the fair Miss Hazeltine. He does all this in the guise of helping Crawford rise politically in the liberal, sinful society of New York City. His motive, of course, is to seduce Miss Hazeltine. Crawford, his ambitions fired, adopts the dangerous doctrine that the end (advancement) justifies the means (hypocrisy and infidelity). He deceives himself and his fiancee, and the result is unmitigated horror. The seduced heroine takes poison; Crawford finds her dying in a brothel to which she has been lured; he stabs the villain, who repents and confesses all with his last breath. Hero kisses heroine (twice) and finishes off the poison. The second scene as well as this last one has overtones of *Romeo and Juliet.* The balcony in this case is the summit of Mt. Holyoke, the point closest to the sun in Judd's personal world, and the lovers swear—not by the sun, the inconstant sun, nor by the "image bearing" river that turns its "bosom to the sky"—but by themselves: "it is enough to appeal/to consciousness within of truth." From this pinnacle the lovers plunge relentlessly downward to the lower depths of New York, the gloom and hellfire relieved only by deathbed repentances and reunion.

Images of falling and of plunging water were on Judd's mind. It would almost seem that Judd's symbolic use of mountains and water was intentional. The heroine resides in "Catskill" but comes to New York to be seduced. In one of the few purple passages in the play, Satanist Geoffrey makes us think of Byron's Manfred and the heights from which men fall:

> I've stood upon the Alps that overlook
> One half the globe; I've looked adown its deep

> Abysses, that make the brain reel—that send
> Up with a thousand echoings, the noise
> Of Waterfalls like sound of many thunders.
> I've looked upon its glacier fields, just like
> The Ocean stiffened when its wrath was up,
> And its rough surges turned to solid ice.—
> Where'er you stand or gaze, the terrible
> And the sublime are blended, and tis awful.
> The mind starts, and chills with a mazy fear.
> The imagination labors, and the senses
> Grow weary, midst the wonders, dark and vast,
> The fathomless of Nature's handy work. (I.i)

Judd had sense enough to make most of the verse on a more prosaic, conversational level than this and to write several scenes in prose. Each of the characters speaks with a distinctive voice. As is usual, Satan (Geoffrey) is the most interesting character:

> The world's a masquerade all deceive and all are deceived. He dupes the world and her. I dupe him and her, and shall be duped in turn. . . . To be honest!—twere to wear a window in ones breast into which every man could look, and see what passed within. Who could endure it! (II.vii)

Judd could have said this about himself in his more despairing moods, but cynicism did not sit easily on him.

"The Deception" was a fairly lengthy work and an advance on anything Judd had done up to that time. Perhaps the most damning thing that can be said about it is that if it had been published it might have been the most popular of Judd's works. Unlike *Margaret,* it had no complexity, depth, or originality of phrase or idea to weary the common reader. The plot was hackneyed, the characters flat and conventional, the verse uninspired. But there was sensation and sentiment, morality and horror, together with the only tight, economical plot that Judd ever achieved.

That this play could be performed at Yale College, and at a time when a revival of religion was in progress,[21] is fact enough to revise our conception of what Yale College was like. Though Yale was the fountainhead of Puritanism in America, it did not exist exclusively for the education of ministers. There were plenty of young Southern gentlemen to counteract the Puritan distaste for the theater. Timothy Dwight had written—concerning Aeschylus, Sophocles, Euripides, Corneille, Shakespeare, and Schiller —that "among all their productions there is scarcely one which an Apostle would even read. How great a part of them are little else than splendid vehicles of vice."[22] The words would have fit "The Deception" perfectly, for despite its obvious moral it was singularly devoid of any pious speeches or saving words of power.

"The Deception" received its only recorded performance on March 31, 1836. The occasion was the annual Exhibition of the Brothers in Unity, one of the three great societies to one or another of which all Yale students belonged. As a combination of debating society, literary club, dramatic association, fraternity, and library, the Brothers in Unity had a vital role in Judd's education. The annual Exhibition was the chief social event of the year, a chance to show off before the "polished and literary society of New Haven," whose ladies were said to be so very beautiful. In a town which had no theater, it was an event to be anticipated.

The handwritten minutes laconically describe the scene. "The President took his seat, at half-past six, the doors were unbarred & an eager auditory instantly filled the room."[23] The records do not disclose to what extent there was embarrassment or hilarity when Sylvester Judd, who played the role of the hero, made his impassioned declarations to a certain R. Dodge, who played the heroine, but the records do show that "the exercises were esteemed uncommonly interesting & good order & good feeling prevailed throughout the evening." In addition to "The Deception," the evening included productions of "The Suspicious Landlord," a farce whose locale was "down South there"; "The Doomed," and another comedy called "Cutting Out." Orations on "Poetry is Connected with Religion," "On Athenian Character," and "On the Causes of our Literary Delinquency" rounded out the program, which ended after midnight.

Presumably, the topic "On the Causes of our Literary Delinquency" had nothing to do with the question of the morality or immorality of plays like "The Deception." That question was also discussed by the Brothers in Unity on July 30, 1836, but the question was phrased, "Is novel reading beneficial?" When the question came up for debate, unusual zeal was manifested in the discussion. Somewhat surprisingly, in view of the enthusiastic support by the Brothers of student theatrical efforts, the question, when put to a vote of the society, was decided in the negative.

The question of the value and place of literature was very much alive. The question about "Literary Delinquency" reflected that concern. It referred to the fact that there was scarcely an American book worthy of the notice of the English critics. If there were to be an American literature, it would have to be a pious literature, and where would a pious literature find its seedbed if not at Yale?

Accordingly, Sylvester Judd was already participating, at the age of twenty-two, in one of the most momentous conflicts in American life: the conflict between art and morality. The conflict would be his concern for the rest of his life, and America's, for Judd had an important role in demonstrating what could be done for American literature by turning the attention from imitation of European speech and European models to the employment of native American idiom and regional materials; thus did he earn the praise of James Russell Lowell for writing "the most emphatically *American* book ever written."

An essay by Judd on the subject of a distinctively American literature still survives, dated April 1, 1834. Judd wrote that a national literature should reflect the particular conditions of the national environment. Art should reflect nature, not in its general character, but in its local manifestations. "Our Climate is rough, cold and stimulating. The Italian soft, mild, and enervating. Our mountains in extent and elevation, and boldness of scenery exceed the Pyrenees." Mountains, rivers, lakes, forests, cataracts should give to American literature something of their character. Judd was saying nothing very original, but he was saying something fundamental enough that it would continue to be said in different ways in the running debate over nationalism in literature that exercised the New York magazines of the 1840's.[24]

Judd's professors cannot be given credit for his later use of native American idiom in his books. They actively discouraged it. Judd's notes on the lectures of his rhetoric professor, Chauncey Goodrich, show that Goodrich cautioned against the use of "Americanisms": words like "breadstuffs," "belittle," "back & forth," "I reckon," "balance of," "I guess," "creek," etc. Judd's student essays written under this sort of tutelage were appropriately correct, pale, and rhetorical. He did not dare to write descriptions for his professors such as the following ones, typical of his 1850 novel, *Richard Edney:*

> Aunt Grint, chromatic, grum, hard-mouthed, who looked as if she had been kiln-dried, and all her natural juices evaporated off,—how she sweetened to the children, and tiddled them, and caroled to them! . . . . Then there was Mrs. Tunny, a sleek, round, fubby piece of mortality, with bunches of ribbons in her hair, and bunches in her neck, who owned a broad-aisle pew in Dr. Broadwell's Church,—had been to a party at Judge Burp's,—hired a piano for her daughters. . . . (140-41)

Even in 1850, the *North American Review* proved to be no

more liberal than the Chauncey Goodrich of 1834 about admitting this sort of language into literature.

Judd did dare to go against the official position of his teachers in at least one essay, however. Yale had, in 1828, taken a firm stand in favor of teaching the classics as the backbone of a liberal education.[25] Judd questioned this emphasis. Could not the mental faculties be as effectively exercised in learning modern languages, he asked. Study of any material exercised the mind. For suitable objects of study, Judd suggested the attention be focused upon "the limitless number and variety embraced in the English language." Judd's interest in foreign languages was intense, but he felt that the failure of Yale to teach the modern languages more aggressively was a mistake. German, in particular, the usefulness of which had been brought home by the advocacy of George Bancroft, was not taught at Yale.[26]

The issue which kept coming to the front of Judd's mind was the question, should he trust himself or submit to authority? He asserted himself on the issue of the classics vs. the modern languages. He advocated originality rather than imitation in literature. And in still another essay he seemed attracted toward an almost Emersonian position about the self and the Soul:

> But that man knows little of himself who has not felt that its elements reside within his own breast. . . . It is the Soul revelling in an unseen world. . . . Revelations multiply such as mortal man cannot gainsay. . . . The pride of Man is flattered by an approach to the Divine Essence. In the mass of men it has been difficult to control this principle, and impossible to extinguish it; nor would I see it crushed.[27]

In the light of this nugget embedded in an essay that otherwise is as pessimistic as Ecclesiastes, we should reread the declaration, in "The Deception," that "it is enough to appeal/to consciousness within of truth," a statement which also anticipated Judd's later contact with Emerson. The rest of this statement must be quoted to see the issue in full perspective. Judd's hero said, "If we are true, it is enough to appeal/to consciousness within of truth." If we are true: there was the rub. Judd was living a lie. How could he give himself over completely to trusting himself when he saw himself illustrating the depravity of man? The argument doubled back on itself and left Judd in a maze of contradiction. In such a state Judd was cautious about asserting his own thought against the authorities. He kept on at Yale, despite his despairing thoughts of giving up, hoping that he would find the folly of individualism and trusting himself. Professor Fitch took years to complete the cycle of doctrinal exposition in Sunday chapel;[28] the least Judd could do was hear him to the end.

In such a mood Judd continued to write papers that reflected popular clichés. "There is nothing new," wrote Judd in one paper, repeating the phrase throughout the essay like a litany, it being the same essay in which he said a good word for mysticism. He spoke of the "perverseness of the human heart." "The flattering Theory of the Perfectibility of Human Society," he said, "appears visionary." Moderation was the great lesson in all things. It was a mistake to try to "rear their goodness or their schemes of benevolence too high." "Men in avoiding one error fall into another." He became angry at the believers in Manifest Destiny: "The impiety which supposes a governing Providence to have been raising up nations and destroying them for 6000 years, all to prepare a substructure for *our* greatness and glory ought to tremble aghast." Like a world-weary Ecclesiastes Judd pronounced that there was nothing new under the sun.

As if to illustrate his point he wrote an oration full of puffery and oratorical gloss. He delivered it before the Phi Beta Kappa society, to which he had been elected, in November, 1835. He chose to discuss monuments, and he showed that they were A Good Thing. "They will endure," he concluded. As Judd's pen raced on, making careless errors in forming letters, his mind seemed to be somewhere else, and his concluding sentence was somewhat lame. He could turn out competent, imitative prose by the yard, but it sounded manufactured, and he knew it. At the conclusion of his address on monuments, he penned the comment, echoing his father's word, "Rather shammy."

This whole question of the relationship of the individual to authority, or originality and novelty to the immutable can be seen running through Judd's work from the beginning of his life to the end. "What is man's nature" and "what is man's destiny" were the great questions. One question looked backward to the childhood Eden and the other forward to the millennium. The destiny of nations engaged Judd's mind when he was a student in Westhampton in 1831, when he wrote his oration on the eternal verities and the ravages of time. What shall stay time's power, was the question behind his speech on monuments. In his "Peep into the 20th Century," the issue was progress and social perfectibility. Judd wanted to be modern and original, but he kept concluding that "there is nothing new" and falling back in submission to authority. The whole system of instruction at Yale, as elsewhere, emphasized authority and rote learning: "The prevailing idea of government was that of repression, of rules and laws, of force and the display of authority."[29] Judd wanted to know, Could man be trusted? If human nature was not depraved, then the whole philosophy of authoritarian repression was wrong. If human nature was good, then progress by man's own efforts was possible. Judd began an essay showing the evils of repressiveness in handling children, but broke it off unfinished. Perhaps he wasn't sure of what he believed. By the time he wrote *Richard Edney,* however, he had made up his mind. One of the delightful aspects of that book is the portrayal of the indulgent Richard, whose handling of the children succeeds when his sister's strictness fails.[30]

In the Brothers in Unity, as in other debating societies, the tradition-centered curriculum found a counterweight. The Brothers did more than produce plays once a year. The weekly debates encouraged men to think for themselves. Questions like abolitionism, capital punishment, temperance, anti-Masonry, and politics were discussed. Judd, of necessity, took his part in these debates and in June, 1835, was one of three students elected to the office of "Orator." That fall he was elected treasurer. As there were twenty-four offices and only thirty-six seniors, we should conclude that he was only moderately popular. By his senior year his doubts about Calvinism were becoming sufficiently definite that he had probably learned to stop his officious meddling and to appear to his classmates as a more seasoned, moderate, and world-weary personality. His letters home at this time support this impression. Intensity had given way to a matter-of-fact and somewhat reserved tone that sounded more normal. His counsel to sister Apphia in April, 1836, was worldly, not religious, and he told her:

Yes, "open your soul;" but take care, in the first place, *who looks in*; and in the second, *what you expose*. Never expose a weak spot; but rather make show of your strength, if you have any.

Judd had almost learned the wisdom of the world, which makes its peace with deception. This would not be the last time.

The Brothers in Unity was not the only stimulus to Judd's more original, creative efforts. The year 1836 was notable in American literary history as a year of beginnings: at Harvard people were talking about Ralph Waldo Emerson's *Nature*; at Yale the event was the founding of the *Yale Literary Magazine*. The *Lit* is the longest-lived student publication in America, and is proud of a tradition that includes such editors as Sinclair Lewis and Archibald MacLeish. Other literary magazines had been started at Harvard and Yale, one of them at Yale during Judd's freshman year; but they lasted a few months or years and died. The moving spirit who served as one of the first editors of the *Yale Literary Magazine* was William M. Evarts, later U.S. Secretary of State.

Sylvester Judd's first published works, an essay and a short story, appeared in the *Lit* that spring of 1836.[31] The essay asked, "What is Truth?" Judd found the way of the truthseeker beset with difficulties and contradictions. Part of the trouble, he said, was the inadequacy of language and ambiguity of terms, which made truth "for all practical purposes . . . often found inconsistent with itself." The traditional reliance on creeds as a basis of authority assumed that language could be cleared of ambiguity and that truth could be expressed in words. The Unitarian contention was that words and creeds could not be the test of truth. Judd went on, however, in a way that did not sound Unitarian: "In theology the doctrines of decrees and free agency are both true, but who can reconcile them?" Who indeed? Predestination and free will were both, paradoxically, true, taught the professors at Yale. In Judd's opinion all their millions of words spilled to reconcile this one contradiction at the very heart of the Calvinist system had not succeeded. Yet he was not ready to declare publicly that the doctrines were wrong; he called the contradiction only apparent: "This apparent inconsistency of truth is the origin of scepticism, and is the occasion of many unhappy dissensions among men."

Judd went further in his skepticism. He was not confident that truth would prevail. In regard to the "litigated points in history," for example, "how is it possible, that, without a revelation from heaven, the truth shall ever be disclosed?" Regarding metaphysical truth, "Who does not feel that there are doubtful points in himself that he will never understand, at least this side of the grave?"

Judd spoke from bitter experience. At this stage of his development, we might infer, he had not found a satisfactory alternative to the Calvinism that was crumbling in him. He was still groping along the lines of logic described earlier in this chapter and had not received, as yet, the key that opened Unitarianism to him. The most astringently skeptical sentence in Judd's essay asserted that "Many points lie equally balanced between truth and falsehood."

Judd was tending along the same line that Horace Bushnell was taking, toward questioning the use of language and logic, doubting that they could be used precisely, mechanically, and mathematically to reveal truth. This was the sort of relativism that could lead to Unitarian toleration and made heresy trials or exclusion from pulpits impossible.

The second of Judd's publications was a tale, "The Outlaw and His Daughter." An exotic but pure Mexican flower, the daughter of an outlaw, blooms beside a lake in the wooded hills of New England. The situation and scene are like those in *Margaret.* In both stories pond and girl are kindred spirits, and water is associated with free, joyous movement. The following passage from "The Outlaw's Daughter" comes after a good deal of the most stilted prose that Judd ever wrote and shows how the thought of the pond seemed to release some hidden spring in him:

> When the wind was high, so lightly and fearless did she skim over the curling tops of the waves, and so shrill and clear she sounded her notes on the air, that her father called her his Bird of the Lake. When the summer's sun was shining hot, she would oar her boat along the shore, under the archway of the trees; here she

twanged her guitar, or decked her hair with flowers from the banks, or filled her basket from the grape vines that twined among the low hanging limbs.

The function of such flowers as the outlaw's daughter is to be plucked. Just as in *Margaret,* two genteel suitors vie for the privilege, the villainous one being tumbled down a precipice in a fight, the honorable one getting the girl. The passage describing True Love's First Flowering shows the worst qualities of the liquid style and of gift-book romanticism:

> She dropped her oar, and taking her guitar, touched its chords. Its notes blended symphoniously in the sylvan recess with the sweet sounds of the young stranger's flute; while their hearts were awakened to thrill in more exquisite melody. The ravished Clermont ran down to the water's edge, and with a rich bouquet of flowers, which he held up to her view, prevailed upon her to approach the shore. He kissed the deep blushes from her cheek, as he assisted her to debark; and the stranger lovers sat down together upon the moss covered bank.

When his imagination was less molten than this, Judd relapsed into the leaden prose that was expected of a proper gentleman:

> Velasque did die. Foiled in his chief design, his spirits sunk, and he had not sufficient energy to counteract the effects of his wounds, which soon terminated his existence. . . . Herraras cheerfully yielded his daughter to his noble deliverer, her devoted lover; stipulating only that he might love her yet, for the sake of her mother.

Judd did not usually write like that. He was an excellent mimic and could adopt a variety of voices when he wrote. In both his essay and his story of 1836 he seemed conscious that they were to be published and therefore required a greater formality of phrase than usual. When Judd tried to be genteel he became awkward and formal, like a young man in coarse clothing who is invited to a New Haven drawing room. He always did better when he wrote dramatically, especially when he transcribed the speech of lower-class persons; and "The Outlaw's Daughter" contained no dialogue.

Judd's intention, apparently, was to combine native New England scenery with the exotic romanticism that Byron had made popular in tales like *The Bride of Abydos;* but he had not yet learned to name the flowers and the birds and to make the scene real and ideal at the same time. When he tried again at a prose tale, he had learned that lesson. In 1843, as he wrote the opening scene of *Margaret,* he seemed to be thinking again of the Bird of the Lake, who this time was only eight years old:

> The process of disrobing being speedily done, she waded into the water. She said, "I will go down to the bottom, I will tread on the clouds;" she sunk to her neck, she plunged her head under. . . . A sandpiper glided weet weeting along the shore; she ran after it, but could not catch it; she sat down and sozzled her feet in the foam; she saw a blue-jay washing itself, ducking its crest, and hustling the water with its wings, and she did the same. She got running mosses, twin-flower vines, and mountain laurel blossoms, and wound them about her neck and waist, and pushing off in her canoe, looked into the water as a mirror. (8)

Judd learned not only to specify the birds and flowers but to individualize actions with verbs. With three words at the very beginning of his first book—"weet weeting," "sozzled," and "hustling"—he broke loose from the bonds of conformity and effected a literary revolution. Professor Goodrich would not have approved.

Among the Judd manuscripts are two one-act dramas that show the comic spirit was not dead in Judd. The handwriting indicates that they were most likely written between 1834 and 1837, but there is no record of their being performed by the Brothers in Unity. The first, called "Enthusiasm, or Quodlibet for Quolibet," is a pleasant but flimsy little satire on the cloud-striding Empyrealist, for whom "mind rides in triumph over matter." He has discovered that "orbiculation is the sovereign principle," "sphericality is the tendency of all things." The rainbow is a "pitiable victim of fate, which itself, did not the unspiritualized Earth intercept, would be a revolving orb." Empyrealist wants to make orbicular horseshoes.

His friend the Poet is equally ethereal and can speak only in rhymes, but is often undercut by the more earthy characters:

> *Poet:* Oh for a simile. Clear as——quartz—no—no—
> *Simplex:* We always say clear as a potato Bin in the spring—If you'll allow a plain man to speak.

The play has something of the quality, without the cleverness, of the Christopher Pearse Cranch cartoons on transcendentalism and reminds one of Emerson's Uriel, who said, "Line in nature is not found;/Unit and universe are round." If Judd did indeed write this play before he had heard of Emerson, he had his eyes open and was satirizing a trend before most people were aware that it existed. Yale may have been behind Harvard in its awareness of the Germanic school of philosophy; but it had its Porters and Bushnells, to whom Coleridge was the new revelation.

The second comedy, "Modern Education," is more substantial and the humor more successful. Miss Flirtiletta Aster writes home from Mount of Delight Seminary, where the chief subjects are poise, poetry, and waltzing, with occasional lectures in chemistry and botany:

> First comes Madame Maniere to teach us how to point the toes in walking, and how to courtesy, and how to sit. O there are so many modes of sitting. I never *can* learn them all. There is the mode negligent, the mode erect, the mode conversational, the mode laughing—&c. &c.

Mr. Simpleswift promotes textbooks that simplify abstruse works by cutting out all difficult passages, condensing the rest, and supplying visual aids:

Simpleswift: Here is an illustration of the passage—"So we find that means very undesirable often conduce to bring about ends in such a measure desirable, as greatly to overbalance the disagreeableness of the means." That is illustrated by some boys playing at see-saw. Well you see one end of the board, or the means, being overbalanced. The boys on that end are all falling into a measure set to catch them,—very desirable.

Mr. Charles Exquisite, who found the air of the recitation rooms at college prejudicial to his health and who was confused by geometry so that he could not "tell a side from an angle, or a circle from a square," is home by special permission of the president. He describes a new "Celestial science which cannot be taught in Books. It can only be learned from practice":

Charles: Orbiculation, with an advancing motion, is the first principle of the sublime—
Simpleswift: Precisely the principles of Astronomy. You see the illustration from this . . . (shows from a book) where the Sun is the center, and—
Charles: Yes. We seek for a centre bright and beautiful as the sun.—
Simpleswift: What say you squire, to commencing the system at once. Perhaps this gentleman would give us a course of lessons.
Charles: With a world of pleasure. If I had the squire's neice to practice with.
Simpleswift: What, both sexes learn! So much the better. Notice shall be read from the pulpit to-morrow. What do you call the new Science?
Charles: Waltzing.

These dramas offer refreshing evidence that Judd was still sane during the years of his ordeal. He could still poke fun at his own tendencies toward extremism and ethereality. He had advocated modern languages against the classical ones and had questioned authoritarian strictness in dealing with children; some people would have called Judd a dangerous modernizer, a Simpleswift. The Judd family was one that enjoyed lively humor on occasion, and Judd could laugh at himself. Under the tense seriousness of this rainbow-chasing Judd was an earthiness that was as clear as a potato bin in the spring.

Arethusa Hall's biography mentions nothing of Judd's literary efforts prior to *Margaret* except for the poems he wrote at Hopkins Academy and an unfinished tale about "The Philosophy of the Affections." Poems, if the right kind, were respectable; fiction and drama were not. She was anxious to show, despite the clear evidence to the contrary, that Judd had no "aspirations for personal fame." She wrote,

> Never, from his earliest student-life, had Mr. Judd that inkling, often existing in the youthful brain, of seeing himself in print. His ambition never led in the direction of notoriety; but, on the contrary, his natural sensitiveness and diffidence impelled him to shrink from it. . . . He never went through an apprenticeship of newspaper paragraphs and poetry, or of magazine-essays and tales.

She said this about the Judd who had been concerned with the erection of monuments and who had written in 1830 to his father, "Had I known half as much of myself years ago as I *think* I do now, instead of handling the yard-stick, I might now be treading my way, at least to *some* distinction in the paths of literature and science." In his poem on poverty, in lines that were quoted in Arethusa's biography, Judd had written, in 1832,

> Where Science leads I wish to go,
> And soon to reach Fame's temple too,
> Where mind's choice pleasures grow
> I wish to tread, and there to sow
> The seeds of influence and esteem.—
> Regard not these as airy dream
> But say God speed thee in thy way.[32]

Judd had, possibly, one other stimulus to encourage his literary ambitions besides the Brothers in Unity and the *Yale Literary Magazine.* His letter of June 6, 1836, concerning the "polished and literary society of New Haven" with which beautiful ladies were associated suggests immediately the name of Miss Delia Bacon. Delia Bacon, a sister of Leonard Bacon, a New Haven minister, conducted a girls' school at the parsonage across the street from Yale. She was two years older than Judd. According to her biographer, "Yale boys jumped at the chance to meet New Haven's beauties at Miss Bacon's soirees."[33] Miss Bacon, who had already defeated Edgar Allan Poe in a short story contest, became one of the most knowledgeable bluestockings of her day, famous for lectures on universal history, and later infamous for originating the theory that Francis Bacon wrote Shakespeare's plays. Although she was, in the 1830's, orthodox in her theology, Delia Bacon was one step ahead of Yale. She had her students read Coleridge and Victor Cousin, two of the chief foreign sources of the transcendentalism that was just emerging in New England. If Judd did indeed come in contact with Delia Bacon's circle, he would have received one more push towards the philosophy that said, trust in one's own consciousness, not in words and formulas and externals.

Nothing is known about what other feminine inspiration Judd might have received from his mingling with New Haven society, but the jocular comment about Judd printed in the record of his class reunion in 1839 hints that he was not known among his classmates for monkish habits. Since Judd did not attend the reunion, the scribe, who included a comment on affairs of the heart for each class member, was reduced to wild surmises when he came to Judd's name:

Mr. Judd. . . . our epitome of his course is derived from the hundred tongued monster, who says the star of love has ever been the star of his destiny, swaying his feelings, his actions and his *faith*. His love and his polemics have been equally erratic and mysterious.
"He could raise scruples dark and nice,
And after solve 'em in a trice,

> As if Divinity had catch'd
> The itch on purpose to be scratch'd.
> Or, like a mountebank, did wound
> And stab herself with doubts profound,
> Only to show with how small pain
> The sores of faith are cured again;
> Although by woful proof we find
> They always leave a scar behind."[34]

Judd's actions contributed perhaps to such guesses about the source of his troubles. As he appeared to his family, in his sorrows he was sometimes the very picture of a young Werther. In 1837 Judd described the way he had formerly acted:

> In the lap of the grave I would gladly have pillowed my aching head, my burdened heart. Thoughtworn, careworn, I would gladly have relieved my crazed brain anywhere. I used to sing, or rather groan out, you know, "There shall the wicked cease from troubling, there shall the weary be at rest." I felt it all to my inmost soul. I have few such feelings now.[35]

Judd was indeed stricken in the heart, but his disappointment was a religious one; he felt compelled to restrain his family from making false inferences about the source of his odd actions. He wrote to his sister-in-law, Elizabeth, that these oddities "did not originate, as you perhaps conjectured, in————. No, it was something else. Nothing in particular, —partly of a religious nature." To his brother Hall, he wrote that "This had nothing to do with ———, but was a *religious affair*." Arethusa Hall's dashes indicate that delicacy forbids inquiring whether the excised words pertain to anything more than the conflict between Judd and his father over money matters that fall of 1835. In 1837, after he had confessed his religious secret to the world, Judd wrote to George Lyman that, to free himself of the religious doubts that "hung about me like mill-stones,"

> . . . I sought every kind of diversion. I was willing to talk about the ladies, to laugh with my fellows, to ramble in the fields, or any thing else.

If Judd was not quite a young Werther, perhaps he was something of a Hamlet. As he moaned about the house, rather dishevelled, his family possibly feared for his sanity. And what would some Polonius have thought if he had come across Sylvester writing love poetry? He could hardly be expected to see that there are things deeper than love that make a young man forego all custom of exercises, see the world as an unweeded garden of philosophical ambiguities, and turn for relief to banter "about the ladies."

A love poem does in fact survive among the Judd manuscripts that seems to fit the circumstances and emotional mood of Judd in the period from 1834 to 1837, although the handwriting would suggest a date between 1836 and 1840. The relationship with the unnamed girl to whom it is addressed seems to have begun in childhood and has not ended yet. The poem pulses with Byronic melancholy. "This wasting heart" still throbs, and memory burns for the girl, whom he has not seen for "a long year." Hopes and ambition are dead. "When Childhood's pulse beat high and fast,/Our hearts insensibly entwined." In youth, although admirers thronged around the girl,

> We cared not for the village crowd,
> Its smiles, or frowns, its Halls' gay sound.
> Within ourselves our social good,
> We sought, and there 'twas found.
>
> We sauntered when the star-light thrills;
> We traced the brook along the glen;
> We gathered blue-bells on the hills,
> Away from haunts of men.

But now, though "that last kiss burns" and "passion kneels" to her, the sun is setting, and fear lurks.

> As heavy clouds thronged to the West,
> Sealing in black the golden sky
> A sudden fear throbbed through thy breast,
> And tears o'ercast thine eye.

In the long year since they have met, "Time writes his lines across my brow" and fears press in:

> Oh did we love too young:—too young
> Did our affections bloom, the blast
> To meet, that fiercely on us sprung,
>   Ere years were rooted fast?

In the most Byronic gesture of all, the poet, brushing a tentative tear from "this seared eye," turns on the world— the World is to blame:

> Knowest thou thy dread account O World?
> How'lt answer for the spirit's wreck!

The Byronic convention may have dictated a good deal of this poem—the poet's "gray hairs" are doubtless imaginary —but still, the strength of feeling and the solidity of specification suggest at least a core of personal experience behind the lines. Judd was approaching the bottom of his downward plunge.

8

Unitarianism vs. Orthodoxy

In July, 1836, the young enthusiast who had entered Yale so eagerly, but whose eyes had grown seared and tired under the pressure of realities, graduated. His family drove down in a carriage, an unaccustomed luxury, and heard Sylvester deliver the English oration at the commencement.[1]

His first concern was a job to pay his debts. Thought of the ministry was, in his state of mind, painful. Perhaps he considered going to the West, as his father had done in 1819; he made a collection of college catalogues from a number of distant colleges about this time.[2] He even received an offer of a professorship from Miami College in Ohio, "an Old School Presbyterian College in Ohio," as he phrased it. It was a flattering offer, and Judd was tempted to accept it rather than puzzle and disappoint his family and friends.

Judd gave "prayerful consideration" to the offer but decided that he could not lend his influence "to bind more closely the yoke" of "superstition, intolerance, and bigotry," nor could he wear the yoke of the "restriction in religious thought and feeling which would necessarily be imposed upon me in the contemplated circumstances." In that winter of 1836-1837, Judd had to wrestle with the doubts that had long been crowding in upon him, and find a way out of the labyrinth. A teaching position at a private school in Templeton, Massachusetts,—between Fitchburg and Greenfield—opened up, and he took it. There he had a chance to think, away from the pressures exerted on his mind at Yale.

Judd had been putting off the moment of decision. The easiest thing to do had been to continue in the direction that was expected of him. But something had to be done. In Templeton he reached his crisis. In Northampton, Unitarians were a tiny, if influential, minority. In New Haven there was no Unitarian church at all. In Templeton the situation was reversed. The Unitarians represented tradition, respectability, and majority opinion; the Trinitarians were a tiny group of dissidents who had split off from the main group in 1832 because they could not put up with the Unitarianism which had taken over the church. The Rev. Charles Wellington was something of a church statesman who had won most of his church to his liberal views and had held them all together for twenty-five years before the split. In him, Sylvester Judd saw Unitarianism in its mildest form. Wellington had a tolerant spirit towards those who disagreed with him, disliked theological hairsplitting, and told his congregation in February, 1837, that if the Trinitarians "have been better edified, more exemplary and happy Christians, under a different administration, I rejoice in the measure." He fully acknowledged, as did Unitarians generally, Jesus to be "Messiah, the Christ, the Son of God, the Saviour of the world," thus disposing of the argument that Unitarians were infidels who reduced Christ to a mere man.[3] Christ might not be God Himself, but he was the Son of God, and there was no need to support Christ's claim to authority by the Trinitarian absurdity of asserting that God is simultaneously one God and three Gods.

The Trinitarian party that employed Judd as a teacher in their school made, then, a rather ragged appearance in contrast to the smooth, kindly parson Wellington. As supervisor of the Templeton public schools,[4] Wellington would have had much to talk about with Judd. We know that they were in close contact, for Wellington and his son called on Sylvester in Northampton on July 26, 1837, at the height of Sylvester's personal crisis.[5] Judd liked to think that his decision was a rational one and dictated purely from within, not by any outside influences, and wrote a few months later that "I did not become attached to Unitarianism from any acquaintance with its men, but from what I supposed were its principles."[6] This may be so, but we can at least say that Judd was strengthened psychologically in his decision by the contrast he saw between Charles Wellington and the orthodox minister in Templeton.

This minister, the Rev. Lemuel P. Bates, had a rather dubious past. He had been dismissed from a pastorate in Whately, Massachusetts, five years earlier under mysterious circumstances. The fact that a council had been called at that time suggests a case of discipline that had been handled discreetly without ruining Bates' reputation. And while Sylvester Judd watched, fascinated, he saw Mr. Bates' indiscretion again get him into trouble. Mr. Bates, among other failings, had a habit of loitering in stores and speaking disparagingly of other ministers.[7]

Meanwhile, Judd was thinking, reviewing the arguments that had been swirling through his head. He was involved in one of the great philosophical debates of all history, the struggle between supernaturalism and naturalism. The Calvinist emphasis upon God's Sovereignty and God's Providence carried with it the inevitable corollary that man's will was not free. Nature was wicked, and only God was good. Only a divine, supernatural intervention could change the inevitably downward gravitation of man's nature. Was it true, asked Sylvester Judd, that God had created man evil and that the natural man hated God "with a fixed, natural hatred," as the Calvinists taught? At this point, said Judd later, "I looked into my Bible." "On its first page was written, 'and God made man in his own image.'" Judd considered the wisdom and benevolence of God and concluded, "The thought is appalling, that the Deity should have created man . . . to hate him." He considered the "practical tendency of Calvinism"; this was ironic, for a favorite argument against Unitarianism was that it contributed to moral laxity and worldliness. Judd concluded that Calvinism drove men to distraction, and he spoke with a peculiar authority upon this point:

> I have seen anxiety intense, troubled, hopeless, pouring itself out in tears and sighs. I have seen despair with its darker horrors, settling upon the countenance, paralyzing the heart, and spreading its midnight hues over life itself. I have seen men hastening from the family altar to the church, from the familiar friend to the pastor; but obtaining no relief; with natures crushed, and souls sickened, they have gone into life, hopeless men, coldly sceptical, to religious sensibility as lifeless as a rock.[8]

No, he concluded, Calvinism was not natural and did not lead to healthiness of soul.

Judd considered "the analogy of nature," as disclosed by science. Here the question formed itself thus: Is nature good? Does it give evidence of God's hand or of the devil's? When Judd put the argument in these terms, the very books he had been given as texts at Yale became arguments against orthodoxy. Indeed, the same books were used at Harvard. The problem was not geology, with its challenge to the literal truth of Genesis; Judd's professor, Benjamin Silliman, had resolved that point and had shown science and nature to be in harmony with the Bible.[9] The argument

Judd seized upon was the one given to him by William Paley, whose books had been studied by every Yale senior for thirty years past as the keystone of his education. Paley had intended to reconcile religion and the new naturalism by proving the existence of God with rational, scientific arguments. His *Natural Theology* (1802) brought the old argument from Design up to date with a fascinating array of scientific examples. The entire biological world gave evidence of the admirable "contrivances" of God. Gill was adapted to water and lung to air, stomach to food, and ear to sound wave. The very air testified to God's glory. As Judd summarized the argument, in his *A Young Man's Account of His Conversion*:

> Philosophy and Science are demonstrating what the Scriptures have long ago revealed, that this earth is "good;" that nature, in the complexity of its laws, and infinite variety of its operations, is one unbroken system of beneficial adaptation. Our physical frame attests the same truth.

"Beneficial adaptation," the basic idea of biological science, which would shortly become the theory of evolution, proved that God had created the earth in His image, that the world was good. This was all Judd needed. It was only a step to the next conclusion, though few at Yale had perceived that step. If everything is beneficially adapted to its objects, Judd argued,

> The soul we should *infer*, would be fitted to its objects. These are Truth, Religion, God. The Calvinist denies that there is any congruity, any sympathy, any adaptation, here. He says the soul hates what it should love, and only loves what it should hate.

In other words, human nature is good, not evil.

At this point, Judd was brought back to the crucial question of the observed nature of children. Nathaniel W. Taylor, in his book *Concio ad Clerum* of 1828, had based everything on the observed *fact* of the universal sinfulness of man from his earliest stage of moral accountability. An important debate (1820-1822) between Unitarian Henry Ware of Harvard and Calvinist Leonard Woods of Andover had turned on the question of the nature of the child.[10] Ware had argued that children were naturally good, though sometimes bad. Woods had argued that children were naturally bad, though sometimes good. Ware said that "wickedness, far from being the prevailing part of the human character makes but an inconsiderable part of it,"[11] and Woods replied that the natural simplicity, artlessness, and kindness of children could not be considered evidence of true holiness. Amiable affections, said Woods, might exist in completely godless persons if they were brought up properly.[12]

At this point, the candid critic would have to say that Ware took Woods over the barrel, for he had made Woods admit that children were not so bad after all, that they had impulses toward kindness and generosity. Nathaniel Taylor based *his* whole argument for original sin on the point of the observed fact of everyone's sooner or later exhibiting a natural tendency toward sin. Woods had already given this case away by admitting that such signs of sin in children might not be observably universal. Ware could thus say that if evidences of goodness in children were no sign of an inherently good or holy character, neither were evidences of bad in children a sign of an inherently evil character. In other words, children were born morally neutral, though inclined toward good, especially if society did not teach them duplicity, calculation, and selfishness. Thus, according to the Unitarians, a proper interpretation of the Lockeian philosophy, to which the Yale theologians also subscribed, was that proper environmental influences could be brought to bear on the child that would develop his own natural tendencies toward goodness and holiness.

Even if Judd did not read the original documents in this debate, he could hardly miss the reverberations of so important an exchange. After 1820, the nature of the child was central to any discussion of theological issues. Judd saw this, and told a story to show how the problem was brought home to him in a personal way, trivial but significant. Judd was at home—whether as early as 1833 or as late as 1837 we do not know—and "a little girl," doubtless the same sister Pin whose shining apple had come in the Thanksgiving box in 1832, "came tripping in, with the freedom and glee of youth." Here was the chance to put the theory to the test. This girl had not, so far as Judd knew, changed from her original nature.

> I called her attention and read to her the verse, Blessed are the pure in heart, &c. and asked her if she thought it was good in God to bless only those who had pure hearts. "O," said she, "I wish my heart to be always pure." Then she added, with a look between a smile and a thought, such as you sometimes see pass over the face of a child, "I should not be happy, in Heaven, with God, if I had a wicked heart." . . . it was a hint, a blessed hint, to better things.[13]

Judd had the key: Out of the mouths of babes cometh wisdom. That one key opened the door to Unitarianism, to romanticism, and to transcendentalism. *Margaret* was merely a dramatization of that one principle. Judd's child-centered church was an embodiment of it. Nature was good. The self could be trusted.

Judd did not have to wait for Emerson to tell him that the self could be trusted. Father Judd had been telling his sons all along to think for themselves, though he did not expect such disastrous results as Sylvester's change of faith.[14] And, ironically, Nathaniel W. Taylor, in the very process of proving that man is totally disabled and sinful, had followed the lead of the Scottish Realists in elevating "the decisions of Common-sense and sound reason" to the status of "infallible judgments."[15] In other words, to put a construction on the words that Judd was now ready to adopt, "consciousness" (i.e., intuition) was the final court of appeal. "Consciousness," said Judd, "is the eye of the soul," and as such "is a primary, incontrovertible, unequivocal source of evidence."[16] Judd, looking around him, instinctively felt the world to be good. Looking within himself, he instinctively felt that he loved God and had always loved him from the very beginning, despite his sins and the forcing of his nature from its true channel by the tortuous windings of Calvinism. Judd instinctively wanted a religion which came, not in spasms of revival emotion, but in waves as gentle as breathing or the blowing clover or the falling rain. Revivals achieved their emotions by grinding the mind to powder between the inexorable opposites of the Calvinist paradox. Judd was tired of all that. It left a fever in the spirit, a burning in the eye, and then a dry, dusty sensation in the soul; and he wanted water.

Judd was not the only one who was thirsty. The Rev. Lemuel P. Bates, whose need for rejuvenating spirits outran the resources of his pocket, got in trouble from his habit of loitering in stores and from saying things about "Christian ministers and brethren" that left him a bit dry in the mouth. In the spring of 1837 he was dismissed from his charge in Templeton "after confessing to his Church that he had violated his pledge of total abstinence in circumstances peculiarly aggravating, which circumstances were that five times he had slaked his thirst by secretly drawing liquor from a cask in a public store. . . ."[17] Theological arguments about "observed fact," "moral tendency," and "the practical tendency of Calvinism" were taking on a wry, humorous twist.

Judd had already been, perhaps, in trouble because of the conflict between his developing beliefs and the demands of an orthodox school. In *Margaret* he would tell of Margaret's dismissal from her job as school teacher because of her refusal to teach the catechism. Now he said, "I have been employed by the Orthodox party; but, alas for me! I am too liberal." A month later he was ready to make the break, and wrote to J.W., "Away with faint-heartedness! Let the cry of heresy come. Let persecution come. Only let *truth*, God's own truth, prevail." With the disclosures in April, which led to Mr. Bates' dismissal from the pulpit, Judd received his signal. He got out on April 22, 1837, as the structure of orthodoxy crumbled around him. Enoch Hale, whose mind had collapsed years earlier and who had gazed at friends unseeingly "with an idiotic stare," had died a few months before, in January.[18]

Back in Northampton, Judd went through a season of torment. His convictions were now clear in his own mind, but the thought of making an open avowal of Unitarianism drove him to despair. At the moment he was less concerned with doors opening than with those which were closing behind him. Northampton took its religion hard. Zealous Calvinists scattered tracts, "sometimes of a very bitter and offensive character," among their Unitarian neighbors.[19] Lydia Maria Child wrote about her Northampton neighbor, a former Southern slave auctioneer, who prayed so loudly and contentiously that his Unitarian neighbors had to drown him out with accordion music in self-protection.[20] The public announcement of Judd's Unitarianism was sure to antagonize his friends and grieve his family. He could expect public censure and perhaps expulsion from his church. Arethusa Hall said that a change to Unitarian views was at that time "almost like a change of caste among the Hindoos," that it was regarded with a "horror" that orthodox people forty years later would not even feel for an avowed "infidel."[21] Judd could expect to be shut out by his friends and regarded as the carrier of a communicable disease, a fatal one.

Judd was sensitive, and in his excited, unbalanced state probably expected worse than he got. He read a pamphlet, Bernard Whitman's *Letters to Moses Stuart,* perhaps about this time, that dramatized the conflict between Unitarians and the orthodox and pictured Unitarians as victims of relentless persecution. Judd marked passages that told how the orthodox called Unitarians "Emissaries of Satan" and how the orthodox associated Unitarians with a party that included "every infidel, and disorganizer, and sabbath-breaker, and debauchee, and gambler, and every haunter of grogshops and theatres in the land." He marked with special emphasis a passage describing how the orthodox were fighting among themselves and accusing each other of Unitarian tendencies.[22] Judd said later that in all his reading of polemical pamphlets, he was particularly struck by a controversy between a Dr. Miller and Dr. Moses Stuart of Andover concerning the Trinity, in which each charged the other with a tendency to Unitarianism; Judd concluded "that all intelligent Trinitarians *are* Unitarians," at least in their views on the Trinity.[23]

Old School and New School Calvinists were fighting among themselves; Lyman Beecher was being tried for heresy that very year of 1837; the Presbyterian church was in a nationwide furor that split it irretrievably down the middle before the year was out. The bubble of Jacksonian prosperity burst in 1837 and the country was in an economic panic. Judd looked around himself and saw an atmosphere in which the parent could devour its offspring. He trembled at the consequences, but he wanted out. Calvinism was a prison house, and he wanted out. His doubts had been like millstones, and he wanted to run, dance, fly—anything to get out. He wrote to J.W. on March 24:

> A spiritual nature was given us, by which to mount up, as on eagles' wings, to an elevated existence, to an assimilation with the

Deity. We dash in pieces our heavenly image; we sink from our high estate; we become the slaves of one another. Yes, man is the most abject slave of his fellow-man. He dare not think for himself; he dare not speak or act for himself; and, more than this, becomes the slave of himself.

It was the old fight, the fight against the shackles, the iron teeth of Poverty that he had sworn to break in 1832, the World that he had brought to book for its "dread account" of frustrated love and the "spirit's wreck." Now he had an enemy that he could assail in more concrete form: the slavery of Calvinism. He could release all these tensions in one smashing stroke:

> Away with faint-heartedness! Let the cry of heresy come. Let persecution come. Only let *truth,* God's own truth prevail. I anticipate the day when truth shall ride forth, conquering and to conquer. I cannot say when; I only pray for nerve and resolution to urge on the chariot-wheels. I cannot rest. The Lord has been leading me by ways that I thought not of.

Judd read the Bible through once more, from Genesis to Revelation. It confirmed the testimony of nature, reason, and his own consciousness. With a deep breath, Judd made his announcement to his family. It was spring, 1837.

Father Judd "was a man of much liberality of feeling. He had always encouraged freedom of opinion, and had therefore not much to say condemnatory." He had in fact been associating on closer and closer terms with Bancroft and had been won from political orthodoxy. "Suspected of Jacksonism" [sic] because he did "not choose to put on the whig collar and do their dirty work," he had sold his newspaper rather than conform as was expected of him or be a turncoat to the other party, as his Democratic friends wanted of him. He had even been casting about from church to church and had, a few months earlier, attended the Methodist, Baptist, and Universalist meetings for worship.[24] Therefore, he did not condemn Sylvester, "much."

Arethusa Hall was home from her travels and spent 1837 around Westhampton and Northampton. She had had a nervous breakdown a few years earlier, had never completely recovered from the effects, and had acquired from her life of suffering a strong sympathy for the sufferings of others. She was especially qualified to understand and sympathize with young Sylvester, whom she called "particularly interesting and dear to me from his earliest years." How did she react? She said, forty years later:

> There was an originality, a quickness of perception . . . which, added to a loveliness of nature, especially attracted me to him. And now that he had struggled through the difficulties of his college course, and was about to enter upon the sacred work of the *Gospel* ministry, all our expec[ta]tions were to be blasted! I felt that I would rather see him *dead,* so much was I dominated by traditional theology.[25]

The discussion of such a love-hate relationship is best left to a psychological critic. We can surmise that Arethusa told Sylvester how she felt, because on May 6, 1837, he echoed her sentiment in his journal:

> Go to the Unitarian Church. Oh! 'tis misery to think of it. It is an *open* step, which I have not yet taken. . . . "Had rather see me in my grave." I ask not your pity; I ask not your charity even: only do not grieve. But the emotion,—this unmans me. One tear weighs more than a folio of arguments.

The conflicting emotions in Judd's mind during May and June reached extremes of despair and passionate exaltation. He went moaning around the house "sometimes humming in heart-piercing tones, 'Oh, where shall rest be found?' or 'Hast thou not *one* blessing for me, O my Father?'" He said that he envied the cartman, the blacksmith, the shoemaker, "anybody whose life was so private that he could enjoy his own opinions in obscurity and peace." In June he wrote a note to Arethusa, in which he confessed his mental and moral powers to be totally paralyzed.

Take, if you please, this scrawl, not of my thoughts, for I have none; not of my feelings, for the "mire and dirt" of those troubled waters I would not put upon paper. I would ask to be remembered to my friends, if I were what I might be; but such a thing as I am, how can I care to be held in remembrance?

The accent, the rhythm, the tone were exactly those of the melancholy Hamlet.

At the other extreme, and at about the same time as this note to Arethusa, Judd composed a long, vivid, passionately eloquent account of his conversion to Unitarianism. He wrote it for his own family and called it "Cardiagraphy," his analysis of the heart. Judd found his tongue again. In one sustained release of electricity, he discharged the accumulated tension. He surpassed anything he had ever written up to that time. Brief quotations can give no conception of the cumulative power. He demolished Calvinism with stroke after stroke, then went on to his own declaration of faith. It was an ecstatic mysticism in which he looked forward to "an assimilation with the Deity." He spoke with transparent simplicity, like a child:

My soul bursts from its prison-house; it walks forth, buoyant with freedom; it treads upward towards its God.

Love, "love is the fulfilling of the law." "God is love." "He that loveth is born of God." To love is godlike. To love is to be happy. We should love all men, because there is something lovely in man. We should love God supremely, because he is infinitely lovely. . . . Love is the cincture of heaven, and the golden chain that may raise earth to the skies.

His motto, said Judd, was "liberty, light, love"; and the greatest of these was love. The highest end of man was to "reflect, in unobscured lustre, the full-orbed glory of his God." Five years earlier, addressing the Lyceum in Hadley, he had walked among the "rolling orbs, the central suns," confident of his future. Now he looked for "the full-orbed glory" again.

All he needed was something, or someone, to love. But in Northampton that summer, doors shut along the street as he walked by. "Every object was an emotion, and every feeling a pang. Man frowned me from his presence. Nature, my mother nature, chided my sorrowing. Self was a dashing sea," he wrote to Arethusa. Judd's wild turmoil of ecstasy and despair that summer was an emotional climax, an end. At times the sun that burned him seemed close enough to reach. At times the abyss of self overwhelmed him. Love and death seemed different aspects of the same thing. The end was also a beginning. In his "Cardiagraphy" Judd said,

> I look forward to death with calmness, yet with some exhilaration. Death is only the vestibule of heaven. Its threshold may be easily crossed. Our bodies are the furnace of the soul, from which it will issue at death, defecated and polished, to mingle in communion with the Holy and the Infinite.

In September, in another mood, Judd wrote to Arethusa,

> There are abysses of feeling which we know nothing about till we are plunged into them. I shudder as I look back upon the past. Man knows not the heart. It is a thing of mysteries. It is the mystery of mysteries.

By that time Judd was at the Harvard Divinity School, studying for the Unitarian ministry. His family had read his "Cardiagraphy," had been silenced, and had, in Arethusa's words, "stood back in reverence before the integrity of feeling evinced." But Judd, for all his intense self-examination, had not solved the mystery of the human heart. He had only stretched and enlarged his own. He had learned how close are heights and depths: "The process of disrobing being speedily done, she waded into the water. She said, 'I will go down to the bottom, I will tread on the clouds. . . . A sandpiper glided weet weeting along the shore; she ran after it, but could not catch it; she sat down and sozzled her feet in the foam; she saw a blue-jay washing itself, ducking its crest, and hustling the water with its wings, and she did the same. . . . 'I will jump to that girl,' she said, 'I will tumble the clouds.'"

"Aim at the stars," said Arethusa to Judd, and he replied, "What if, in a dark night, I catch a glow-worm?"[26] In his dark night of the soul, Judd had caught a glow-worm. He had not solved the mystery, but he was moving eastward toward the sun.

Part IV

The Ideal

and the Real

9

Harvard, Emerson, and Judd

Wordsworth was thinking of the French Revolutionary ferment when he wrote, in Book XI of *The Prelude,* "Bliss was it in that dawn to be alive,/But to be young was very heaven"; but the words might well be applied to Greater Boston in 1837. Sylvester Judd had the good fortune to be in the right place at the right time. Only eight years earlier Boston's pontifical *North American Review* had pronounced: "Intellectual science is now fixed. . . . the conclusions of Locke and Aristotle, which . . . exhaust the science and leave no room, on essential points, for the farther progress of real discovery, must form in all ages the creed of judicious men. . . ."[1] Then a sense of expectancy developed. Young men and women here and there grew restless, impatient with Lockeian rationalism and the smugness of counting house and pulpit. They waited for a Moses who would smite the rock and set the waters free.

In 1837, a year after the first salvo from Concord, the intellectual revolution received its declaration of independence. Emerson's "American Scholar" address put New England on notice that a new age was at hand. Young men talked about "The Newness," and "The Spirit of the Age." Northampton organized a Lyceum and Horace Mann a state board of education. Father Judd scratched his head over the new phenomena of animal magnetism and spirit rappings; he took up biology and nature walks, sometimes with his son Sylvester. Young ladies enclosed anemones or mallow blossoms in letters, and Sylvester Judd pressed a red leaf between the pages of Andrews Norton's attack on Emerson.[2]

Prophets grew thick on every bush. In Boston Sylvester Graham of Northampton fought off mobs of butchers and bakers to preach the millennium of Graham bread and vegetables; in Northampton, ex-editor Judd helped organize antislavery meetings and a temperance society; his son Hall Judd became secretary of a utopian community in nearby Florence that, between 1842 and 1846, raised silkworms and spun tenuous threads but did not get very far toward the millennium.[3] The Devil himself, as portrayed in Sylvester Judd's *Philo,* caught the spirit. Emerson had said "Things are in the saddle,/And ride mankind." Judd's Devil preached to a crowd, "Your customs need to moult, come out bran new;/Mankind are saddle-galled, put on green leaves," and looking very much like Dr. Sylvester Graham, shouted,

> I am excited; I go for reform.
> . . . .
> Down, down, below what you can see or hear,
> The wronged ones quake with cold; let in the sun. (p. 166)

The flower flexed, not yet ripened to its inmost leaf.

On August 27, 1837, as Sylvester Judd, twenty-four years old, walked across Harvard Yard, he had not yet seen this Emerson, who was shortly to play the role of Lucifer at Harvard. But Judd wrote to his mother that day:

> My dear Mother,——You see I am on the heretic's ground. Strange as it may seem to myself, unanticipated as it has been by you, it is nevertheless true that I am here.

The fact that he could speak lightly about the heretic's ground shows that Judd's relationship with his family had not deteriorated beyond the point where it could be joked about. Three days later Judd saw the whole company of heretics assembled at the Harvard commencement exercises. He had a certain liking for shams and shows and would not miss seeing the famous faces; he had driven over to Amherst for the commencement whenever he could.[4]

Prominent among those on the platform at Harvard was old Henry Ware, whose appointment as Hollis Professor of Divinity in 1805 had been the signal for the Calvinists to get out of Harvard and found Andover Theological Seminary and who had bested Leonard Woods of Andover in the theological warfare of the 1820's. His son Henry sat nearby, a professor liked by Divinity School students, whom he invited to his home for breakfast and sermon polishing. John Gorham Palfrey, Dean of the Divinity School and editor of the *North American Review,* was there. Andrews Norton, dubbed the "Unitarian Pope" by Carlyle, doubtless walked over from his Shady Hill retreat, where he wrote biblical criticism after an early retirement from Harvard. Awarding the degrees was President Josiah Quincy, whose autocratic methods in handling the student rebellions a year or two earlier had been answered by such pranks as an explosion in chapel and the strange device on the wall, when the smoke had cleared, "A Bone for Old Quin to Pick." The warriors of 1820 were the old guard of 1837—Dr. Ware seldom referred to books less than forty years old. But there also was young Professor Henry W. Longfellow; and down among the graduating seniors were Richard H. Dana, who made an eloquent, Coleridgian graduation address; and one Henry David Thoreau, who waited for the morrow, when a real man would speak.[5]

The next day, August 31, Ralph Waldo Emerson gave his Phi Beta Kappa address on the topic "The American Scholar." It is a safe assumption that Sylvester Judd, who was a member of Phi Beta Kappa and who had come to Cambridge early to drink in the local color, was in the audience. A week later he was writing to his mother in a staccato style, brisk and masculine-sounding, that seemed to owe something perhaps to the Emersonian tonic:

> There is the aristocracy of the lower orders, and the aristocracy of the higher. Who would fillip a copper for the difference? Man is aspiring. That is his glory. If he were not so, he would be of the brute. The world would stagnate. Give each man all the influence he can get, and we shall all have our proper influence. The scholar looks down upon the farmer, the farmer upon the shoemaker, the shoemaker upon the chimney-sweep. All, in my estimation, are good enough.

Mrs. Judd, whose son had previously written coherent, straightforward letters to her, must have been bewildered by this new tone, this strange set of disjunctions and dartings about, with its central epigram teetering precariously somewhere between truism and profundity: "Give each man all the influence he can get, and we shall all have our proper influence." To Arethusa, the same day, September 7, Judd wrote, "If we stand still, I have heard it said, the world will come round to us," echoing Emerson's ". . . if the single man plant himself indomitably on his instincts, and there abide, the huge world will come round to him," a phrase Judd was still repeating two years later in a letter to his brother Hall. Again, Judd wrote, in a letter of September 15, 1838: "Sunsetting still comes to you, and midnight and the stars," which in "The American Scholar" had been "Every day the sun; and, after sunset, Night and her stars."

As the brass band and the 215 Phi Beta Kappa members marched across the Harvard Yard and into the First Parish meetinghouse that noon, few were prepared for the electric intensity of the hour that followed. Emerson's college career had been desultory, his abbreviated stay in the Divinity School broken and disappointing, his pastoral career abortive. The power that had then come welling up in him was evident enough in his little book *Nature,* published the year before, but few professed to understand it. At least one elderly listener reported he did not understand Emerson that August day in this, his most lucid address: "It was to me in the misty, dreamy, unintelligible style of Swedenborg, Coleridge, and Carlyle. . . . It was well spoken, and all seemed to attend, but how many were in my own predicament of making little of it I have no means of ascertaining." As Emerson had said, in *Nature,* "Most persons do not see the sun. . . . The sun illuminates only the eye of the man, but shines into the eye and the heart of the child." But another listener, Oliver Wendell Holmes, who was no child and no transcendentalist, testified, "But the young men went out from it as if a prophet had been proclaiming to them 'Thus saith the Lord.' No listener ever forgot that Address." James Russell Lowell wrote, thirty years later, that it was

> an event without any former parallel in our literary annals, a scene to be always treasured in the memory for its picturesqueness and its inspiration. What crowded and breathless aisles, what windows clustering with eager heads, what enthusiasm of approval, what grim silence of foregone dissent![6]

As Sylvester Judd listened, it must have seemed that Emerson's words had a significance especially for him. In his "Cardiagraphy" Judd had said that he discovered "in the laws of his nature the laws of God" and that "man's *intellect* looks through universal nature, and discovers beauty, uniformity, design,—in all things a God." Now he heard Emerson saying that "nature is the opposite of the soul, answering to it part for part. One is seal and one is print. . . . Its laws are the laws of his own mind." Judd had said, "Religion does not consist in 'going to meeting,' or in any formal exercises. It is the soul communing with its God. I would strive, then, to make the 'world my temple.'" Emerson said that each man should believe himself "inspired by the Divine Soul which also inspires all men," and inveighed against formalism repeatedly: "When he can read God directly, the hour is too precious to be wasted in other men's transcripts of their readings." Judd had said that man should "reflect, in unobscured lustre, the full-orbed glory of his God." Emerson replied,

> There is never a beginning, there is never an end, to the inexplicable continuity of this web of God, but always circular power returning into itself. Therein it resembles his own spirit, whose beginning, whose ending, he never can find, —so entire, so boundless. Far too as her splendors shine, system on system shooting like rays, upward, downward, without centre, without circumference. . . .

Judd's mind echoed with the word "boundless" and the thought of infinity. In "Cardiagraphy" he had spoken of "rapturous unison" with the "one infinite, changeless heart of love." His discourse on astronomy five years earlier had pictured the spirit going on "from sphere to sphere with the speed of light forever" and had reverberated with the word "boundless" and the thought *what are we?* in this immensity.

Emerson was there to answer that question. "Man is one." Each man is a microcosm: "In going down into the secrets of his own mind he has descended into the secrets of all minds." The fact that Emerson was expressing Judd's own half-formed thoughts gave to Judd immediate confirmation of the truth of Emerson's point about the microcosm: in each man is the image of God, and therefore man is one; or, as Judd had put it, "Man, discovering in himself the image of his God, learns the true idea of his own dignity." From that fact could be deduced Emerson's great principle of self-trust. Man, said Emerson, must throw off all slavery to books, to "the courtly muses of Europe," and to the decorous society that fosters the "decent, indolent, complaisant" yes-man. If a man trust himself, stand on his own feet, "plant himself indomitably on his instincts, and there abide, the huge world will come round to him." There was the radiant word that Judd had been waiting for. He had gambled everything on the proposition that he was right and everyone around him mistaken, that man had innate dignity and could be trusted, that he could trust his own instincts. Judd had felt alone. Now the world was coming round to him.

It will give some idea of the extent to which Judd had anticipated some of Emerson's ideas if we quote the entire passage from Judd's "Cardiagraphy" which has hitherto been quoted piecemeal:

> Man, discovering in himself the image of his God, learns the true idea of his own dignity. I abhor slavery in all its forms; that of the body and of the intellect, but chiefly that of the soul. Confidence is the great bond of society, and I learn the true grounds of it. *Man is to be trusted.* Religion is the soul loving its God. . . . Religion does not consist in "going to meeting," or in any formal exercises. It is the soul communing with its God. I would strive, then, to make the "world my temple, and life itself one act of devotion."

Two ideas here require further comment. "Confidence is the great bond of society" contains the germ of the reform movements of the day, which rejected repression, vengeance, force, and authoritarianism as principles of society. Judd's rejection of formalism in religion anticipated the basic emphasis of Emerson's Divinity School address of 1838: that religion cannot be received at second hand and that much of what passes for worship is a fraud. But more important to Judd than such specific resemblances between his thoughts and those of Emerson was the general tone of Emerson's address that Phi Beta Kappa day. It was a trumpet call to a new life, to the thinking of great thoughts, to becoming a man. Judd had just declared his intellectual independence, and here was a rationale for revolution presented to him.

If Emerson touched chords in Judd that were prepared to respond, that fact was not notable. If Emerson is right, all people whose religion is living and vital understand each other because it is one spirit that speaks through them. And both Emerson and his audience met on the common ground of Unitarian assumptions.

Furthermore, it must not be imagined that Judd heard Emerson's address and went forth fully an Emersonian. He did not talk about Emerson in the letters that Arethusa Hall printed. His prose style, after a few tries at Emersonian granularity, relapsed into coherence. For one thing, the whole point of Emerson's plea was that a man should be himself, not a disciple. For another, there was a disturbing omission amid Emerson's vague talk about the divinely inspired soul. He had talked much of man and nature, but not once had he mentioned Christ. That fact might have gone unnoticed in a purely secular address, but Emerson had kept talking about divine inspiration, which traditionally was mediated through Christ. Emerson had emphasized the dangers of subservience to books. Could it be that he meant The Book? That way lay the specter of infidelity. Sylvester Judd did not want his Calvinist friends to gloat, to find the fulfillment of their predictions that Unitarianism was but a way station on the road to infidelity. Years later, in 1848, when Judd got up to deliver an address to an academic audience, he spoke not of the American Scholar, but of the Christian Scholar, and he dwelt on the superiority of Christ to Socrates. Judd's theology was Christocentric, and he never let himself forget that.

It would be a mistake to emphasize the influence of Emerson on Judd as if he filled the sky. There were other transcendentalists, and there were those who tended in that direction without crossing the line. Neither Henry Ware, Jr., who visited students in their rooms and whose lovely wife invited them constantly to tea and cared for them in their illnesses,[7] nor the great William Ellery Channing, whom Judd visited in Boston, in April, 1838, could be called a frostbitten rationalist. Channing, the acknowledged leader of the Unitarian movement, had said, in his most transcendental utterance, "We see God around us because He dwells within us." "Whence do we derive our knowledge of the attributes and perfections which constitute the Supreme Being? I answer, we derive them from our own souls."[8] Both Ware and Channing were active in support of reform and philanthropy, had a spiritual ardor that stopped just short of transcendentalism, and held fast to Christian revelation and the personality of the Deity. Their Unitarianism had not gone all the way over to naturalism, and they believed that the miracles of Christ were necessary proofs of his divine nature and mission. Much in Judd's writing that has been pointed out as Emersonian could be as easily traced to such a man as Channing. When Judd later got up in the pulpit to preach, he looked to such men for inspiration more than to Emerson.

Judd was not always in the pulpit, however, and he wrote more than sermons. Emerson had the vitally important function of encouraging the other side of Judd's nature, the earthy element. In "The American Scholar" Emerson applauded the new tendency of the romantic movement to explore "the near, the low, the common" and make it into poetry. "What would we really know the meaning of? The meal in the firkin; the milk in the pan; the ballad in the street; the news of the boat; the glance of the eye." The Emerson who spoke thus found his answering chord not in the cloud-striding, orbiculative Judd, the Empyrealist, but in the Judd who wanted things as "clear as a potato bin in the spring."

Judd needed someone to bring him down to earth. His style was often saccharine; Emerson's was chewy and sinewy as beefsteak. Judd's writing was all soul, too often, and

Emerson's was body instinct with soul. Judd's "Cardiagraphy" was a cry of the heart in the shudder of a great convulsion. In romantic artistic theory, poetry came from the cry of the heart, but Wordsworth insisted that emotion, to become art, must be recollected in tranquillity. Emerson's speech, unlike Judd's apologia, had the serene command of a person who had been through tribulations and had distilled them into a bracing tonic. Emerson had a sense of balance that Judd needed to learn.

The secret of Emerson's prose was that he held the real and the ideal in tension with each other. Neither Empyrealist in the clouds nor Simplex in the potato bin was enough by himself. Emerson admired Thoreau, who could construct a house or a sentence with almost equal skill. The trick was to find a fact and make it flower into a truth, for, as Emerson said in *Nature*, every natural fact was a symbol of a spiritual truth. Emerson taught this to Judd as he did to Thoreau, and without this principle *Margaret* would be a mere sermon. Judd insisted on the beauty and truth that lay hidden inside dirt and homely things. Look at the root of a pie-plant, just before it shoots from the earth in the spring, says Margaret. Remove the soil and you will find a "'rose flesh color, deepening into the purest carmine, and alternating with vermilion and gold.'" From this fact Judd, in the best Emersonian manner, extracts his truth, but with a rhythm and diction more colloquial than Emerson's: "'Children that germinate with a plenty of mother earth about them, come out in the fairest hues'" (441). Mr. Evelyn, who speaks the language of pulpit and polite society, manages at least one earthy touch: "'Yet if I could crack any man as I do this stone, I should lay open beautiful crystals'" (240). In the revised edition Judd cut out the soft adjective and used a more vital verb, making the sentence even more lean and Emersonian: "'Yet if I could crack any man as I do this stone, I should open to crystals.'"

Judd's greatest success in uniting the real and the ideal in a homely way was in the rhythms and metaphors of Deacon Ramsdill. Here, he went beyond Emerson.

> "There now," responded the Deacon. "I tell you children have nater, and you can't help it, no more than you can being a cripple when your hamstrings are cut. When they first come to school they are just like sheep, you put them into a new pasture, and they run all over it up and down, shy round the fence, try to break out, and they won't touch a sprig of grass, though they are hungry as bears. You send the youngsters of an arrant, and they climb all the rocks, throw stones at the horse-sheds, chase the geese, and stop and talk with all the boys and gals in the way, and more than as likely as not forget what they have gone upon."

As a philosopher of nature, Deacon Ramsdill is one step ahead of Hosea Biglow—more homely than Natty Bumppo, more shrewd and wise than the Jonathan figure of American tradition. The kitchen and the barnyard are his province:

> "We old folk must keep patience, and remember we did just so once. It's sheer nater and there's no stoppin on't, no more than a rooster's crowing a Sabber-day. . . . nater must have its course. Don't keep them too tight. When the tea-kettle biles too hard, my woman has to take off the cover. 'Twon't do to press it down, it's agin nater, you see." (197)

Nor was Judd's earthiness limited to finding sermons in stones, sandpipers in brooks. He could render unvarnished and unimproved reality in a way that illustrates Jacques Barzun's point, in *Romanticism and the Modern Ego,* that the romantic novel represented a movement toward realism. In the following scene, Margaret, having just met Mr. Evelyn for the first time, returns from a tête-à-tête by the pond in which the pagan state of her heart has been explored. She gets a good teasing by her irreverent family:

> "What springal is that, has kept you from helping me?" said Brown Moll, coming to the window with a tray full of hot potatoes. . . .
> "A fox after the goslin, hey?" said Hash, who with his father arrived at the same moment. "I saw you on the Head."

"I guess he has lain out over night," said Pluck. "He looks soft and glossy as your Mammy's flax of a frosty morning.—Now don't take pet, Molly dear."

"She swells like a soaked pea," added the old woman. "What's the matter, husy? I should think he had been rubbing your face with elm leaves."

"Never mind, Molly," interposed her father. "Better to play at small game than stand out. You are the spider of the woods. Spin a strong web; you are sure to catch something."

"She looks as if she had been spun, colored and hung out to dry," said her mother.

"Gall darn it!" exclaimed Hash. "I smell potatoes. Give us some dinner."

"Speaking of spinning," said Pluck, when the others were gone in, "you know how to use the wheel-pin—keep the thread taught and easy in your fingers, mind the spindle, then buzz away like Duke Jehu;—only if he is a dum spot of a Lawyer or a Priest, weave him into a breeches-piece, and I'll wear him, I be blown if I don't; and when he is past mending, I'll hang him up for a scarecrow, blast him!" (237-38)

Judd went even farther than this in his improvement upon Emerson. Emerson used a sturdy Anglo-Saxon vocabulary but observed the proprieties in his diction. Judd, released from restrictions by the license of the novelist, strewed his pages with Anglo-Saxonisms. In the following description of children sliding down a hill, vivid action verbs that had seldom, if ever, seen print spewed from Judd's pen in Elizabethan profusion:

They started off at the same moment, those in the crates standing up, swinging their caps, and echoing the cheers of the spectators. They skewed, brustled and bumped along, the crates wabbled and warped from side to side, the riders screamed, cross-bit, frumped and hooted at each other; they lost control of their course, their bows struck, they parted with a violent rebound; one went giddying round and round, fraying and sputtering the snow, and dashed against a tree; the other whirled into the same line, plunged with its load headlong into the first. It was a regular mish-mash; some of the boys were doused into each other, some were jolled against the tree, some sent grabbling on their faces down the hill, some plumped smack on the ice, some whisked round and round, and left standing.

Judd was trying to return to the origins of language, where grubby words smack of the soil. The childhood of language, the childhood of man were closer to truth than were the euphuisms and euphemisms of effete civilization. This romantic primitivism seemed to be the linguistic program and the moral message of at least the first section of *Margaret,* although Judd wavered from it as he wrote on. Judd was trying to show that one could be down to earth and yet soar at the same time. He found a successful expression of this in the image of Margaret's sled, "Hummin' Bird," whizzing down the hill in a race:

> The signal was made, and they flushed away. Soon separating, some went crankling, sheering, sidewise of the hill; some were tossed in somersets from the rocks; some ran into each other, and turning backwards channeled and ripped their way through the hard crust; on, on they went, skittering, bowling, sluice-like, wave-like; Margaret curvetted about the mounds, she leaped the hollows, going on with a ricochet motion, pulsating from swell to swell, humming, whizzing, the fine grail glancing before her and fuzzing her face and neck; her hood fell back over her shoulders, her hair streamed bandrols in the wind; she reined her sled-rope as if it had been the snaffle of a high-spirited horse. . . . Margaret was evidently foremost and farthest.
> "You hitched," said Seth Penrose, somewhat angrily.
> "No I didn't," said Margaret, somewhat excited.
> "She didn't hitch," said little Job Luce. . . . (174-75)

With the bump at the bottom, the dazzling spray of verbs ends.

In the same scene, and in others, Judd flirts even more dangerously with vulgarity. At the bottom of the hill one of the boys picks himself up and says, "I shall take it knee-bump, next time"; another boy replies, "Try bellygut, you'll like that better." Brown Moll, in another scene, yells at her husband, Pluck, "Panguts! . . . what do you do? lazy-ing about here like a mud-turtle nine days after it's killed" (30). At a Bacchanalian Thanksgiving dance, the preacher tries to stop the sinful proceedings:

> *Preacher.* ". . . And here I espy the arch-adversary of souls, the con-triver of your eternal ruin, the very devil himself in your midst."
> *Nimrod.* "The devil you do."
> *Preacher.* "Young man, you will have your portion in hellfire."
> *Nimrod.* "I go to hell if I do."
> *Preacher.* "The deep damnation of God is prepared for you."
> *Nimrod.* "I be damned if it is." (66-67)

Some critics were shocked, dared not refer in print to Judd's worst offenses, and spoke vaguely of the book's "vulgarity." W.B.O. Peabody, in the *North American Review* (Jan., 1846), said of Hash's vocabulary, "If such words as his were ever spoken in reality, they never should have been written down" (p. 118). Even Dexter Clapp, Judd's friend and fellow-Westhamptonite, criticized *Margaret*'s coarseness in the *Southern Quarterly Review* (April, 1846). In his preface to the revised edition Judd, obviously smart-ing, defended himself and said that illiterate, common peo-ple were not vulgar in a bad sense. But he quietly omitted "knee-bump" (Victorians had no legs, only "limbs") and "bellygut," changed "panguts!" to "trencher-worm!" and omitted the profanity. He wrought havoc on his splendid Halloween orgy with its pumpkin-god and its overtones of the mad scenes in King Lear, that Peabody had called "the greatest failure in all the work," and he cut down other scenes of drunken delirium, not always to the novel's det-riment.[9] But in most cases, where vulgarity was clearly an artistic success, Judd held out against his critics, even though the mask of anonymity he had imposed on the first edition had been pierced; and Judd, who, it must be remembered, was a minister, stands as one of the most courageous and original artists of his time.

Emerson could not teach Judd how to write a novel about vulgar life, although he gave him some useful precepts about language. Transcendentalism, for all its talk about getting out of the pulpit and into the fields, was always at the stretch. If not always in the pulpit, it was at least always on the lecture platform or in the study, or the school, or anywhere that a person might be pulled up to full height and challenged to live the nobler life. Such a mentality, when not actively hostile to fiction, was not very likely to express itself in fiction.

Entirely ignoring fiction like Judd's or Lydia Child's, as perhaps not sufficiently transcendental, Lawrence Buell, in his *Literary Transcendentalism* (1973), says that, although transcendentalists "composed a fair number of literary dialogues, in the manner of Landor's *Imaginary Conversations,* which Emerson, Fuller, and Alcott all admired," still, "none is of much literary consequence, partly because the language is too stilted to sound conversational, partly because the writers are less interested in drama than monologue." For all his advocacy of the common, the low, even the vulgar, Emerson "even grew away from" the colloquial style, comments Buell. True, as both Buell and F.O. Matthiessen demonstrate, Emerson was capable of a colloquial vigor in his syntax and diction. Matthiessen collects such examples of Emerson's "bullet-like words" as "the potluck of the day," "a gang of friendly giants," "an Age of Reason in a patty-pan," "Truth is such a fly-away, such an untransportable and unbarrelable commodity," and "I call it bilge-water." But such phrases tended to come from the journals, more than the published essays, illustrating that Emerson was under the same genteel pressures to conform as Judd and that he conformed more than Judd did. Harvard's young instructor Francis Bowen, who led in the attack on Emerson, included in his disapproval such "coarse and blunt" phrases as the following, culled from Emerson's

Nature: "the affairs of our pot and kettle" and "I expand and live in the warm day like corn and melons."[10]

With eminent Unitarians jumping on Emerson for putting in print such mildly relaxed language as this, it can be easily seen that Judd's coarseness must have created an almost seismic sense of shock in the polite world of the Harvard educated. Judd had to find out for himself how to write the fiction he wanted to write. Not even Cooper, Scott, or Burns could teach him. He had to look at the world and use what he saw. That was what Emerson told him to do, although Emerson did not quite have Judd's results in mind. Emerson asked his disciples to surprise him, and the best ones—Thoreau and Whitman—did.

To learn a thing or two, Judd might have profited from Harriet Beecher Stowe, had her major writings come earlier. "Life among the Lowly," her subtitle for *Uncle Tom's Cabin,* suggests but one of the interests she and Judd had in common; her later books *The Minister's Wooing* and *Oldtown Folks* dealt with the life of the New England town. Like her, and unlike Emerson or Thoreau, Bronson Alcott or Jones Very, Judd required dramatic expression, fiction as well as essay and poem. Like Stowe, Judd mixed humor, satire, sentimentality, earthy realism, reforming zeal, and Christianity. The sense of the ideal and the real, the millennialist urge, was deep in the bones of both. The Dream, the perfected soul and the perfected village, haunted and tantalized him. The Fact, which follows a man wherever he goes and shuts doors in his face, both repelled and fascinated him.

Life was a paradox and a state of tension, and the holding of real and ideal in creative tension with each other was the key to success in life and art. Emerson understood this principle of Undulation or Polarity, as he called it, and it was the assumption that underlay the "American Scholar" address, and indeed all that Emerson wrote. Life was not a mechanism but an organism and expressed itself "in the inspiring and expiring of the breath; in desire and satiety; in the ebb and flow of the sea; in day and night; in heat and cold" and in the tension within every atom. Each thing required its opposite, and the principle of Compensation required that each thing received must be paid for by something given. Therefore consistency was a hobgoblin and truth was dazzling as it turned its many sides to the seeker. Action and reaction, love and hate, the cycle of the seasons, good and evil,—"There is never a beginning, there is never an end . . . but always circular power returning into itself."[11] All were part of the circuit of God.

> Line in nature is not found;
> Unit and universe are round;
> In vain produced, all rays return;
> Evil will bless, and ice will burn.

As Judd responded to this principle of microcosmos, circularity, he, in *Margaret,* caught up in one chant Emerson, Jonathan Edwards, Wordsworth's Immortality Ode, and his own astonishing experience as a developing writer:

> "Yet," said Margaret, "all that is lies secretly coiled within our own breasts! All Beauty, I am persuaded, is within us; whatever comes to me I feel to have had a pre-existence. I sometimes indeed doubt whether I give or receive. A flower takes color from the sun and gives off color. Air makes the fire burn, and the fire makes the air blow; and the colder the weather the brisker the fire."

Then, after such preliminary generalities, facts began to flower into truth:

> "A watermelon seed can say, 'In me are ten watermelons, rind, pulp and seeds, so many yards of vine, so many pounds of leaves.' In myself seems sometimes to reside an infant Universe. My soul is certainly pistillate, and the pollen of all things is borne to me. The spider builds his house from his own bowels. I have sometimes seen a wood-spider let off a thread which the winds drew out for him and raised above the trees, and when it was sufficiently high

and strong, he would climb up it, and sail off in the clear atmosphere. I think if you only begin, it will all come to you. As you drain off it will flow in." (245)

As Judd wrote *Margaret*, drawing the many-colored silk of reality out of his mind, he must have marveled at what he found there. There was a tenuousness in Judd, an evanescence of floating silk, catching the sunlight. He was air and fire. But his flights were artistically successful only when they began with a strong sense of earth. "The book was written for the love of the thing," said Judd, in explaining himself in his introduction to the revised edition; "each item has been introduced with a love of it. Every bird has been watched, every flower pursued, every foot-path traversed." He loved the commonplace, the vulgar, just as he was repelled by them.

The apostle of harmony was tormented by tensions. Life was organic, not mechanical and neat; disorderly, and the pressures of the heart pushed outward toward expression. In June, 1839, Judd wrote from the Divinity School to an unnamed correspondent, rather obviously female, with whom he shared his intimate feelings for over a year.*

I have seized my pen; but the ink, that comes flowing from my inkstand, glimmers and is quenched in the utter despair of my

---

*In one of these letters, dated April 10, 1839, a reference to "your sex" and "ours" clearly identifies this correspondent as female. Letters to the same person followed in swift succession: April 14, 18, 21, 23, suggesting something rather intense was going on. Possibly, other unidentified letters in this period could be to other persons, but the intimate tone and subject matter are consistent with the theory of the single confidante. It could even be Arethusa, who, although identifying some letters to herself during this period, might have wanted to draw the veil lest the letters reveal an excessive intimacy. Such a conjecture—admittedly mere guessing—seems to me at least as persuasive as the theory that the mystery friend was Jones Very, as Francis Dedmond argues. It also could have been Robert Waterston, who left the Divinity School at about the same time as Very, in 1838. Waterston seems more like the type to keep Judd's correspondence than Very. Waterston attended Judd on his deathbed in Augusta and supplied Judd's pulpit thereafter, giving Arethusa Hall ample opportunity to copy Judd's letters; but there is no record of contact between Judd and Very after 1839.

heart, of my life. Felt you ever so, when the wildest impulses of your nature tempted and urged you to an act, which a still stronger impulse would not suffer to be done? Rosalie [Allston's painting],[12] Corinne, and then the vile admixtures, the obstinate interference of this mechanical world, the imperiousness of expediency, the impudence of discretion, and then my own faltering, tameless nature.

This profession of despair must not be taken as the literal truth about Judd at this period. Even as he made the statement, a sinewy vitality pushed through the sentence. The impulse toward manliness, whether coming from Emerson or elsewhere, was beginning to toughen up his prose. The world was mechanical in its frustrating aspects and dragged a man down toward the dirt of expediency, mere discretion, and faltering nature. But even hog-philosophy had its attractions. Judd wrote again three weeks later, probably to the same person, and his mood had swung to the opposite pole; he had just had a good dinner:

Your gastronomer,—is he not the true philosopher? This three times a day, table-gathering and beef-eating, butter-spreading and tea-drinking, and friendly chat, and free laugh, makes one wonderfully content with life. . . .Why not centre all life in that? Why trouble one's self about the philosophers?. . . . Did you ever look into a swinefold? "So I can but get meal-mixture enough," says the hog-philosopher, "and mud-mixture for a siesta, I am content." "Amen!" says the hog-moralizer, who sees no end but the butcher's knife and the salt-barrel. "Amen!" adds the hog-sentimentalist, who settles his fair proportions still deeper in the heterogeneous compound that forms at once his bath and his bed. "Amen!" respond all the little piglings, who scamper at their feet's end up and down the straw and the mire. . . . This is the genuine gastrosophy. . . . So plates and spoons urge us to our immortality. I would soar, but I am clogged. Shall I to my bed and sleep?

Judd's moods swung widely, even as he struggled to hold together earth and heaven in a fruitful, organic tension. Coming from the regular prayer meeting of the students, he seemed melted in tenderness and calm: "Our souls

seemed very near heaven. We melted into love and holiness."
In the spring he tended to be manic; in November he entered the depressive phase. Of course there were fluctua-
tions within those larger movings of the tide, but in the
three years from 1837 to 1840—the only ones for which
we have sufficient materials to generalize—that seemed to
be the case. The fact that he was forced to go home for a
month in December, 1837, by "the old disorder in his
teeth & face," and that in December, 1838, he was again
home, sick for three months, explains some of this tendency. Even in his sadness, however, there was often an
austere warmth. To his mysterious correspondent he wrote:

> All Things sadden me. Mr. —coming in, and talking about "these
> views," makes me sad. Philosophy, theology, poetry, make me
> sad. Coleridge, and Ripley, and Norton make me sad. My Father's
> presence with me now makes me sad. The snow, my rose-plant,
> the cold moon, produce the same effect.[13]

This tendency to swing from manic to depressive phases
is one of the chief characteristics of the romanticist's psychology. It can be seen particularly in Poe and Shelley, but
also in Byron, Keats, Coleridge, and all the rest, from
Felicia Hemans to Harriet Beecher Stowe. In certain of the
greatest writers—Wordsworth, Emerson, Thoreau spring to
mind—the extreme swings of the pendulum were held in
check; the tension produced a calmer, more subdued and
satisfying fire. The pendulum swing stretched the soul and
enlarged it; without the heights and depths a person would
sink into humdrum and gastrosophy. At the same time the
commonplace had its attractions and was necessary to the
establishment of sanity and balance. The greatest art came
from the dynamic tension between real and ideal.

As long as Judd was able to maintain this tension, he
was an artist. But he was never able to maintain it for a
whole book, and sometimes not even through a whole paragraph. Usually, it was when he forgot himself and wrote

as a man inspired that the words fused into poetry; when he went back to rewrite later, the spell was lost, and the reviser, trying to heed the critics, often made things worse than before. Furthermore, mechanical efforts to impose ideality upon the real from outside were foredoomed failures. When, at the end of *Margaret*, Judd tried to create a utopia by a *deus ex machina*, the novel fell apart. The reader gets the impression, despite Judd's protestations to the contrary, that the drunken villagers have been reformed by a little preaching, a little new-fashioned philanthropy judiciously applied, and a few statues strewn over the landscape. The transformation is mechanical, not an organic growth from what has gone before, and the result is a bit ludicrous. Only when Judd found the ideal already inside the real, peeled back the mother earth from the pieplant roots, did he find the vermilion and gold. The elusive rainbow that he sought was not in the skies where he looked for it; it was down under the earth that intercepted its perfect orb.

In a letter that he wrote to Arethusa Hall in June, 1838, Judd said,

> Our hearts *do* make us sin.
> Aim at the stars, you say. What if, in a dark night, I catch a glow-worm? . . . Elevated society has its drawbacks. I love sometimes to escape to the low, home-spun realities of common life. Its rudeness only provokes an agreeable humor.

This is our first very definite indication that Judd had begun to cultivate the soil. In a way it was an escape from frustration: "In it you expect nothing, and never run any risk of disappointment," Judd added. In a letter to Arethusa on June 3 Judd said that he had gone into Boston every day the previous week, and that spring had burst "in all its beauty and attractiveness," calling him much from his room. He confessed that his external being sometimes so "staggers and reels, that I fear some observer will detect the hidden cause. 'Tis strange how I, that is, one like myself, catch the sympathies of longing hearts." Arethusa at this point draws the veil with an excision, after which Judd goes on, "There is now and then a person in the world 'charged;' and you have but to touch them, and the fire of their souls is at once emitted." He concludes, "You will not think but that other and higher thoughts engage my attention. With you alone do I take the liberty of writing freely." Arethusa, in her reply, evidently twitted Judd with his "total depravity," and he responded, "'Total depravity,'—well, so be it. Heart *is* every thing, with or without husband or child. With,—perhaps 'tis more than every thing."

Arethusa left it to the reader's imagination to guess at the nature of the experience Judd was talking about. The word "sympathy" was a highly connotative word to Judd, and implied the emission of fire from the soul when touched by another person, an instantaneous release of electricity. He used the word often in his letters to Arethusa and his unnamed correspondent, rarely with other people. The most interesting use of the word is in a poem that survives in manuscript, entitled "Oh ask not, hope thou not, too much of sympathy below." The handwriting suggests a date between 1837 and 1839. It may have been written within a year or so of the other love poem discussed earlier. In this poem the "burdened heart" finds momentary solace before loss. There is a chance encounter on a moonlit seashore with a young lady, who opens her heart in "sympathy," then flees. The poet searches for her in city throngs, hoping to see her face, her form:

> Return, Mysterious One, to me!
> How this heart pants, oh didst thou know,
> For thee, . . .
> . . . .
> We walked by the deserted shore

> Of the dark sea, while evermore
> Its gloomy song broke on the ear—

Their hearts echoed "the waves low moan":

> One ear, one heart, one heaving breast-
> We sat us on a sea-mossed rock to rest.

The moon

> . . . beamed down on us in sorrow.
> Faintly it flushed the rippling waves.
> A crimsoned surf the beach sand laves.

Both have suffered; they recall the past with "stifled sighs."
The moon, the rock, and the waves blend together.

> But when I asked that we might tell
> *What* thoughts our histories contained,
> She left the rock, the strand she gained;
> She hurried on, as modest maid;
> I would have gone, her hand forbade.

If he does not find her again, "then die/ My heart! deceived by mockery."

There is no particular reason to connect this poem with the letter just quoted or with Judd's mysterious correspondent, although the careful reader may have caught certain flashes of an occult sympathy between the poem and the letter. Another clue, only the faintest suggestion, is provided by the nature of the imagery in Arethusa Hall's statement in her biography of Judd, a statement introducing her discussion of his Divinity School years.

> His spirit yearned for sympathy, for companionship in all its recesses, in all its weaknesses. . . . He himself found it difficult to trace the clew of light through the labyrinth of darkness in which he had wandered. . . . He needed the tender support of a strong mind that had itself *suffered* as he had, that had gone down to the silent abyss of unutterable sorrow, that knew all its devious ramifications, and that understood how to remove the garment of sadness so gently, that the change would be known only by the refreshment which succeeded. With him were longings for the in-

finite, the unattained. . . . He descended into the depths of the loneliness of his own spirit; he sounded its profoundest recesses, and drew up thence fountains of knowledge. . . .

Yet the sunlight of joy gilded the tops of rocks that rose above these troubled waters.

Rocks, waters, the abyss, fountains, "the labyrinth of darkness"—the mind echoed with the word "boundless" and the thought of "circular power returning into itself."

A few years later, as Sylvester Judd wrote *Margaret*, the same images flowed into his mind. Margaret and Mr. Evelyn stand on the Head overlooking the pond, the cliff from which the Indian chief will later plunge. Margaret, who is now a young woman and in love, says,

> "Look down *into* this water. . . . I have wished to drop into that splendid cloud-flowing abyss, and perhaps I shall be missing one of these days. . . . look off into the mountains yonder. That is Umkiddin. You will not blame a passion I cherish for climbing that sunny height, and laying hand and heart in the downy Blue." (233)

The symbol of *climbing* toward some ultimate consummation in the heavens links Margaret's yearning with one of the basic archetypal images. The ascension symbol is almost universal in the mythologies of primitive societies as an expression of mystical experience.[14] Heights and depths, climbing and falling are related to each other. For Margaret the thought of Umkiddin and the pond gives birth to Orphic mysteries:

> "Lost, gone, vanishing, unreachable, inappropriable, anagogical!— I used to sit here in my merry childhood and think all was mine, the earth and the sky. I ate my bread and cider and fed the ants and flies. Through me innumerable things went forth; the loons whooped me in the water, in my breath the midges sported, the Sun went down at my bidding. . . . In the darkest night, with our red tartarean links, Chilion and I have rowed across the Pond, and sniggled for eels, and so we conquered the secrets of those depths." (233-34)

The passage reminds us of Whitman's "There Was a Child Went Forth" and "Song of Myself." The external world is the symbol of the internal world, says Emerson. "'I seem to myself to be deep as our own bottomless Pond,'" says Margaret. *Margaret* teems with what a Jungian might call "symbols of transformation." The pond and the fountain of Helicon which feeds it are Orphic mysteries, and Orpheus is a symbol of Margaret's Beautiful One who comes to her in a dream and reveals all truth to her subconscious, and the Beautiful One is Christ. The pond is Margaret's own subconscious mind: "'Yet, yet, the sun swims through me, and I hear Jesus walking on the troubled waters above.'" Down the long the lonely light rays comes Jesus walking, walking on the water. "'I knew not that I had any depth. Now shaft opens into shaft, and the miners are still at work,'" says Margaret. She is a cave, a Cave of Music. Then with a start, she comes out of her trance: "'I hear my chickens peeping, and I must go feed them.'"[15] Infinite and finite meet and burn in rainbow hues in the pool at the bottom of the waterfall. We return to the commonplace. In defending his use of the vulgar, the low, the "unequal, grotesque, mermaiden, abrupt" in his book, Judd said, "Have we not seen or heard of a cascade that starts, say, from the blue of the skies, pours down a precipice of rusty rock, and terminates in drift-wood and bog?" And, he asked, is it bathos to plunge from the ideal to the real, as so many of the critics had charged?[16] As Judd implied, by close juxtaposition, even interfusing of the two, they would fecundate and enrich each other. Judd was unlocking the rich resources of the subconscious and pouring them prodigally over the landscape of the barren New England mind.

The essence of Judd's achievement in *Margaret* is that he accomplishes, often, a fusion of the real and the ideal.

The fusion is imperfect: much of the book is flat and uninspired, much is sentimental and moralistic. But, in the passage just quoted, homely details become symbols of inner
reality. The ants, flies, loons, and midges unite Margaret
with the real world around her and yet reveal a depth within herself. The pond becomes a gateway to a wonderworld
within, a "splendid cloud-flowing abyss." The gates of the
wonderworld swing open and grand, hooded phantoms fill
the sky of what Judd calls "this illimitable, whale-bearing,
sky-cleaving Nature" (432). The "downy Blue" of Umkidden
cleaves the sky and suggests the heights of human experience. Opposite to it are the Tartarean depths and the black
night. The oarsmen with their "red tartarean links" row
across into the night and conquer "the secrets of those
depths." "A princely offering are we to Annihilation," says
Margaret (239). In the depths of the pond, she and her brother Chilion sniggle for eels. The homely detail and the homely word bring us back to reality, yet seem symbolic. The
depths harbor dream-like beauty and at the same time
black, snakelike denizens of the underworld.

In another scene, Margaret looks down from the hilltop
on "an entire firmament of purest white clouds. . . . like
sea-waves." "They were an organic lustre, sublimated wool,
spiritualized alabaster; they glowed like snow-flames." The
fog seems like a dream, filled with "fair shapes of Ideal
Beauty." "A new Venus, of whom she had read, was indeed
sprung from this foam . . . and she would run down and
embrace her." Then, suddenly, out of the dream "a great
black crow flew up from the depths of the white waves, a
true make-shift for Vulcan." The imagination contains
more than dreamlike beauty; it sends forth croaking ravens
from Vulcan's smithy. A black-whiskered villain material-
izes from the fog, attempts a seduction, and is foiled (218-
21). Later, in another context, Margaret, having found genuine love after much tribulation, says, "Has a volcano burst
within me; has a tornado prostrated me? . . . . I am in ruins,

and so are all things about me. Yet in the windfall some trees are new-sprouting; invisible hands are rebuilding the shattered edifice" (387).

The death-rebirth archetype is suggested not only by such individual lines and scenes, but by the whole structure of *Margaret*. Margaret's brother is unjustly executed by the Calvinists; the town is destroyed by fire; Margaret flees to the city in confusion. Then she is found to be a missing heiress and returns in triumph to find a happy marriage and to assist in the moral and physical rebuilding of the town in a pattern closer to the ideal. In the closing paragraph of the book, Judd sums up the archetypal movement of his story with the myth of Orpheus, whose music "subdued the rulers of Hell," but who was torn in pieces by the Thracian women. "The river Helicon, sacred to him, hid itself under ground." Margaret's pond is the "Lake of Orpheus" from which the Helicon flows. Christ is the new Orpheus. "His music was quenched; he was torn in pieces; his waters, hid under the Earth, as I would fain fancy, have appeared on Mons Christi! Whither now shall the Christian Helicon flow?" (460). At the end, Judd loses his hold on the earth and flies off into foggy, symbolic realms. It is a Shelleyan flight to the intense inane, from which "gastrosophy" would be a relief. Nonetheless, Judd launches his flight to the sun from a firm base on earth. Coarse, grubby reality becomes beautiful in his hands. "Nature is not shocked at toads," he says, answering his genteel critics.[17] Margaret turns over rocks and logs in the spring to let the light in upon the lizards, beetles, sow-bugs, and ear-wigs that have wintered there. Then she watches the toads: "Toads, piebald, chunk-shaped, shrugged and wallowed up from their torpid beds, and winked their big eyes at her" (186-87). Spring gives birth to more than dreams. More than any other author of his time and place except Melville, Judd wrote a "source-book for plenitude."

10

Controversy at the Divinity School

In the years Judd spent at Harvard from 1837 to 1840 his maturing was being gradually accomplished. It was an organic development, not a cataclysm. The conversion experience of the Calvinist was mechanical, thought Judd. Similarly mechanistic, thought Emerson, was the philosophy behind what he called "the corpse-cold Unitarianism of Brattle Street."[1] In contrast was the quiet maturing and deepening as a person discovered his own inner resources and the fecundity of the world around him. The blowing clover and the falling rain, without the flash of lightning, were the symbol of Judd's discovery of romanticism.

The richness of the mind that wrote *Margaret* was not yet perceptible in the theological student who was learning the value of "home-spun realities of common life." Imagination was still coiled within the seed, like "so many yards of vine, so many pounds of leaves." Except for the two poems already discussed, which were imitative and sounded like something written by Byron or perhaps by Felicia Hemans, the poet so much admired by Andrews Norton,[2] none of Judd's creative work during this period survives for our inspection. Arethusa Hall tells us that he was writing something, however, "a tale, chiefly illustrative of 'The Philosophy of the Affections,'—the deep things of the heart,

246

its yearnings and disappointments, its aspirations and its sufferings," but that he broke off the project, after writing "quite a number of pages," upon "regaining a more healthful tone of feeling, and entering upon the duties and interests of his profession."[3] Although Judd's mental state improved almost immediately after he went to Harvard and received his dose of the Emersonian tonic—Judd became more objective and interested in reporting the world around him to his correspondents—he also continued in his self-centeredness, dissecting his mental states of ecstasy and wretchedness. He probably began his long tale before going to Harvard, during the period of what Arethusa calls his "despondency and nervous wretchedness" and continued writing at it until 1840. Perhaps of significance in dating this long tale is Judd's letter of October 28, 1839, to his unknown correspondent. In it he talks about the value of autobiographical writing and seems to write with an air of authority about the advantages of such self-revelation. Already, as later in *Margaret,* Judd was concerned with analyzing organic development of the mind.

Further evidence that Judd was fictionalizing his own experiences in 1839 is his journal entry for July 29, 1839, one of the few entries Arethusa Hall gives us from Judd's now-lost journals. The passage, describing a walk from Northampton to Hadley, begins with matter-of-fact description in the first person, but gradually takes flight:

> The water was trembling in light. The dark, shaded banks enclose it like a gem. From the high heavens I fancied it looked earth's night-jewelry. Walked the thoughtful quickly on. The burying-ground,—its white monuments stood up like the sheeted dead, new-risen from their graves; and its black monuments, like the wasted skeletons of a hundred years. As he hurried by, these dead seemed to move.

As the "I" becomes "he," we can see that a switch has been thrown in Judd's brain and he is turning experience into "literature":

> They joined in dance over the hillocks, in the dim moonlight, the black and the white, under funereal pines and elms, with tall, gaunt weeds that grew there. They danced noiselessly, as the dead must dance. They danced to no music; for they needed none, save the silent wind.[4]

If this is a fair sample of Judd's "Philosophy of the Affections," or at least of the sort of writing that went into it, we might conclude that Judd was wise to give it up. It is rhythmic, but shadowy and bloodless. It lacks grit.

Later, in *Philo*, which he began writing in 1845, Judd proclaims that grit is the very stuff of poetry, that "grit is steadfast." Judd's character, the Poet, has learned to cling to rock:

> David his harp enjoyed, I thrum a rock;
> Petrarch his Laura had, I have a rock;
> Our Pastor loves a horse, but I a rock.
> When speculation wearies me, to thee,
> O Rock, I come.[5]

When the Poet, under the stress of praising the fair Wynfreda, relapses into romantic bombast, she reminds him that "Youth's first emotions need/A stint; must oaken up to manliness." Sentimental softness is not the way to mature love: "The frost must pinch the nut, or 'twill not sprout." The tightness and vigor of "pinch the nut" and "oaken up to manliness" are refreshing islands in the grey sea of Victorian poetic propriety. Again, in *Philo*, Judd defies convention in the character of the Devil, a coarse but engaging fellow who has "muckered round in lanes,/Ditches, and garrets, hovels, hospitals" where "maidens never smile, but glout,/And stare at you like stupid walruses."[6] This is a dumpy Devil, not heroic at all, owing little to Byron or Milton. He is a bit of a junk dealer, who trades in bruised hearts. The lumpishness of his verbs "glout" and "muckered" is reflected in the incongruity of "maidens" and "stupid walruses." There is a muckiness of mild vulgarity here in which Judd took public delight.

Whether Judd "muckered round in lanes" collecting data for his artist's notebook during the years he spent at the Divinity School it is impossible to say. He appears to have preferred conversing with the moon in Mt. Auburn cemetery.[7] But we do know that he later saw no incongruity between his role as a minister and the sociological investigation that went into the production of his major works. We still have his notebooks, and we know how he compiled them. He made his own thesaurus and dictionary of words and phrases that didn't get into dictionaries. When he heard a racy bit of talk, out came his pencil and folded slip of paper. He talked to people with notebook in hand.[8] No wonder people called him odd. For example, while his brothers played a game of cards, Judd eavesdropped and took down their entire conversation.[9] Refashioned and improved, the Judd-family card game became part of the Halloween revel in *Margaret.* In Augusta, Maine, he visited lumber mills, cultivated the common man, drew him out, and jotted it all down. He had heard Emerson say in his "American Scholar" address that "the clergy . . . are addressed as women; . . . the rough, spontaneous conversation of men they do not hear, but only a mincing and diluted speech. They are often virtually disfranchised; and indeed there are advocates for their celibacy."[10] Judd seems to have set out to remedy the situation. He turned up words that others of his calling didn't know existed or that they thought "never should have been written down."[11] Judd delighted in writing them down. How he could record such profusion of aphorism, humor, dialect, folklore and also write *Margaret* plus a weekly sermon in the short space of three or four years is a mystery. One is forced to infer that he began his notetaking even before 1841, the date he began working up his material for *Mar-*

garet. Arethusa Hall supports this conclusion with her comment that it was one of his early habits to take notes, that it "was one of the most common things" to see him doing it, and that his notes included, among unusual words and expressions of wit, "sometimes a broad truth, uttered by his father."[12] Along with "broad truths" he also recorded the following live bit of language (cut in the revised edition), addressed by Brown Moll to her husband, Pluck Hart: "'Don't deary me with your dish-cloth tongue'" (30).

We would guess none of this from the extracts from Judd's letters during the Divinity School years that Arethusa Hall printed. Perhaps such things do not get into letters. The Judd we see there seems to have lived in the clouds or in the dumps more often than on level ground. Judd was in love with light. He was in love with love. Writing to his unidentified confidante on April 2, 1839, he began on an Emersonian note but swiftly rose to a more rarefied atmosphere:

> We grovel too much. We take our flight beneath the clouds, and become immersed in their shadows and drippings. If we would but mount above them, we should see these gloomy masses permeated and transparent with the light of the all-enlightening sun. As we approach that luminary, we become light ourselves, and all things glow with light about us. To an inhabitant of the sun, there is not a dark spot on the face of the universe.
>
> Truth is light, love is light, God is light. Truth, Love, God—O my soul! By what art thou surrounded! To what canst thou attain! How glorious may be thy life! Yet how dost thou fold thy wings, make feet of thy hands and claws of thy feet, and crawl about in the dark caverns, the slimy pits, of this nether world!

Beginning with Emerson, Judd undertook a Shelleyan flight to the sun, and ended up sounding like Carlyle's Teufelsdröckh. "Love is light." "We become light ourselves." Marvelous. Judd had spent the day before communing with nature and perhaps with someone else at Mt. Auburn. Judd was a bit light-headed.

Meanwhile Judd was living a life on earth as well as in the mind. He boiled sausages and potatoes in his room at the Divinity School and was troubled with headache and dyspepsia afterwards.[13] He was kept awake with the rituals of coffee and tea drinking in polite society—something of a novelty at father Judd's, where they were still fighting the Revolution and tea was considered "English," and a butt of the ebullient Judd humor.[14] Sylvester taught a class of boys at a local Sunday school, and in his senior year conducted the meeting for Sunday school teachers, also taking his turn with the other seniors preaching in the college chapel. He paid off his debts, having received aid from a Unitarian philanthropist in Boston that made up for his loss of support from home.[15]

The prodigal returned to Northampton to find that he was still welcome: He took long walks in the country with his father and talked with him about local history. He delivered an address on "Childhood" at the Northampton Lyceum in January, 1838,—"Town Hall full. Unitarians most all there," noted his father. In August of that year he came back to the town hall to deliver a rabid abolitionist address, which he had earlier given in Hartford. In February, 1840, he was invited back to lecture on Northampton history—a subject "which he knows little about," commented his father sourly.[16] The outsider was at last getting the recognition he craved. The great world was coming round to him—a little. He was discovering that being a Unitarian had its advantages. The doors leading to carpeted rooms and elegant music were swinging open to him:

> I recollect a lady, whom I asked to sing, once said to me, "You don't care for me, but only for my singing." Well, she insinuated a truth. . . . Sometimes a lady's whole being is her singing. But this lady had another self. "Care for *me*," she said.[17]

Judd, who craved masculine sympathy as well as feminine, thought for a while he had found his "man," as he put it,[18] in the person of Robert C. Waterston of the senior class at the Divinity School. Waterston's father was a wealthy Boston merchant, and Judd was often entertained at his home. Through Waterston, who later married one of

President Quincy's daughters, Judd received at least two invitations to visit the president, his wife, and his daughters, "who combine elegant accomplishments, and solid worth in an eminent degree."[19] Judd also met Deborah Taylor Taft, who in December, 1845, then a "sedate matron of 25," wrote him a coy letter from Uxbridge, Massachusetts, as "a tribute to the 'days of lang syne,'" inquiring if he were indeed the mysterious author of *Margaret* and asking if she and her husband might become "one of your company" at the community described in *Margaret,* if indeed such a community existed. As the letter hints at no particular degree of intimacy other than friendship, it should not be given too much emphasis, except insofar as it happens to be the only letter from a female correspondent outside the family preserved among the Judd papers. The friendship with Waterston was of more moment, although Judd wrote in April, 1839, "Is there no friend for me?"[20] and found his contacts with Waterston somewhat less frequent in later life. At Waterston's request Judd wrote him a series of long letters describing his conversion that were made into a powerful and persuasive Unitarian tract in March, 1838, called *A Young Man's Account of His Conversion from Calvinism,* also published in the *Christian Register,* the official Unitarian newspaper. Judd was beginning to create a minor ripple in the great world.

He still was not satisfied, however. He found Unitarians a little cold and wished that with their enlightened theology they might combine some of the fervor of the orthodox. Most Unitarians, he wrote, "do not seem to appreciate the full value of their own principles." To correct the situation he helped set up prayer meetings at the Divinity School, where he held forth with appropriate fervor.[21] The "corpse-cold Unitarianism of Brattle Street" and the polite tea-sipping in starched collars were not quite what Judd had in mind when he talked about a flight to the sun.

Emerson didn't like such coldness either. The transcendentalist revolt was not just a philosophical squabble about ontology and epistemology. As the enthusiasts saw the matter, it was a flight from State Street finance, routine living, routine theology, mechanical preaching by rules, the city of the dead. The clockwork world of eighteenth-century rationalism, run by a watchspring, was *dead,* felt the transcendentalists. Sylvester Judd was inclined to agree, although he had not had the experience of growing up in such a world and listening to the dead, formalistic preaching in the Concord church that irritated Emerson so much.[22] Judd had already had his revolt against the fathers, and one revolt is all that most people can manage in three years; Emerson had studied at the Divinity School under Andrews Norton, "the old tyrant of the Cambridge Parnassus," as Emerson called him, and Norton's dogmatic ways in the classroom were, to a man like Emerson, only an encouragement to rebellion.[23]

Emerson's comment was not quite fair to Norton, an eminently moral man who also "read and wrote poetry fairly dripping with tender affection." Rationalism and common-sense empiricism were not incompatible with cultivation of sentiment and sensibility.[24] But for Norton truth was in the word, the final word was in the Bible; the ultimate truth had to be revealed by supernatural means; therefore close attention to every textual detail was the supreme duty of the truth-seeker. He labored for over twenty years to write the six volumes of his *Evidences of the Genuineness of the Gospels.* Emerson was much more interested in the book of nature and the testimony of his own consciousness, and he scornfully brushed off "the restorers of readings, the emendators, the bibliomaniacs of all degrees."[25] Judd, who believed the standard Unitarian doctrine that consciousness, nature, and revelation must necessarily harmonize, sought a middle ground between the extremes of Emerson and Norton.

In Henry Ware, Jr., and in William Ellery Channing, but especially in Ware, Judd found a middle way that he could admire. He liked Ware from the start. Dean Palfrey he described as "nicely critical, inconveniently punctilious, yet just such a man as we need." Henry Ware, Sr., he called "a fine specimen of the Old School of Divines." But Henry Ware, Jr., he called "excellent beyond what I shall attempt to describe."[26] Ware was fervent and spiritual; he was no dead formalist. Like Judd, he believed religion to be "essentially evangelical," and he emphasized the emotional aspect of religion. Unitarians regarded him as "the finest example of what their movement could produce," and Emerson, who had been Ware's colleague-pastor at the Second Church in Boston, said at one time that he "thought *le bon Henri* a pumpkin-sweeting."[27]

Ware had provided Unitarians in 1831 with their devotional manual, *On the Formation of the Christian Character,* which some called a sort of "Unitarian *Imitatio Christi.*" Ware said that religion consisted in "cherishing the sentiments and performing the duties which thence result." Daniel Walker Howe concludes that "Religion, thus defined, was a means of self-culture," with the Christian character to be achieved gradually through "long training" of the conscience and "cherishing the sentiments," toward the end of "balanced development and harmonious integration of the faculties." Looked at this way, religion was less a matter of being accepted by God and achieving rapport with Him than a matter of conditioning and fine-tuning the sensibilities through systematic application. Thus, Unitarians of a serious intent were among those who kept count of pages read in "worthy" books and who worked at morality as systematically as Benjamin Franklin, keeping records of resolutions, worthy projects, and results.[28]

Most important to Judd were Ware's views on questions of social ethics. Ware was no profound theologian or biblical scholar; his title was "Professor of Pulpit Eloquence and the Pastoral Care," and he was eminently practical, telling his students to make the closing prayer after a baptism brief because the water sometimes made the baby cry. Judd, in his preaching, followed Ware's example by emphasizing practical piety and social issues at the expense of haggling over doctrines and textual details.

Judd's views on social issues resembled very closely those of Ware. Both preached reform, the chief evils to be eradicated being war and slavery. Philanthropic work among the poor and the besotted was also important. Ware was instrumental in founding the Philanthropic Society at the Divinity School in 1831 with the initial purpose of assisting convicts to readjust to society. This concern for the reformation of criminals was one that Judd felt for the rest of his life and expressed in his sermons, his actions as a minister, and in *Margaret.* The Philanthropic Society, which became a debating club of such liveliness that outsiders often attended and the newspapers sometimes carried accounts of the debates, was a seedbed of radicalism during Judd's years in it. Topics in earlier years had included, for example, the treatment of lunatics, the influence of the factory system on pauperism, the moral influences of the drama, and liquor license laws. During Judd's first year at the Divinity School, pacifism and abolitionism became subjects of intense interest.[29]

Judd had been against war for a long time, had written essays on the subject in 1832. Two weeks after entering Harvard, he wrote to his mother, as if telling her something new about himself,

> War is a most unnatural, inhuman system. I am a peace-man, ultra as need be. I am withal so great a *coward* that the consistency of my principles will probably never be hazarded.

Judd acquired a number of antiwar pamphlets: three by William Ellery Channing, dated 1835, 1837, and 1839; one by Henry Ware, Jr., dated 1834. Channing stopped short of a completely pacifist position, but Ware's condemnation of war was more uncompromising.[30] By June, 1839, Judd could write to his brother Hall thus:

> The anti-war question has been pretty thoroughly discussed in the seminary; and we are perhaps surprised to find that our whole school, with scarcely an individual exception, sustains the position, that all war, offensive and defensive, is inconsistent with the spirit of Christianity. This is a result, which, as I am aware, has not been reached in any other seminary, literary or theological, in the country. It is in no way of boasting, when I intimate that Unitarianism is most peculiarly fitted for such a conclusion. Its idea of the worth of man, as man, and its faith in the indestructible principles of human virtue, render such a decision comparatively easy. We see that the man is too valuable to be shot down for the capricious and "honorable" ends of government.

Disputes, he added, should be settled "by appeals to the exalted sentiments of the soul." This was an easy pacifism, not yet tried in the furnace of affliction, the Civil War, depending upon a soft, romantic doctrine of human nature. It was admirable and a bit naive and far from the pacifism of the 1950's preached by Martin Niemöller and André Trocmé, who had been through Nazi concentration camps. But in its day it was new and daring and looked attractive even to a man like George Bancroft, no pacifist, who wrote an idealized account of the Quakers in his second volume of the monumental history. The volume appeared in 1837, just in time to give added glow and authority to the pacifist views that Judd was espousing. In the spring of 1839 Judd and most of his classmates read several volumes about the Quakers, including some of William Penn's works. Judd, like Emerson, continued after that to entertain a kindly feeling towards the Quakers, whose social views and whose belief in the Indwelling Christ so much resembled his own.[31]

An antiwar position was not likely to arouse any great furor in the late 1830's, when there were no standing armies of any consequence and no power elite dependent on military contracts. There were no immediate prospects of a war, although the Maine boundary dispute and the Aroostook War of 1839 were matters of some small excitement. "Nonresistance" did not arouse opposition to the extent that abolitionism did, except insofar as nonresistants tended also to become abolitionists.

Judd did not have to go to Harvard to become an abolitionist. His father had been one of the leading promoters of an abolition meeting in Northampton as early as January, 1836,[32] and had served as Secretary of the Northampton Anti-Slavery Society that resulted, just as he was also deeply involved in temperance reform activities about the same time. But young Sylvester had pointedly stayed away from the huge meeting of 1300 people that January 13, and had taken a jaunt to Amherst instead. At Harvard, however, he could not escape the antislavery ferment.

At Harvard, antislavery became entangled with another concern that had a long Unitarian history: the issue of free speech. Unitarians in the 1820's had smarted at the refusal of orthodox ministers to exchange pulpits with them and had called it persecution and denial of free speech. Northampton Unitarians had especial concern over this issue. Unitarians, they were proud to point out, did not exclude anybody for his opinions. Freedom had been the great Unitarian rallying cry: let every voice be heard, and truth will prevail. Now, however, abolitionism was particularly dangerous. Boston's shipping and textile interests were not anxious to stir up trouble with the South. The burning of the Charlestown convent, the ugly mobs that swirled around Sylvester Graham and William Lloyd Garrison, the killing of Elijah Lovejoy in Illinois were all fresh memories. In Amherst an abolition meeting in 1837 had been annoyed by cannon fire. Father Judd noted, "shot off the hand of one of the disturbers! 'He that diggeth a pit shall fall therein.'"[33]

When, therefore, the Philanthropic Society at the Harvard Divinity School decided to agitate the antislavery issue in May, 1838, conservative Boston was concerned. General invitations had gone out for a public meeting on May 25th. The question of faculty control over outside speakers at the Divinity School became involved, as the students were giving platform space to antislavery agitators. President Quincy took decisive action. He fired a letter to Dean Palfrey, Dean Palfrey convened the faculty, the faculty voted "that the Dean be directed to request the Philanthropic Society to defer their proposed meeting." The students assembled amid the furor. Every issue dear to the student heart was at stake: presidential dictatorship, freedom of speech, freedom of the student, freedom of the slave, freedom of the pulpit, Unitarian toleration. *Unitarians* could not exclude others. The students voted to consider the faculty resolution merely advisory. With Judd, in a dramatic last-minute switch, casting the deciding vote, the students decided to assert their right to invite outside speakers. The words "outside speakers" and "exclusion" took on a nasty ring. The records do not show, however, that the outside speaker actually came, despite the brave resolution of the students.[34]

This is the story that did not get told in Samuel Eliot Morison's *Three Centuries of Harvard.* Perhaps it was not important. The other side of the coin, President Quincy's defense of faculty freedom, is perhaps more significant. Henry Ware, Jr., who had founded an antislavery society in Cambridge which had died after about a year, kept his job. And, reported President Quincy, the University never even considered asking Ware to moderate his opinions. Still, Carl Follen "had lost his Harvard professorship of literature after becoming vocal on antislavery," which could have caused Ware to tread softly, although he occasionally expressed his antislavery views.[35]

Sylvester Judd's abolitionism was advanced enough in 1838 that he was ready to risk public exposure of his views. His lectures in Hartford and Northampton that August reveal a young zealot, standing firm for principle, pure principle, spurning all attempts to support abolitionism by appeals to expediency: "Get right, each of you," and the world will then find abolitionism an irresistible power. The address was marred by the oratorical tone and by Judd's persistent addressing of his audience as "thou," and it did not get down to specifics. Judd wanted to blur the issues that separated abolitionist, antislavery man, and colonizationist. Individual purity, not political action, suited Judd's temperament.

Later, Judd drew back from radicalism on this issue as he saw a spirit of denunciation and hate in the antislavery movement. Lydia Maria Child, who was living in Northampton in 1838, presumably heard Judd speak, as she was a Garrisonian abolitionist; but she found the Judds no kindred spirits and complained bitterly that she could find none around her who would go the full way.[36] Judd did not want to go the full way if that involved denunciation and questioning of people's motives. One of his earliest sermons, in November, 1840, was devoted to criticizing the methods of so-called reformers. Questioning a man's motives arouses his resentment, he said, and "you cannot amend a man whom you cannot approach." "And when you have knocked a man down, and bruised his character, and thrust your feet upon his motives, he will be slow to believe you when you tell him you love him, and only wish his good." Truth, he said, should be uttered in love and not in rancor.[37] Mrs. Child's husband, striking up the accordion to drown out the praying of the rich slave auctioneer next door in Northampton, cried out, "'Hear him! Hear the pious old thief, trying to come paddy over the Lord!'" Mrs. Child noted the baskets of vegetables and fruit carried from the pious old thief to the complaisant minister, "a part of the price for which the Judas betrays his master."[38] This was the "truth as a knife," as Judd put it in his sermon, and knives had a way of becoming swords. Judd continued to support freedom for the slave with generalities, but he considered peace the overriding issue.

The knife of exclusion and separation came down at Harvard in still another way that summer of 1838. Emerson, who had been to a discussion meeting with the Divinity School students in April and perhaps on another occasion or two that spring,[39] was the man of the year. Sylvester Judd, in a class that numbered only seven students, could hardly have missed coming into close contact with Emerson on these intimate occasions. Philip Judd Brockway, in his study of Judd, has sufficiently demonstrated the affinity between Judd's writing and Emerson's, and it is pointless to try to prove how many times they saw each other. Judd did not arrive home in Northampton until four days after the momentous "Divinity School Address" that Emerson delivered July 15, 1838, and of course Judd was one of the hundred or more privileged listeners who packed the tiny chapel that July night. His friend Waterston, who was tinged with transcendentalism,* was one of the seniors who per-

---

*Waterston's published lecture *On Moral and Spiritual Culture in Early Education* (Boston, 1836), which Judd bound into his collection of sermons, anticipates Judd's most transcendental utterance, the watermelon-seed passage from *Margaret*. Waterston says, "The mind of a child is not empty. It is not blank paper. It has life and power. It is full of the seeds of things. The work of the teacher is not to pour in, but to draw out. . . . The moral and the spiritual already exist within the child's mind, as the flower exists in the bud, and education is as the sun, and the air and the dew to call forth its beauty and fruitfulness" (pp. 5-6). Judd's *Margaret* says, "A watermelon seed can say, 'In me are ten watermelons, rind, pulp and seeds, so many yards of vine, so many pounds of leaves.' In myself seems sometimes to reside an infant Universe. . . . The spider builds his

formed the important function of requesting Emerson's manuscript for publication.[40]

In print, Emerson's address became a two-edged knife that divided Unitarians as they had never been divided before. It aroused rancor that must have pained Judd, who was willing enough to take a stand where principle was involved, but who longed for a spirit of harmony that would end divisions and strife. Love was the controlling principle to Judd, throughout his life; the irony was that the pursuit of truth involved him in some of the major controversies of his day. No wonder that as he surveyed the pamphlet warfare that ensued upon Emerson's challenge, Judd wrote that "Coleridge, and Ripley, and Norton make me sad."

Emerson, on July 15th, did nothing less than attack the very basis of Unitarianism and weaken faith in divine revelation. It was a sermon in support of undisguised naturalism. Emerson spurned the traditional Unitarian appeal to Christ's miracles as a prop for faith and declared that faith was its own validation. Consciousness and nature were the test of truth; the Bible was true insofar as it agreed with consciousness and nature. Emerson did not argue that the Bible was wrong; he merely implied that it was unnecessary. And all of this was made to sound appealing, right, pure. How could Sylvester Judd disagree with Emerson's eloquent attack upon the mere formalist who usurps the pulpit and drains it of life? How could he disagree with the

---

house from his own bowels" (245).

In another Emersonian passage, Margaret writes: "Could we understand the Philosophy of a single moment, or a single atom, we should understand the Philosophy of Infinity. . . . Could I understand God in the structure of a single head of fox-tail grass, I should know more than all theosophists." Nature, not speculation, gives her the meaning of things; "The Germans . . . surprise the age with the novelty of their views, and the grandeur of their speculations." But, "What avails speculation in this slouched, vagabondish world? Eternity is made up of moments, let me live the present moment well, and I shall live forever well." By working "the work of Nature, so shall I work the work of God, and be above all schools" (450).

plea for firsthand religion; the injunction to become a "newborn bard of the Holy Ghost"; the prose poem in which all nature sang a divine chant, "man's life was a miracle," and became "one with the blowing clover and the falling rain"? Judd had heard nothing like it before. Emerson had surpassed even Emerson. It was Emerson's most eloquent and heartfelt performance, like a lambent flash of summer lightning that discharged the pent-up electricity of years. Emerson was Uriel, with a station in the sun, whence he watched the motions of the planets moving in perfect harmony around him. In that light, man seemed "a young child, and his huge globe a toy."[41] Judd had waited years for this; it was as if Emerson was explaining Judd to himself—his thirst for nature, his wild imaginings and communings with the holy spirit. Judd wanted to suck the breath of life deep, feel the refulgent summer but a revelation of the divine love, and see a perfect law of harmony binding all things to each other.

Viewed in this positive aspect, Emerson's address might have seemed a call to renewed dedication in the ministry. Judd, who was no formalist, could not have felt personally affronted by Emerson's attack on the dull ministrations of dead preachers. Judd's early sermons, probably written at the Divinity School, showed, in their solidity of substance and richness of rhetoric, how deeply he had been stirred by Emerson's way of speaking. Also, Judd profited by Emerson's plea for more "personal reference" from the pulpit, and some of Judd's sermons drew from personal experience in a way that must have seemed novel to his listeners.

But the aspect of Emerson's address that received publicity and aroused controversy was the paragraph rejecting miracles, that said all life was a never-ending miracle. Here, in a Carlylean concept of "natural supernaturalism," was the sword that divided. The crux was the question of pantheism. Emerson seemed to be implying that God lacked personality, that he was nothing but a vague spirit of nature. Emerson did not say this, but his enemies quickly put his case in its most unflattering terms. Henry Ware, Jr., who discreetly avoided all personal reference, rushed into print without seeming to rush and attacked Emerson without seeming to attack. "There is a personal God, or there is none," he said.[42] Emerson, turned upon by his former colleague pastor, held his tongue and did not reply. Andrews Norton, less cautious than Ware, in an unprecedented[43] act of public rage dragged the case into the *Boston Daily Advertiser* of August 27, 1838, calling Emerson's address an "insult to Religion" and a "personal insult" to the "highly respectable officers of that Institution," the Harvard Divinity School. He went on to call Waterston and his fellow seniors "accessories, perhaps innocent accessories, to the commission of a great offence," and added, "the public must be desirous of learning what exculpation or excuse they can offer." It became clear that people like Emerson were henceforth to be excluded from Harvard. The ugly words "exclusion" and "faculty dictatorship" suggested themselves to the student mind, still smarting over the antislavery affair. Norton went on to name the enemy for the benefit of those who did not already know: "the atheist Shelley," "that hasher up of German metaphysics, the Frenchman, Cousin," "that hyper-Germanized Englishman, Carlyle," and "the German pantheist, Schleiermacher." From this time on, "pantheism," "transcendentalism," and "German metaphysics" became dirty words wherever all sober, true Christians gathered.[44]

Sylvester Judd, of course, proceeded to do precisely what he had been warned against: he read the German philosophers, as we can tell from the record of books withdrawn from the college library. First he had to learn German, for translations were not easily available. In June, 1838, he wrote to Arethusa that he had commenced the study of German and was continuing his reading in French every day. He must have picked up some Spanish somewhere too, for among his extant notes are some transcriptions in Spanish. By March, 1839, Judd was far enough along in his German studies to attempt two of Kant's major works in the German. Then he read two anthologies of German poetry and the next fall tried Boccaccio in the Italian and Fichte in German. Most ominously, he read Schleiermacher, who applied the new ideas specifically to religion. Judd read Schelling, Schlegel, Rousseau's *Emile,* and even began to study Arabic. Reading Tieck and Fouqué introduced him to German romanticism in fiction and prepared the way, perhaps, for the dream episodes in *Margaret,* in which the child seems to float through her dog's expanding saucer-eyes into a wonder world of lakes and silver pipes and silver ladles pouring magic liquids to create a beautiful woman (132), to mention just one passage which seems to come from the realm of archetype and fairy tale.

None of his classmates followed Judd in his dizzying pursuit of knowledge. How much of it all he understood is a question. His sermons reveal no tendency toward subtle speculation. But he was breathing an atmosphere. Emerson and Carlyle at least he understood. Arethusa Hall mentions that at about this time or perhaps a little later she began to have access through Judd to Emerson's books, and Judd's father, perhaps under the son's influence, became quite absorbed in Carlyle in the summer of 1839.[45]

The Unitarian movement, which only a few years earlier had been enjoying the spectacle of the New School-Old School controversy among the Calvinists, now found the laugh turned on itself. The Calvinists had charged for twenty years that Unitarianism was disguised infidelity, that Unitarians were a stealthy crew who concealed their worst opinions from the public, and that the whole tendency of

Unitarianism was to follow the German philosophers and biblical scholars down the slide into undisguised denial of the divine authority of the Scriptures. If not infidelity itself, Unitarianism at least *led* to infidelity, they argued. Unitarians had replied with some heat that they were firm in support of the principle of miraculous revelation, that they believed in the historicity of the miracles reported in the Bible and that they believed in the divinely appointed mission of Jesus and his resurrection, though not his divinity. This explains the vehemence with which Harvard repudiated the transcendentalists: Emerson was giving the whole Unitarian case away by confirming the Calvinists' predictions.[46]

Sylvester Judd, who wanted Unitarians to be more evangelical and spread their faith,[47] saw the movement split disastrously at the outset of his career. The real world never seemed to match the dream. The student scribe at the Harvard Divinity School reported in 1839 that the faculty was down to two members temporarily, that the student body was down in numbers.

> The aspect of the School is dull enough. So that our Zion is well nigh desolate, & ye room for prayers presents but a dismal spectacle of a dark cold morning. What is worse, there seems as yet but little prospect for ye future.

In 1840 the scribe reported that "the School has suffered very much from. . . . ye misunderstanding between what has been called ye old school and ye new school of Unitarians."[48]

It is difficult to give a definitive answer to the question of how Judd reacted to all this. He acquired the pamphlet missiles that flew between Andrews Norton and George Ripley, the transcendentalist minister of a Boston church.[49] He left Norton's pamphlets unmarked, but marked, probably with approval, some of Ripley's comments on Norton's "looseness of reasoning" and want of candor. Ripley put the case on persuasive grounds. He did not deny the miracles of Christ or the divine origin of Christianity. He merely questioned the practice of making Christianity stand or fall on the miracles. He insisted that there were other proofs. Christianity was self-validating.

As Emerson had put it, "man's life was a miracle," "God is, not was."[50] The trouble with the followers of Locke was that they talked as if God were dead. They could not see the miracles of the flower and the sun and hear the interior, small voice in the soul. They required vulgar signs and wonders for the multitude before they would believe. Religion for them had to go from the outside in, be written by a magic hand on the tabula rasa of the mind. They were materialists, sensate men. They did not know that there was an interior fountain, that the soul was the seed ready to respond to the divine sun, that God was still alive and speaking to men who would listen. The issue could be stated as a matter of external evidence vs. internal evidence, of events in the past vs. events that were repeatable in the present, of historical method vs. scientific method, the vulgar understanding vs. intuition. Ripley did not state the case in precisely this way, and his pamphlet was a reasoned argument rather than an Emersonian rhapsody, but he hammered away at the point that internal evidence of Christianity was important, almost burying Norton under the sheer weight of his assembled authorities and his detailed knowledge of German theology. A quotation from Martin Luther was particularly effective:

> It was necessary to bring over the ignorant with external miracles, and to throw out such apples and pears to them as to children; but we, on the contrary, should boast of the great miracles, which Christ daily performs in his church.[51]

The image of Andrews Norton as an ignorant child, a doubting Thomas who needed external evidence before he would believe perhaps occurred to Sylvester Judd as he read. Norton had said, "The denial of the possibility of miracles must involve the denial of the existence of God." He was making it impossible to reconcile religion with the growing trend toward naturalism. George Ripley, pillorying Norton, perhaps unfairly, made him look like a reactionary who was trying to impose his own opinions on others, assassinate men's characters, and stifle free speech. Ripley later conceded that Norton was a man of "stainless purity of purpose, of high integrity of life, with a profound sense of religion, and severe simplicity of manners." Norton was well liked by many of his students and colleagues and was an outstanding biblical scholar.[52]

The issue of external evidence vs. internal consciousness as a test of truth was one that Judd had confronted before. In his "Cardiagraphy" of 1837 he had said that "consciousness" (intuition) "is a primary, incontrovertible, unequivocal source of evidence." This sounded suspiciously transcendental. Although Scottish common sense philosophy, an epistemology on which Yale and Harvard agreed, went beyond Locke and found some role for intuition, it was basically "a way of restoring faith in Lockean empiricism after Hume's devastating skepticism";[53] and the heavy emphasis with which Judd leaned on the words "primary, incontrovertible, unequivocal" showed a "dangerous" tendency toward an intuitive religion of the heart.

Unitarians, in accepting "natural theology" and embracing the argument from design in nature as the chief proof of God's existence, had had to fight off an attack from the deists on their left, who in the name of natural theology and science were undermining the authority of the Bible and of Christ. Faith in miracles had become a litmus test differentiating a Unitarian from a deist. And now came the attack from another group of naturalists, the transcendentalists, who were also weakening the authority of the Bible, this time by an appeal to mysticism and intuition. Ironically, transcendentalism fed on the very attitudes and concepts used by Unitarians as an argument against deism: the sense of wonder concerning nature's mystery. Developing a preromantic tendency in Unitarianism encouraged by Bishop Joseph Butler's *Analogy of Religion* (1736), William Ellery Channing and Henry Ware, Jr., spoke of the "impenetrable mystery" in nature and the "inexplicable" marvels of leaf and flower that drew a person to God. Trying to find the golden mean between deism and orthodoxy, Unitarians argued simultaneously for "the truth of natural religion from the stable order of nature, and the truth of revealed religion from the breakdown of that order," and did not find these ideas incompatible.[54] Emerson, like Thomas Paine, did. Judd, intrigued and yet bothered by Emerson's naturalism, found in Ripley a more attractive and Christian statement of the transcendentalist case.

The same debate over naturalism was working to the fore among the orthodox. Lyman Beecher and Nathaniel Taylor had already been accused of weakening the doctrines of original sin and predestination and enlarging the role of man's free agency and "natural ability." Now came along another Yale man, Congregationalist minister Horace Bushnell, who like Judd was turning from Thomas Reid and Dugald Stewart, the common sense philosophers, to Coleridge and the Germans for inspiration. Though neither Judd nor Bushnell would allow the influence of Schleiermacher, Coleridge, and Carlyle to take them along with Emerson into what even Unitarians were calling pantheism and infidelity, Bushnell was directly contributing toward acceptance by the orthodox of the concept of Divine Immanence, the indwelling of God in the creation. The assumption Judd and Bushnell shared was that the natural world had the seeds of redemption in it, that this world was not so corrupt as Calvinism had made it out to be. God's grace came from within, by organic growth, not through supernatural invasion from outside. As Judd and Bushnell developed their ideas during the 1840's, three parallels between them became evident.

The first one concerned the relation between Christ and human beings. In *God in Christ* (1849), Bushnell wrote that Christ "enters into human feelings . . . to re-unite the world . . . to the Eternal Life." Christ "comes to renovate character; to quicken by the infusion of the divine life. . . ."[55] In *Margaret* (1845), Judd spoke words remarkably similar: Christ was sent by God into the world to "restore us by the infusion of himself, by re-uniting man with his spirit, his holiness, his love. His wish and prayer were that we together with him might become one with God. . . . As he was a sacrifice, so are we to offer our bodies living sacrifices. He suffered, leaving us an example" (259-60). Such words represented a large step toward a religion of the heart, with Christ an "infusion," his purpose to "re-unite" God and the world, his atonement "an example" to man. Similarly, Bushnell's "moral influence" theory of the atonement brought Christ's theological balancing of the accounts down out of the sky and into the heart of man, moving man to recognize the eternal validity of the principle of sacrifice, Christ's giving man an example.

A second contribution of Bushnell, contained in *Christian Nurture* (1847), a book Judd bought when it first appeared,[56] was also an idea Judd emphasized in his preaching. Judd's sermons on the subject of "training up children" to be Christians, published after his death as *The Church* (1854), agreed with Bushnell that the child should be encouraged to grow up a Christian, never knowing a time when he was not. Judd's sermons did not seem so romantic in their epistemology as Bushnell's book, having about them an odor of mechanism and Lockeian tabula rasa psychology, illustrating the point that Judd's expression of transcendentalist ideas was confined to the period before

1845; but in *Margaret* at least, Judd was saying that growth is organic, not mechanical, that Christ acts upon this world from inside man and by a process of gradual development.

Among Unitarians the concept that regeneration was a matter of gradual growth was far from novel, their whole movement stemming from an antipathy toward revivalist conversions. For Unitarians, as Daniel Howe points out, conversion was regarded as "character development," was a "never-ending process, and described in natural rather than supernatural terms."[57] Creeping naturalism had already invaded even the revivalist camp. Charles Grandison Finney, the chief revivalist of the period, said, "There is nothing in religion beyond the ordinary powers of nature. It consists entirely in the *right exercise* of the powers of nature." A revival "is not a miracle or dependent on a miracle, in any sense. It is a purely philosophical result of the right use of the constituted means." Suppose, he asked, a farmer were to expect a crop without plowing and planting: "Why, they would starve the world to death." Though a revival was not "*caused* by means," being ultimately produced by "the blessing of God," it found its "*occasion*" in human means as surely "as a crop does from its cause."[58]

Though Finney, Bushnell, Judd, and the Unitarians were all tending, therefore, toward an enlarged role for natural agency, they differed on the matter of gradualism and on the definition of what the "constituted means" should be. For Finney, the means included anxious seats, traveling evangelists, and protracted meetings: deliberate efforts to work up a revival. Judd wanted the children to be regarded as birthright members of the church, in the same way that they were members of a family or a nation, and this meant that all children should partake of the "constituted means," including baptism and communion. Judd surveyed with sorrow the situation resulting from the split between Unitarians and Trinitarians: Trinitarians too often had kept the "church" and Unitarians had ended up with the "parish" (also called the "society"), and only a handful of Unitarians regarded themselves as "church" members and partook of communion. In common with many other Unitarians of the period, Judd was urging that open communion should replace close communion and that the distinction between church and parish should be abolished. But in thus urging communion upon his flock, Judd was going against the prejudice of Unitarians against revivalistic enthusiasm, associated with communion and the "church."

What differentiated Judd's sermons on the Birthright Church and "training up the children" from much of the Unitarian literature on the means of character development was that Judd was not writing a self-help manual for individuals, like *On the Formation of the Christian Character,* by Henry Ware, Jr. Judd was emphasizing the organic social unity of the church, with status in it hereditary, just like that of the nation and the family. He was talking to parents about their children's needs. He blamed the weakening state of the church, both Unitarian and orthodox, on the failure to approach children positively with the simple message that they were part of the Christian family. If parents and the church would take that step, throwing off their aversion to a direct, positive approach to children, then it would be "as easy to train up a generation of Christians as a generation of Jews or Mohammedans."

> I suppose we generally put the case problematically, and tell children, if they grow up good they will be Christians, and God will love them. The Jew begins just the other way. He says to his child, you are a Jew, and you must act like one. He never says, If, as you grow up, you do right, then you will be a Jew.[59]

As Daniel Howe concludes, Protestants of both the orthodox and Unitarian camps, whatever their differences in theory, came to the same conclusion in practical matters: "religious experience could be psychologically induced."[60]

A third parallel between Judd and Bushnell is their interest in the theory of language. Here, both perhaps owed a debt to Emerson, particularly to his dictum in *Nature,* section IV:

1. Words are signs of natural facts.
2. Particular natural facts are symbols of particular spiritual facts.
3. Nature is the symbol of spirit.

As Judd put it, in the 1840's, in his lyceum lecture on language, words were no accidents created by man through a social compact; they came from God, in the nature of things. Coarse words rooted in the soil, in the childhood of a people, being of divine origin, should not be banished from books; they should be recaptured for literature and restored to their original innocence. Judd wrote, "Once no words were vulgar; all were common, all divine. Now, disagreeable associations belong to some words, and we discard them; not for any vice in themselves, but because, like the dog in the spelling-book, they are found in bad company. Adam and Eve saw no vulgarity in any thing."[61] Judd's "vulgar" diction in his books was thus no accident; it was a deliberate program, as much an aspect of his romanticism as the emphasis upon the folk and the supernatural was an aspect of German romanticism.

Bushnell's treatment of language in relation to theology, in the opening section of *God in Christ,* had similar romantic overtones. For Bushnell, words were not rigid and dry, as he felt rationalists had made them out to be; they were plastic and warm, living, flexible. This meant that the Bible and the terms of theology had to be taken symbolically at certain points, uniting the spiritual and the natural worlds through the process of metaphor. Judd's essay of 1836 on "Truth" had argued the "barrenness of language" and the "ambiguity of terms" which, combined with the difficulty of establishing historical facts, conspired to limit our efforts to discern truth, so that "Many points lie equally balanced between truth and falsehood." Like Emerson, who said, "A foolish consistency is the hobgoblin of little minds, adored by little statesmen and philosophers and divines," Bushnell also valued paradox: "The same essential truth may clothe itself under forms that are repugnant." Indeed, two forms, by contradicting one another fill each other out, keeping us in a state of suspension so we do not fall into the error of thinking *either* form really expresses the complete truth. As Bushnell concluded, "Poets, then, are the true metaphysicians. . . ." Here was something that could be compared with the transcendentalist ideal of the poet-prophet. Bushnell's significance for orthodox theology was that he released its thinkers from the habit of treating words as if they were numbers, to be fed into a logic machine to reveal truth at the end of a computation. He saw words as suggestive and releasing, not strait jackets fastened on the mind. Like the transcendentalists, he was critical of that literal-mindedness of the conservative Unitarians which he thought tended to destroy mystery, paradox, wonder, and the sense of the indefinite or infinite. Unitarians, said Bushnell, "decoct the whole mass of symbol, and draw off the extract into pitchers of their own; fine, consistent, nicely-rounded pitchers, which, so far from setting out anywhere towards infinity, we can carry at pleasure by the handle, and definitely measure by the eye."[62] Bushnell thus held on to his orthodoxy by using some of the resources of romanticism to soften the harsher elements of his inherited theology.

One of the tantalizing but unanswerable questions that suggests itself is whether Judd would have been so ready to embrace Unitarianism if Bushnell's books had been written in the mid-1830's or if Judd had formed a continuing relationship extending beyond the year they were together at Yale. The romanticism that Judd found attractive in Emerson he could also have found in Bushnell, a middle way between the extremes of Calvinism and polite Boston Unitarianism—and he could have avoided the dilemma of being attracted toward Emerson but being repelled by Emerson's lack of Christ-centeredness.

The effort to connect Judd with Emerson and the transcendentalists leads to some frustration, although Octavius Brooks Frothingham, in his reminiscent history of the movement, in 1876, testified that Judd "in the dress of fiction set forth the whole gospel of Transcendentalism in religion, politics, reform, social ethics, personal character, professional and private life."[63] But Frothingham let it go at that and did not demonstrate in detail what he meant. Judd did not write for the *Dial*, although he apparently subscribed to it,[64] and we have few records of his contacts with the transcendentalist circle. Margaret Fuller, in 1846, wrote that she had never met Judd, although she reported that she had received a letter from him saying "that he wished me to know I had one admirer in the State of Maine, a distinction of which I am not a little proud, now that I have read his book."[65] Her words would seem to indicate that his letter preceded her reading and favorably reviewing his book. At the same time her lack of acquaintance with Judd, plus the lack of any positive evidence, would seem to raise doubts about the rumor which is abroad to the effect that he attended meetings of the Transcendental Club.[66]

There is no indication of any contact either in person or by letter with Emerson between 1838 and 1852, although Emerson, who addressed a lyceum in Augusta in 1852, spoke familiarly of his talk there with "Judd." (See above, p. 95.) When Judd, in response to Emerson's question about who his companions were, replied "Sunsets," he was giving a not-unexpected reply. Emily Dickinson, confronted in 1862 with the same question by Thomas Wentworth Higginson, gave the same answer: "You ask of my Companions   Hills—Sir—and the Sundown—and a Dog—large as myself, that my Father bought me." Judd, in responding from the book of transcendentalist gambits to Emerson's question, was laying himself open to a lesson in conversational chess from the master. If Emerson's account seems to bristle a bit with self-satisfaction as he records his put-down of Judd's pertness about sunsets and of his exaggerated lugubriousness about being a "priest," who "conversed with the sick and dying," we should balance Emerson's apparent coolness against other evidence. He apparently admired at least one of Judd's works. Edward Everett Hale, writing to Judd in 1850 about the reception of *Philo,* asked, "Has Mr. Phillips told you of Mr. Emerson's enthusiasm about it?"[67] Still, despite the obvious whimsy of Judd's statement to Emerson that he was isolated from the healthy portion of mankind, there was some truth in it. Augusta, Maine, for all its bustle, was not exactly Cambridge or New Haven or Concord. And Judd had always been something of a loner. To the intellectual movement which has been his chief claim to fame, Judd, as in his other relationships, was an outsider.

Two links, besides the relationship to Emerson, tie Judd in with the transcendentalist circle. Caroline Healy Dall, who wrote one of the best inside accounts of the movement, married one of Judd's classmates at Harvard; and Judd mentions seeing them in Boston in 1847. More important than this very tenuous link is Judd's friendship in the years 1837-1839 with Jones Very, the poet whom Emerson encouraged and called his "brave saint." Very, who was a tutor at the college and a student at the Divinity School, hovered on the borderline of insanity and imagined himself a newborn bard of the Holy Ghost. Emerson was too earthy and selfish for him, and Emerson listened, impressed.[68] Very gave his friend Judd at least three poems, now in the Judd papers at Harvard: "Hymn,"

"The Measure of Wheat," and "The New Birth," the last one dated Sept., 1838, and inscribed by Judd, "By My Friend Jones Very."

Judd seems to have been impressed too, for he wrote a lengthy review of Very's poems, in which he said, "Why should a man who speaks from the impersonal, boundless, authoritative depths of his own nature trim and palaver to public taste?" It was a thoroughly transcendental statement. The *depths* were now "boundless"; the mind swam inward upon itself and found the immensities of space reflected in its own being. This review, written while Judd was still at Harvard, applied Emersonian standards of criticism:

> What springs from the soul has a meaning agreeably to that soul. If it be a genuine production, there will be found to exist a correspondence, and a reflection of lights from one to the other. It is in vain that we seek to detach a work of genius from its author. Its design is alone appreciable through, and it can alone be understood by, knowing what he is. There is, in all minds, an instinctive propensity, an insatiable longing, to trace back a production to its source.[69]

The insatiable longing to return to the source of being, the thirst for childhood, Eden, and simplicity warred against the necessity to be an individual, to assert oneself against the mass and never "trim and palaver to public taste." The impulse towards harmony and simplicity and freedom made one a pacifist or an abolitionist or a transcendentalist and got one into continual trouble with society. How could one reconcile society and the soul?

Jones Very solved the problem, apparently, by ignoring everything except the soul, a thoroughly antinomian solution. In a conversation with Very, September 22, 1839, which Judd thought important enough to transcribe at length after Very left, Very advocated "unconsciousness."[70] "When you are wholly unconscious, then shall you rise and go to any mans house, and he will make you welcome."

Very got up to leave: "You think you see me, but you do not. You can only see me by finding me in yourself. And if you find me in yourself, you will not wish to see me." He might have added, with Whitman, "If you want me again look for me under your boot-soles. . . . I stop somewhere waiting for you." Judd asked Very if he would write to him. Very replied, "A letter may be written but I shall be wholly unconscious of it. If I find a piece of paper and your name is written on it, I shall not know it. —I cannot tarry about these things." Apparently there was an air of authority about young Very that made these statements other than ludicrous when delivered in the flesh; and Judd seemed to be saying that Very's poems had value because of their source.

Having read the above paragraph from my dissertation of 1964, which is his source of information about the incident, Francis Dedmond concludes from it that Judd was making "a parting plea" to Very that "they might at least correspond with one another," but that Judd's "plea" for continuing friendship "failed."[71] This may be, but then again it may not. Dedmond makes an interesting effort to nail down Jones Very and attach him to several of the letters that Arethusa Hall identifies as "To —," but he gives mere spectral evidence, and the wraithlike poet glides out of the grasp. The "me" of Very's oracular statements to Judd is clearly the Self, the Oversoul, the universal Christ whom Very identified with. The "me" and "I" say, with Emerson, "They know not well the subtle ways/ I keep, and pass, and turn again," or, as Very puts it, "You think you see me, but you do not. You can only see me by finding me in yourself." Very's words can be read as an exhortation to see the divine soul according to the transcendentalist gospel and need not be read as a rejection of Judd's friendship. Very is saying that a person who becomes a "transparent eyeball," to use Emerson's words, rises above the world and its particulars and achieves universality. A person who achieves unconsciousness spends his time gliding through walls, being welcome at any man's house, and "cannot tarry about these things," such as mere letters and pieces of paper.

Jones Very was enough to make the mind dizzy. To talk with him was like plunging into a bottomless pond and returning to the source of Being. In the words of Judd's Margaret, "'I have wished to drop into that splendid cloud-flowing abyss, and perhaps I shall be missing one of these days, and you will know where to find me'" (233). Jones Very, like Margaret, stops somewhere waiting for us, and we will have to look for him under our boot soles.

Judd could not ignore particulars, and mysticism was not enough. His mind was blood-warm. Judd wrote novels, not just wraithlike abstractions in oracular form. The problem of the Many and the One would not leave him in peace. It was the ultimate problem, the problem of the real and the ideal, the artist and the critics, the fathers and the sons. It was the problem of progress and primitivism, in which one left Westhampton and pushed out into the complex world of Yale and Harvard, only to find trouble, and long for harmony and simplicity again. George Bancroft, who wrote admiringly of Quaker simplicity, now dispensed party patronage from the customs house in Boston and would end up ordering the troops into Mexico. Sylvester Judd could not be content in Eden. He had to know. And he loved apples. They appeared and disappeared. "You think you see me, but you do not." The apple his sister Pin had offered him was full of perplexity. The orbs were swimming in his head, and he was a little dizzy.

When he had come to Harvard, Judd had solved his theological problems and was ready to begin the work of evangelizing the world. Unitarianism was simple, rational, free of distressing paradox. Now he was not so sure. On March 5, 1840, having just finished Schelling, Schlegel, and Fichte, Judd wrote to his brother Parkman, "I am not insensible to what you say about the unsatisfactoriness of metaphysical studies. In all the horrors of their perplexities, my own mind has been involved." A year earlier, on April 18, 1839, he had written to his mysterious confidante about his struggle with the One and the Many. He had just heard a lecture by Dr. Carl Follen on atheism, and in his comment Judd revealed the extent to which he was attracted by transcendentalism.

> Are we not confounded when we would tell what God is; what Nature is? Is Pantheism a system unnaturally unnatural? Do we not discover Pantheistic tendencies working in all minds?. . . . The tendency of philosophy is to generalize, *ad infinitum,* which is, to reduce all things to the one. . . . And then our religion does sometimes lead us to the confession of universal absorption,—God in us, and we in God. Our hours of reverie also do carry us away from our individuality.

Judd's mention of hours of reverie reminds us how much time he spent with his imagination and that the preparation of an artist consists in more than taking notes in the streets. Yet he was wary of mysticism insofar as it involved becoming "unconscious," after the manner of Jones Very, and having one's identity "swallowed up in the infinite abyss of the One"; Judd called this a "horrible sensation":

> We follow in the track of some principle,—existence, extension, life, heat,—pursuing our course through men, trees, the earth, sun and stars, till we have made the compass of universal being. We discover an inexorable oneness binding together all objects and creations. We begin to lose ourselves in the vast conflux of existences to an indistinguishable identity; and then, for fear of an irretrievable perdition, to be sure that any individuality remains, I pinch my hand, get up and walk, feel proud, any thing, that I may return to my identity, and rescue myself from the horrible sensation of being swallowed up in the infinite abyss of the One!

The combination of mysticism and worldliness was Emersonian. Though Judd's imagination sometimes ran to thoughts of drowning, he was repelled by it, just as he was both attracted and repelled by the World, where grit was steadfast. Judd both loved and hated the imaginary village he created in *Margaret*. It was coarse, drunken, cruel, and Calvinistic; but as it grew in his mind the picture took on a quality of ecstasy that betrayed his love. Judd both loved and hated old Pluck, the unregenerate drunkard who was the secret hero of *that* book, just as the Devil was the secret hero of *Philo*. And though Judd professed to love the perfected village at the end of *Margaret*,—sanitary, genteel, prosperous, filled with art and music—he could not make it real, and it fell dead in his hands. Judd's books always started well and ended miserably, always started with the real and ended with the ideal, began with a living world and ended with it theoretically redeemed or more happy, but actually dead.

Judd may have been involved in perplexity during his years at Harvard, but the phenomenon of transcendentalism did not touch him with the same intensity as his earlier struggle, and it left no scars. His mind was slowly healing, growing toward more objectivity about itself and the world. Hell was no longer a reality to him. He faced the world with confidence in his principles and in his powers. His basic principles were simple, and his mind shrugged off metaphysics when it became too perplexing: "I am persuaded that any system of theology which is sustained merely on metaphysical grounds must ever prove unsatisfactory," he wrote to his brother Parkman, in the letter quoted above. His early sermons, written at the Divinity School, showed a mind that was growing up, sounding more mature; Judd received the honor of giving the first Austin Beneficiary Lecture at the Divinity School on July

8, 1840, stipend $15;[72] his powers were being recognized
by the world.

As he graduated that July and prepared to look for a
pulpit, he wrote in his journal that his health was good, his
energy vigorous. "I am a better and a calmer man. I have
few agitations, know few griefs. Could name one or two
things, but they are trifles. I enter the theatre of the world
to act my part."

A few months before, he had been in Northampton, sliding down the hill on a sled with his brother J.W.'s six-year-
old son. The letter he wrote to J.W., January 15, 1840,
revealed a Judd who had learned that unconsciousness did
not mean retreating from the world into the soul, necessarily, that it might mean losing the self in the world around
him. Judd's letter struck a new note and showed him well
on the way toward becoming a novelist. He was ready to
leave behind the disembodied spirits of the Empyrealists,
those oracles of abstract truth, and dig into the real world,
where boys played with sleds:

> Your boy is doing admirably. He and his uncle go out to slide every
> morning. It would please you to see him fagging up the hill, with
> a red face, panting breath, his feet pressing with a short, quick,
> divergent step, into the snowy path; his arms swinging up and
> down like a young bird on the ice. He is on the sled; and hurrah!
> down he goes! His sled shies off into a snowbank, and over he
> goes. Up he jumps, spitting out the snow from his mouth, pushing
> up his cap which has fallen over his eyes, with—"Well now that's
> too bad, I declare, uncle Ves."

To see why Judd wrote novels and transcendentalists generally did not, one only has to compare this dramatized
description with an entry in Emerson's journal: "That
which is individual & remains individual in my experience
is of no value. What is fit to engage me & so engage others
permanently, is what has put off its weeds of time & place
& personal relation."[73] Judd refused to put off the weeds

of time and place and personal relation, to disappear with Jones Very into unconsciousness and the "infinite abyss of the One."

On July 9, 1839, Judd had written to his confidante, as he stitched together the sheets of his long letter, like a sermon manuscript,

> I am such a consistent piece of mechanism. . . . The student has turned seamster, or, rather, I am the man seamstering. But you would have chuckled. What a bother! The first point is to thread one's needle. I am not altogether inexperienced, yet is it a perpetual vexation. . . . Then, by a due force, I pushed the resolute needle through the quire of paper, have tied the ends of the thread together, and so am a consistent man. Consistency, thou art a jewel.

Man thinking had become man seamstering; he was a mechanism, and consistency was not a hobgoblin. Perhaps Judd was a Teufelsdröckh, stitching together a patched and mended clothes philosophy. Judd went on:

"Oh for a wife,—a great-souled, worth-appreciating wife, —to put on my buttons, and stitch my manuscripts! Shall I never find such a one?"

On July 24, 1840, as Judd set sail from Boston harbor, his first voyage on the ocean, he was exactly twenty-seven years old, plus one day. He was fairly afloat in life.

11

The End of the Rainbow:
Augusta, Maine

Two years earlier Sylvester Judd had written in the book he kept for an annual summary of his state of being, "Still unlinked with all the world." Now, on July 24, 1840, as he embarked for Augusta, Maine, on the steamer *Huntress*, he was looking for what his profession called "a settlement." Theory was now to meet the test of reality. Judd had to come to terms with the world and with himself. The question was, would he remain an outsider.

The trip from Boston to Augusta took little over twelve hours on the steamer, half the time though twice the distance of the trip overland by stagecoach from Boston to Northampton. Space was contracting and time was speeding up its tempo. Augusta was a town that was more conscious of change than most in New England. Twenty years earlier it had been a village in a remote province of Massachusetts. Now it was capital of a state and was developing sawmills and other light industries. A large dam, recently built across the Kennebec River, was expected to bring further industrial growth. Augusta was a boom town, almost a city. In 1830 it was little larger than Northampton; by 1836 its population had increased from 3980 to 6069, while Northampton's population remained virtually unchanged. Land speculation had been feverish; in 1836 prices on some properties doubled in only six months. Fortunes were being made by a breed of self-made men, chief among whom was Reuel Williams, lawyer, banker, land speculator, industrialist, U.S. Senator, Unitarian, father of six daughters. He was one of the utilitarian entrepreneurs of the linear logic; one of his enterprises, appropriately, was the project of throwing the dam across the turbulent Kennebec. His fortunes survived the financial panic of 1837 and the spring flood of 1840 that burst the dam. Such misfortunes, however, reminded a man of limitation.[1]

Sylvester Judd knew a great deal about frustration, but he had not learned much about the acceptance of limitation. His mind often ran to images of moving water. To him, water seemed to suggest freedom, release, infinity, inward depths. In *Richard Edney,* the fruit of his Augusta experience, Judd would write vividly of the hiss and roar of the Kennebec waters. But in *Richard Edney,* there would be no depths as in *Margaret.* The water would no longer seem symbolic of inner experience. The water would be all surface. *Richard Edney* would reveal that Judd had learned to accept limitation. Between 1840 and 1850 Judd would come to terms with what he called, in *Richard Edney,* "bordering."[2] Grit was "steadfast." There was a place in this world, after all, for dams to turn the water's flow to some use. Reuel Williams, dam builder, solid citizen and Unitarian, could tell Sylvester Judd something about that.

On Sunday morning, July 26, 1840, Sylvester Judd stood up in the pulpit of the Unitarian church in Augusta to tell Reuel Williams and the assembled congregation something about life. Although Judd could not have realized it, his sermon topic, "Restrained Religious Emotion," was particularly applicable to the spiritual state of Senator Reuel Williams, who had but recently returned from his duties in Washington, D.C. Perhaps it was also applicable to the state of John Fairfield, Governor of Maine, who was also a Unitarian and who intermittently attended the church when he was in Augusta. The Augusta Unitarian church was full of politicians, especially when sessions of the legislature brought them to Augusta as temporary residents of the capital city; the church was perhaps inclined to the worldliness, rationalism, and dryness that Sylvester Judd had found among the Unitarians in Cambridge and Boston. The Augusta church had, since its founding in 1825, been unable to hold a minister for long; it had quarreled with one pastor over his theology and with another over his politics. As Sylvester Judd began his sermon on "Restrained Religious Emotion," he was merely one of a series of supply preachers who had been filling the pulpit since the former minister's dismissal nine months before.[3]

Reuel Williams had every reason to expect that a sermon about restrained emotions would praise religious restraint. That was the Unitarian, company way. Instead, Sylvester Judd drove home the point that habitual and undue restraint led to indifference, worldliness, and sin. Some men, he said, have religious emotion but consider it undignified to show it. This damming up of outward expression would eventually paralyze religious emotion altogether. Judd doubtless thought of his own father as he described the virtuous but stolid and unmoved churchgoer. His words, however, fit the case of Reuel Williams with equal precision. John A. Poor, in his *Memoir of Reuel Williams,* said that Williams was "naturally reserved," "had few confidants," and had a "talent for silence" that "was seldom equalled." Williams had never been baptized. He refused to join the little group of "church" members who partook of the communion; instead he remained a member of the larger body called the "parish" or the "Unitarian Society," composed of those who had no claim to any special holiness, did not really believe in conversion, considered it undignified to show religious fervor, failed to take communion, and—unlike Sylvester Judd—were perfectly satisfied to remain in their state of emotional restraint and call it virtue.

Judd's first sermon at Augusta, then, dealt with a problem that would continue to be a concern during the remaining twelve-and-one-half years of his ministry: how to shake the outward indifference of such people as Reuel Williams and get them to acknowledge their membership in the *Church* of Christ, how to keep the communion service from becoming a ritual that divided the congregation into two groups. Judd longed for unity, and he wanted the communion service to be a symbol of that unity. He wanted the whole family, children included, to consider itself part of the church.[4] He was still fighting the battle of Westhampton, in which the unworthy trembled on the threshold of the church, afraid to enter into communion lest they "drink damnation" to themselves.

Judd's sermon, though criticizing restraint, was itself restrained and did not arouse antagonism. Reuel Williams did not seem to resent the turbulent, pushing force that he saw in Sylvester Judd, even though it was pushing against Williams' own defensive walls. The senator was a liberal—in fact a Democrat—and he believed in toleration of views different from his own. The next day Judd wrote to his mother that he had already been urged by some of his hearers to stay as their regular minister. Perhaps among them were Reuel Williams' son and two of his daughters, whom Judd found to be among the more enthusiastic supporters of the little church. Young Joseph Williams had much in common with Judd. He was about the same age and had been to Harvard. He had been a hero of the great Harvard rebellion of 1834, when he had led his class in refusing degrees until the seven ringleaders were reinstated.[5]

When Sylvester Judd made his first formal call at the Williams mansion, which was on a high ridge and commanded a striking view of the main part of town across the

Kennebec River to the west, he entered one of the most notable dwellings in Maine. Judd's feet sank into an imported Brussels carpet with a pile so thick that it lasted a hundred years. Perhaps as he entered he heard piano music from one of the parlors, where Reuel Williams' daughter Jane Elizabeth was playing. Oil paintings, including a portrait by Gilbert Stuart of Mrs. Williams' father, Daniel Cony, hung on the walls. There were mirrors from England, a highboy from Japan, a mahogany wine cooler, silver bowls, and all the necessary accoutrements for the Williams family's famous hospitality. The octagon room was notable not only for its shape but also for its French wallpaper showing scenes of Polynesian life, including dancing girls in the background. The Reuel Williams family was to Augusta what the Joseph Lyman family was to Northampton, but on a more lavish scale. The Williams guest book during the 1840's would show such famous names as President James K. Polk, Secretary of the Navy George Bancroft, President Josiah Quincy of Harvard, and John Lothrop Motley, the historian.[6]

Sylvester Judd described, in *Richard Edney,* how a young country boy felt upon being confronted suddenly with such wealth, graciousness, and charm. "Having nothing for his muscular hands to clutch, how could he talk in that drawing-room?" "His perceptions clouded, and his language tripped; his hands swelled, and his face burnt. He was glad to find an open door, and disburthen himself to a draft of air."[7] Judd had been in polite society before, but not with entire ease. His journal entries that first month show a restiveness of spirit upon his introduction to the trivialities of the ministerial profession: "Augusta, as I may have told fifty people, is a very pretty place. But I am somehow un-homed here." "Discussed for the forty-eleventh time the beauties of Augusta. Strong coffee saved me the trouble of going to sleep, and set me into a horrible fantasy."

In *Richard Edney,* the Governor's daughter joins Richard on the piazza and puts him at his ease. Reuel Williams had daughters too. The three oldest were already married, but three remained to be disposed of, hopefully with due respect to the tradition of seniority. The oldest of the three eligible ones, Jane Elizabeth Williams, was slender, delicate, and intensely feminine, but tinged with mild radicalism. Sylvester wrote that in politics she was a Democrat like her father, but of a more radical variety, that in philosophy she was "something of a Transcendentalist," in contrast to her father.[8] The second eligible daughter was Zilpha, who like Jane attended the Unitarian church. Her letters reveal her as more extroverted than Jane, who was high strung and inclined to moods of alternating ecstasy and depression. The youngest was Anne, aged fifteen. Zilpha was eighteen, and Jane was almost twenty-one. The Williams family illustrated the multiplicity of the new age. Reuel's wife, Sarah, still attended the orthodox[9] church presided over by the Reverend Benjamin Tappan. Williams' married daughter, Sarah Bridge, had recently helped form an Episcopal church in Augusta, and her sister Anne also showed an interest in becoming an Episcopalian.[10]

In Augusta the relations between Unitarians and Episcopalians were extremely close, not only because of family ties but also because both groups were started in reaction to the monopoly of the orthodox church. The Episcopal church in Augusta got its start the very summer of Judd's arrival as a result of the Great Dancing Controversy that split the orthodox Congregational church and set Augusta society into an ecstasy of commotion. The whole story was told, with acerbity and wit, by Daniel C. Weston, in a book called *Scenes in a Vestry,*[11] complete with transcripts of the trial in which he and his mother, the wife of Chief Justice Nathan Weston of the Maine Supreme Court, were defendants. Weston's sister Louise was a good friend of

Emerson. Since Weston's mother was sister to Mrs. Reuel Williams, and since Daniel Weston was to become Sylvester Judd's good friend, Judd must have become drawn with horrified fascination into this scene of social strife, backbiting, and censoriousness. Briefly, Mrs. Weston had been caught sponsoring dances in her parlor for the young people. Refusing to repent and be saved, she was expelled from the church after a sensational series of trial scenes reminiscent of those in the Westhampton and Northampton churches in the 1820's. The spirit of censoriousness and division had followed Judd to Augusta. Significantly, the Rev. Mr. Tappan, who consigned the erring ones to darkness, was a nephew of a prominent merchant in Northampton.

Yet Sylvester Judd, typically, seized upon this moment of sectarian division to make a show of church unity. The Weston family, together with others of Augusta's highest society, chose to become Episcopalians; and Judd, scarcely two weeks after his arrival in Augusta, found himself thrown together with them in a way that must have seemed rather unusual to him. Father Judd, writing in 1842 to his daughter, who had married into the Williams family, was capable of saying of Episcopalians, "I feel no respect for these bastard catholics, with their arrogant pretensions."[12] His son, as one of the first actions of his ministerial career, participated with his church in playing host to the Episcopalians at the formation of their new church. On August 9, 1840, nine persons were confirmed as Episcopalians in the little Unitarian meetinghouse at the corner of State Street and Oak Street.[13] Judd approved of this show of the ecumenical spirit. Dominating all his thinking was the idea of the unity of the human race. He looked for a day when wars would cease, when all sects would join hands, when men would no longer enslave each other. Overcoming sectarian strife was thus one of his chief concerns as a minister.

The influence of Episcopalianism upon Judd's conception of church polity may have had its beginning at this time. Notable in Judd's *Margaret* was his use of the title of Bishop in the ideal church of the utopian society.

Judd speedily won the regard of the congregation that he was temporarily serving. After preaching his second set of sermons, one of them a glowing exposition of the mystical element in Christianity called "The Indwelling Christ," Judd received a tentative offer of a permanent settlement. Judd had expected to continue in his travels, perhaps visiting Alabama for the winter, and had an engagement to supply the pulpit in Deerfield, Massachusetts, for a month. "What is duty, what is duty?" he asked himself.

> The next morning, he says, "I went out of the village upon the highlands north, up, up, over granite ledges, through the woods. Was so happy! Could have died. We are always ready to die when we are happy."[14]

After his month in Deerfield Judd also received a call for permanent settlement there. Judd was tempted to accept because of the "proximity of that town to the residence of his father." "The influence which turned the scale was his acquaintance with the family from which he afterwards chose his wife."[15]

Before the month was out, Judd's decision to stay in Augusta was made. On October 1, 1840, he was ordained minister of the East Parish in Augusta. It was the beginning of a pastorate that would continue for the remaining dozen years of his life. Preaching the sermon before the assembled Unitarian clergymen of Maine on that occasion in 1840 was Andrew Preston Peabody. That evening the clergy were again addressed by Frederic Henry Hedge of Bangor, Maine, who was pulling back from transcendentalism because of conservatism in his congregation. Judd would continue to have occasional contact with Hedge and kept in his library Hedge's *Prose Writers of Germany*, which made

German literature available in translation. Hedge's movement from transcendentalism to a more conservative position was a portent for enthusiastic young ministers.[16]

Judd was not a man to tread cautiously. He immediately began a series of sermons designed to make his listeners uncomfortable. It was the month in which the nation waited for the outcome of the "hard-cider" election campaign of 1840. Senator Williams and Governor Fairfield were both Democrats. Judd was not, but had sense enough to profit by the fate of his predecessor and keep his political views to himself. However, he could not resist writing to his cousin, George Lyman, "Hurrah for Harrison!" Neither could he stop himself from uttering some pungent advice from the pulpit to politicians. On October 18, 1840, while Governor Fairfield waited anxiously for results of a recount that would ultimately result in his defeat by less than a hundred votes, Sylvester Judd preached against "Political Strife." Political parties, he said, *strike at the ties of human brotherhood.*

> We send round the town crier with our own sophistries, but start up a lion by every man's door when the truths of others are abroad. All is fair in politics, though it be foul in the market-place. We are false at the caucus, we are hypocrites in the drawing room.

"The impeachment of motives is a proclamation of hostilities," said Judd. "It is but a short step from the State House to the Arsenal. Words have a wonderful affinity to blows." As Judd went on, it became apparent that he had been writing this sermon for a long time. It had a rich, aphoristic quality, as if he had written it by mining his journal, in the same manner that Emerson composed his lectures:

> Ridicule and denunciation shuffle into every man's hands brickbats and clubs. Night, that blends all distinctions, changes gentlemen and boys into mobs. Death is a quick reduction of all majorities. . . . In Mexico they have learned to ballot with balls.

Strife and the rule of force were anathema to Judd.

Judd was not particularly discreet. Having attacked the major diversion of the men in his congregation on October 18, 1840, he went on the next Sunday to attack one of the favorite pastimes of women. His topic was "Social Strife." Vanity, gossip, snobbishness, backbiting were among the evils hit:

> We live in an evesdropping world and must shut the shutters of our actions at early night-fall. We sweep our own house clean, it may be very clean, we see not that the refuse and dirt fall through upon our neighbor's lawn. We have been scandalized, and from our card-rack drops one and another name into the fire.

As Judd went on, the rich stuff of his rhetoric was too much to absorb at a single hearing:

> No housewife shakes any seive half so sturdily as that by which she sifts the characters of others, and that too saving all the bran, while she lets the flour escape; the bran to be scrutinized yet more, which she lays upon the shelf to be reserved for the fingering gabble of her neighbors when they come in. No shop-man uses half so nice a weight as that which graduates his neighbors failings. When virtue dies we are all in at the funeral. Few shafts sink so deep as those of derision and none so poor but his quiver is full of them. And yet indifference kills more hearts than malice.

The Emersonian style of these sermons was unusual; the typical Judd sermon was more flimsy and rested more easily on the ear. Here, Judd spoke with a weight and pith to his prose that showed he had been observing the real world with a disillusioned eye for years and had been storing up aphorisms to express his assessment. Judd, apparently, had been on the outside looking in for a long time, and he had felt lonely; but he had observed a great deal:

> We exchange cards, but keep ourselves at home. We make parties, but dread our visitors. . . . our address is carved on our front-doors; no bell-ringings can summon our sympathies to the parlor. We are separated into clans, coteries, friendship clubs.

Judd had arrived in Augusta too recently to be fully aware of the aptness of what he was saying. Augusta society was particularly characterized by clans and coteries. A reminiscing native of Augusta, the philosopher B.A.G. Fuller, who was related to the Williams-Cony clan, wrote in 1948 that the Augusta aristocracy were closely related by marriage and "formed a kind of close corporation and at the same time mutual admiration society. My mother used to say, that from hearing them talk about one another, one would gather that they were the Lord's anointed." Augusta was a city of boosters. "No city in the world was better than Augusta, and nobody in Augusta, or anywhere else for that matter, was better than they."[17] In this atmosphere Judd's jeremiads must have seemed out of place. Sometimes they hit too close to home. But Reuel Williams was a tolerant man.

The young minister who was not afraid of his powerful parishioners and who seemed, in that fall of 1840, to discover a genius for saying the wrong thing at the right time, was a striking contrast to old Enoch Hale, now dead, who had said the right thing, always. He was also a refreshing contrast to the father of the Williams girls. Jane and Zilpha Williams were much taken with this handsome, fearless, and foolish young man. Joseph Williams liked him too.[18] Reuel Williams, a temperate man of restrained emotions, kept his thoughts to himself. Governor Fairfield, writing prior to the sermon on political strife, decided that Judd was "a young man apparently of first rate talents," and he added that "his sermons today were more than common."[19]

Jane Williams and Sylvester Judd did not take long to fall in love. There were not enough complications and delays in their love affair to make up the plot even of so modest a novel as *Richard Edney,* which paralleled in some respects the story of Sylvester Judd's rise in the social world of Augusta. In December Reuel Williams returned to his Senate desk in Washington, unaware that he was about to lose another daughter. On February 18, 1841, the senator penned a letter to Sylvester Judd in his usual terse, cool style:

> Dear Sir
>
> I recd last evening your letter of 12th inst.—The request you make was wholly unexpected, and involves consequences too important to admit of an immediate answer.
>
> I will however bestow upon it all the consideration which my time and opportunity will allow & endeavor to come to such a conclusion as will best promote the happiness & usefulness of a beloved daughter.
>
> I am respectfully
Your obt servt
R Williams

"Happiness" and "usefulness" were terms which came easily to the minds of utilitarians. One week later, Senator Williams again took up his pen from his desk in Washington and wrote to Judd,

> Unwilling to keep you longer in suspense upon the interesting request made by you some days ago, and having now recd letters from Mrs Williams & had opportunity to confer with my son & others here I am now prepared to communicate to you my full & free consent, & in doing this I am not insensible to the important influence it may have upon the happiness of a dear child as well as of yourself.[20]

Upon receipt of this letter, Judd belonged. He had received an official seal of approval that would be recognized anywhere. He hastened to write to all the members of his family—a stiff, formal letter to his father, assuring him that his future wife "does not like to bow to the world. . . . I do not mean to say there is anything of the Amazon in her character. She is gentle, humble, mild as a lamb." To his mother went a more chatty, informal letter:

Jane is a dear soul. We love each other with an intense love. She has soul, heart, mind and all. The only thing about her that will ever give us the least uneasiness, or that causes her to fall short of perfection is a tendency to sadness. But you know I have that, and so we agree very well.[21]

To Judd, his engagement and marriage were culminating events, an end and a beginning. For years he had been, emotionally, an outsider. He had felt his poverty keenly; now he was a member, though a somewhat awkward and uneasy one, of the inner circle of wealth, culture, and power. He had longed for love. To him, love was the highest value: "Love is the cincture of heaven, and the golden chain that may raise earth to the skies."[22] Now, after much frustration, he had come home. His journal entries, letters and sermons of this period took on a quietness of spirit, a new mellowness. The image of water came naturally to his mind again as he wrote to Arethusa Hall about his impending marriage, but the water was now tranquil:

We have few fears, few trepidations, few movings of the spirit in any way. We are already upon the sea. 'Tis only passing from latitude to latitude. We sail on as goodly as possible. . . . hardly feel the change.

The recurrent image of the plunging cataract was also in his mind as he made a journal entry:

She read my book, took a glance at my former self. *Quam mutatus ab illo!* I can say in the best sense. The stream that rustled and maddened down the mountain sleeps, with a quiet surface, a serene depth, at the bottom.

Sylvester Judd and Jane Elizabeth Williams were married in the north parlor of the Williams house the evening of August 31, 1841. The weather had been, in Judd's phrase, "obstinately dry," but that night rain fell. Judd regarded the rain as a "propitious" sign. Senator Williams, who was on his way home from Washington for the occasion, did not arrive in time to give the bride away; but Jane was nonetheless "assured, calm, deliberate." Judd, who liked to do things his own way, eschewed tradition and prepared a lengthy form of words to replace the usual brief vows:

> You, Sylvester Judd, jun., take Jane Elizabeth Williams to be your lawful and wedded wife. . . —a union of the finite with the finite soul, under the embrace, protection, presence, and love of the Infinite Soul.[23]

After this rather transcendental prologue, the mutual pledge went on to talk of duty: "engaging to one another a mutual and reciprocal submissiveness and authority, deference and honor; subordinating each motive and wish, each action and feeling, to your common happiness and sustenance."

The word "submissiveness" showed a Judd who was prepared to accept limitation, though he had a wild impulse in him that kept asserting itself and that would come back to plague him into writing *Margaret,* a novel that was alternately rebellious and submissive, wild and genteel, a book that he felt constrained to have published anonymously and, when the mask had been penetrated, to prune judiciously in the second edition. For Judd, entering into the Unitarian world was the great rebellion. Once there, he stayed. Ironically, the radical path led through to respectability. Judd was drawn into society, a constricting circle of velvet, enamored of it and yet pulled backwards towards the soil, towards Westhampton and Norwich Pond, the world of Margaret, Pluck, and Deacon Ramsdill, where the children had "a plenty of mother earth about them." Judd's further rebellions were but fluttering flights, oscillations between the poles of the wild and the tame. Judd could not rest completely either at the pole identified with Augusta, respectability, Unitarianism, and Progress or at the pole identified with Westhampton, Calvinism, and romantic atavism.

The tension in him was electrical and, at its most creative discharge, led to the writing of *Margaret*. Judd's tension could lead to the emotive richness that would in one sentence praise the wild, natural beauty of New England, its trees and its skies, and then in the next sentence praise the utilitarian "high calculation" which was improving nature, producing progress, and destroying wildness, which was "ripping up the earth for a Canal from Worcester to Providence" (268-69). Judd's love for the earth mother was perhaps equivocal, at times repressed. He never felt that he could eat a woodchuck raw. And his new wife, Jane, was afraid of lightning.[24]

The wedding ceremony completed on that rainy August evening—the bride, in her husband's opinion assured and calm, despite the agitation of missing her father's return by a day—the couple departed the next morning for a honeymoon to Northampton. For outsider Ves Judd, now married and worldly enough to smoke a pipe, the return home was something of a triumphal tour. With Jane he took the traditional climb to the top of Mt. Holyoke. There, Crawford and the fair Miss Hazeltine, in "The Deception," had once surveyed the world of natural virtue and its opposing world of unnatural vice. The kingdoms of heaven and earth stretched out in the river at Judd's feet; and, for now, both kingdoms were one. The restlessness in him was stilled, temporarily.

To the west of Mt. Holyoke was Westhampton and beyond that Norwich Hollow, where "ignorant Methodists," to use father Judd's phrase, held midnight prayer meetings, "bawling and wallowing," and where herb-gatherers spoke their racy dialect and dispensed folklore along with medicines. In 1843 we catch a glimpse of the Rev. Sylvester Judd, already writing the first part of *Margaret*, actively exploring these woods, returning to the point of his origin to refresh his memories and to gather new material, jotting down unusual words and snatches of conversation, questioning his father closely about costumes, customs, and other "old matters" of the world of 1801. An error, which began with James Russell Lowell and persisted even into the 1968 edition of *Margaret,* is the assumption that the setting of *Margaret* is Maine and that it has "the soul of Down East" in it. But Judd returned to Norwich, his mother's birthplace, for inspiration, and the best part of his book looks backward.

Jane Judd occasionally went along on these rambles into the world of the past, but she was not so much at home there as her husband. That August day in 1843 she and Judd's brother, Chauncey Parkman Judd, tagged along with Judd on a long walk to Norwich Pond. In the house of Mrs. Weeks the herb-gatherer, while Sylvester smoked his pipe and took careful notes on dialect, folklore, and medicine, Jane "cut out of the house and took a stone for a seat by the road-side for fear of bed-bugs in the house." Mrs. Weeks and her son, who were already being transmuted by Sylvester's imagination into characters in *Margaret,* discoursed to their genteel visitors of the virtues of Heal-All, the leaf of which, they said, has two sides, "one which irritates a wound" and another which "cures right off in all hurts."[25]

Sylvester Judd was finding the world like a Heal-All plant: it had two sides. One hurt and the other healed. He was stripping the dirt back from the rhubarb stem and was finding the vermilion and gold at the roots. The new volume of his journal that Judd began on his honeymoon (the only volume, incidentally, that has survived) was full of tenderness, a continuing love letter to Jane that he shared with her, but it recorded also brief moments of hurt. We might surmise this, not only from what it said but even more from the excisions that Jane later made with her sewing scissors. Genteel wives, though intellectually a bit daring and transcendental, busily engage in pruning the hedges of the husband's memory. Sylvester Judd, in *Richard Edney*, called it "bordering." Wild impulse had to be kept in check.

By the time Judd wrote *Richard Edney* and *Philo*, between 1845 and 1850, his submission to domesticity and "bordering" was apparent. Judd was surrounded by women: the women of his church and the women of his family. He had always had a streak of the feminine alongside of his masculine traits. Significantly, he expressed himself through a female persona more than once, and the savior-figure he created was a woman. Arethusa Hall and his sisters Apphia and Peninnah were the ones he felt most at ease with. A contemporary description of Judd by an anonymous reviewer who heard Judd speak at the autumn meeting of Unitarian ministers in 1852 is interesting:

> His face was of exceeding beauty, with light clear complexion, blue eyes, and flaxen hair; intellect and kindly feeling were blended in his expression; his nervous-sanguine temperament rendered his cheeks mirrors to the glow of his enthusiasm, and his voice was rich as the vibration of a wind-swept string. There was about his mouth and eyes an infantine expression, which rendered the great brow almost a surprise; and the writer remembers feeling, when that speaker sat down, as if he had been listening to one specially endowed to renew the ancient benediction upon little children. [26]

Jane's five sisters and his own two sisters, Apphia and Peninnah, hovered around him either as visitors to or permanent residents of the stately Williams family compound on the high east bank of the Kennebec. In 1842 sister Apphia paid Sylvester and Jane a long visit, and by summer an engagement to Jane's brother Joseph resulted. Sylvester playfully gave his sister a bill "for services rendered." It was the sort of humor that came to be known in the family as "Juddy." Included in the bill, among a few nickel-and-dime charges for such things as fetching Apphia from the station, was an item for $25,000: "Negotiating J.W. Williams Esq. $500,000 @ 5 percent." The marriage took place in Northampton on September 26, 1842, and Sylvester Judd became a brother twice over to the future governor of Maine, who was one of his warmest admirers.

Besides sisters, there were Judd's father and his mother as occasional visitors and, by the middle of the decade, a visitor for several years, his "demi-mère," Aunt Arethusa. She had not only forgiven Sylvester his apostasy, she had come home to him. Before long she joined him: she became an enthusiastic admirer and a Unitarian.* Judd's family grew. When he wrote *Richard Edney,* he had already acquired two daughters, Jane Elizabeth and Frances. (He would never live to see his third daughter, Apphia.) In short, the rebel had become rather domesticated, a Mr. Evelyn who had cracked a stone and had opened to crystals. He liked to write with his children playing around him in his study, and he liked to lead the children of his church on picnics and nature walks. He was on the school committee. Children, women, birds, and trees conditioned his life. "I converse with the sick and the dying," he would tell Ralph Waldo Emerson, in a lugubrious whimsy, and his written reactions to the deaths of his brother Hall and the son of his sister Apphia were full of tender pathos. He also talked with cartmen and lumberjacks and sawyers. But when he was away on trips, he sent little notes to his children in baby talk, and when he was home he sent love notes to his wife in the next room, telling her that he enjoyed hearing her sing and play the piano. In the shadow of the Williams mansion he had built a modest brown house with high gothic gables, one of which prominently displayed a stone cross, and was devoting himself to the cultivation of his

---

*Late in life she would go even farther, associating closely with Francis Ellingwood Abbot and the Free Religious Association, beyond the pale of Christianity.

garden, his church, his shrubs and new trees, his novels and poetry, and his chickens. Arethusa Hall, who excelled in landscape gardening, made fun of Judd's "feeble attempts" with shrubbery, reported Judd's daughter Frances, half a century later.[27]

The influence of these activities upon *Richard Edney* is apparent. Judd could no longer count on anonymity and in his subtitle hastened to assure his readers that this would be a cultured yet practical book, with hints about Doing Good and Being Good. At times it sounds as if it were intentionally addressed to children. Despite a few bright touches, this novel of the city and of Horatio-Alger success is, as a whole, uninteresting, revealing a Judd who has become urbane—surrendered, like his heroine Margaret, to gentility. The more sophisticated Judd's style, the less interesting it seems. Smoothing rough edges only robbed it of strength. Margaret Fuller had been right in her 1846 review of *Margaret* when she had identified a certain naive quality in Judd's writing—in the Schiller sense of naive, meaning close to nature—which was its greatest charm.

In *Richard Edney* Judd wrote his implied renunciation of transcendentalism, his acceptance of limitation. Beauty, he said, is increased by a border. View a scene from the mountaintop: it is more beautiful if one steps back from the edge to see it "through the breaks and crevices" in the trees.

> A moss-rose is an instance in point,—beautiful because it is bordered. . . . A house in the midst of shrubbery is an instance; so are islands in a pond; a view through half-raised window-curtains, and distant scenery through a long suite of rooms.

"Bordering" was more than a principle of perception and a principle of art; it was a principle of life:

> But why, if vastness be the ultimate sentiment, is partial vastness more attractive than entire? Why curtain it, to heighten the effect? What has Bebby's head, stuck through those trees, to do with

Infinity? I should call it, rather, Limitation. It is rather the reduction of the Infinite to palpable bounds, than an elevation of the Finite to the immeasurable.[28]

Unlike Ahab, who demanded the Infinite, Judd could accept the wall, shoved near to him, without his former urgent desire to thrust through the wall to the Beyond. In writing *Margaret,* Judd had begun with the finite, a rock or a tree, and had let it flower into truth. Now he was thinking of "reduction of the Infinite to palpable bounds." When he wrote these words, his flirtation with transcendentalism was over. He had already explicitly repudiated transcendentalism in one of his sermons, writing "I am supremely a Christian, being neither pagan nor Jew, unbeliever nor transcendentalist."[29] But then, hardly anyone would answer to the name of transcendentalist. Emerson wrote about the transcendentalists as if they were someone else. Judd went even farther, however. In *Philo* he called the transcendentalists to the bar of judgment, having them submit meekly to limitation, confessing that "too oft on self we gazed," and not enough upon God. They conclude,

> Our fount ran dry, alas! good Lord; and now
> We bring our empty bowls to thee.[30]

The tension between grainy roughness and smoothness gone, Judd's creative productions relapsed into prosiness and sentimentality, grey, flat, and sweet. The change was already apparent in the latter part of *Margaret.* It was enough to make stomachs that demand roughage rumble.

Judd had written, prophetically, in 1832, about the course of the river. It was a real river that he described, but in retrospect it seemed to be a symbolic one that plunged over the cliff into the pool of placidity:

Now dashing precipitous among the rocks that would impede its course, now falling with a tumultuous roar beneath the cliffs that projected over its bed, then boiling up in the wildest commotion, the river then became tame. It returned to its bordering banks, and "the view was charming." "The spray rose high to meet the Sun and receive its rainbow-hue, and then with a graceful curve it fell back to its mother Deep."[31]

Judd's journey outward into the world of time and change was ultimately a search for home, the point of origin. In the "mother Deep" lay unity and peace. *Margaret* was both futuristic and nostalgic. It contained a chapter about Thanksgiving, the festival that in New England was, in the early nineteenth century, what Christmas became in the twentieth century: a time of reunion, of celebration of family unity.* Judd traced Thanksgiving backward toward its point of origin. As a harvest festival it was related to mysterious nature rites in ancient forests "in England, Ger-

---

*"It had been the custom of the Williams family for many years, to gather on Thanksgiving evening at the home of one of the members, for social intercourse with games and dancing, followed by a feast of all the goodies of the season," sometimes a hundred people. "Old and young joined in the figures of the contra dances, Money Muck, Sailor's Hornpipe, Virginia Reel, the matrons with stately bows and curtseys, the children with flying feet and merry laugh. For that evening indeed all were young. Oats peas beans, and fox and geese are obsolete now, and the generations are fast passing away that remember the pretty sight of circle within circle, the innermost including the babies of the family, all singing the familiar words, and imitating the motions of the farmer sowing his seed. What a delight it was to have Uncle Reuel, or Uncle Daniel for the fox, and how they would chase the poor geese, till weak with laughter and excitement they were forced to yield. Battledore and shuttlecock followed, and the dear uncles were never too weary to pit their skill against our youthful agility. Early in the evening, the doors to the big kitchen were thrown open, disclosing a long table fairly groaning with its load of Thanksgiving delicacies. Not the salads and ices of the present day, but big turkeys, whole hams, oysters, (then a rarity seldom enjoyed), mince pies, marlboro pies, pumpkin pies, apple pies, biscuits, cakes, coffee, nuts and raisins, figs and oranges, and other things too numerous to mention. On this evening unmindful of the morrow, the children were allowed to eat not only what they desired, but to fill their pockets, and happy was he who could carry off the most good things. When ample justice had been done to all the good things toasts were drunk, and the evening ended with the singing of well known hymns the lines being 'deaconed' out by Uncle Daniel" (anonymous typescript, shown to me by Richard Hamlen of Schenectady, New York).

many, Sweden, nay, everywhere." Indeed, said Judd, "we must look perhaps for some great Oriental centre, some fountain head beyond the Indus" (60). To find the ultimate origins of the river and the rainbow, one had to travel deep and far. Thanksgiving, as an American invention, symbolized the newness that was America; but as a fertility ritual it joined the American to the earth and to the past.

Down "the dark backward and abysm of time" one went to find the Garden at the beginning of time. In the search for peace and unity one "took the long way round to Nirvana,"[32] pushed down the river in order to find one's way home, because one could not rest in Westhampton. One wrote *Margaret* as a lover's quarrel with the rejected world of the fathers, concluded all one's books with a prophetic vision, a millennial day when evil and strife would be burned away by refining fire. At the end of time was the garden, as at the beginning, its paths now bordered with flowers and inclining toward children and chickens. Childlikeness was the final, blessed state. The fire, the garden, the rainbow, and the rose were one. Judd longed for the Infinite, but settled for domestic happiness. In the afterglow of romanticism, it was difficult for him to distinguish between Edenic peace and Victorian domesticity.

But for Judd the rainbow was elusive and a Victorian, Coventry-Patmore Eden was not enough. The search for simplicity involved him in complexity. Home was not always simple or harmonious. In 1843 Parkman Judd took over his father's journal to record the following domestic scene. This tidbit, plus another page about father Judd's shocked reaction to wine sipping at dinner by seven Williams women, was torn out of a copy of the printed *Memorabilia* placed in the Forbes Library, Northampton. Evidently, someone acted as a censor.

Aug. 20 [1843]. To-day, we are all sad, and at a loss what to do. Father sick, mother tired out, a house full, no help, and Pinny urgent to go off to Maine. Those from Maine wish to go home, but dislike to leave father so sick, and, to crown all, father telling them he is going to die, and they will have to come back soon to attend his funeral. The doctors gave it as their opinion that his heart was not diseased. "Oh well," says father, "you know but little about my disease, and I have lived too long not to know something about it. The disease, I know, is a fever, but it comes from the heart. This fever and I will never part. Now, doctor, you have a certain amount of palaver to tell over to your patients, and it's no use to tell it to me. I know too much about my disease to believe it. Doctors never tell sick folks they are going to die."

As 'Ves was sitting with father, after tea, father began to lament over the sad state the children were in at his approaching death. "Walker has got off from the old track, and is becoming looser and looser. There is no telling where he will stop. Park han't got any religion at all; he don't believe anything, and has no regard for anything good. Hall is stubborn in his ways, conscientious, but an infidel. Hophni is wild, has left the ordinances, seems to be unfixed, and I fear he has no religion. Pinny, I want you should let attend Dr. Tappan's church in Augusta." So he went over us, leaving out Appy, and making no personal remarks on 'Ves. The announcement of these sent us all into a grand consultation, when I expatiated at large on the nature of my religion, and the state of the church in the world, and what constitutes infidelity. 'Ves thought father made him the bell weather who has led us all astray. In former days, when we began to think, father always told us to think for ourselves, not to be trammelled, or tied up to any set of men and dogmas. Now, as we are thinking and breaking away from men and dogmas, he is alarmed, and is constantly checking us, and complaining of our infidelity and departure from the faith![33]

Father Judd survived until 1860.

The Rev. Sylvester Judd's public life was also complex. He sometimes got himself into trouble with his independent tongue. The trouble began as early as the spring of 1842.

While Judd was preaching a pacifist discourse as part of a Sunday-night lecture series in his church, some members of the state legislature stalked out angrily. His lecture, "A Moral Review of the Revolutionary War," was calculated to illustrate the evils of war in general by showing that the American Revolution, though admittedly the holiest war in history, had been attended by great evils, particularly the suppression of liberty, and had not had entirely beneficial results. Judd's intentions were not clearly understood by all of his auditors: it sounded un-American, as if he were singling out the Revolution for particular attack. The next morning the capitol chambers rang with heated denunciations of Judd, who was forthwith discharged from the legislature's group of chaplains. The legislators wanted no prayers from such a polluted source. The newspapers carried full verbatim accounts of the proceedings at the capitol, the town buzzed, and Jane Judd fretted and fidgeted. In the aftermath Judd almost was dismissed from his pulpit.[34] But Reuel Williams, from Washington, commented that "the legislature had more disgraced itself in this affair than Mr. Judd," and his opinion in support would have carried great weight within the little church. Newspapers throughout New England commented on the contretemps, frequently taking Judd's side, and the American Peace Society passed a resolution of support. Judd published his lecture to show that his attack upon war in general had not been an attack upon the founding fathers, and the hubbub quieted.

During the Mexican War, Judd's activities included work with the League of Universal Brotherhood, led by Elihu Burritt, "the learned blacksmith." Judd's friends Edward Everett Hale and Robert Waterston were also taking leadership in this peace movement. Burritt had ideas about sending peace missionaries to Prussia and other countries of Europe. In a public letter to Judd, who had helped organize one of the first statewide branches of the League in 1847 and who served as its Corresponding Secretary, Burritt tried to enlist Maine's support for his plan. Judd endorsed the idea in a letter to Samuel Fessenden of Portland, but nothing further appeared in Burritt's paper, *The Christian Citizen,* about any relationship between Maine and Burritt's peace congress the next year in Brussels, Belgium. One result of the association with Burritt was an all-day peace convention in Augusta in February, 1850. Burritt spoke several times, and Judd was the final speaker, with what Burritt called "some impressive remarks" upon war's "utter inconsistency with all the precepts of religion and the dictates of humanity."[35]

In 1847 Judd aroused widespread newspaper comment, much of it unfavorable, by an odd form of demonstration against the Mexican War. Instead of reading the governor's Thanksgiving proclamation from the pulpit and preaching the usual sermon, Judd treated the occasion as a fast day and proceeded to read to his congregation the Book of Lamentations, entire. As a rural legislator commented, somewhat admiringly, after hearing Judd preach, "he is death aginst war." Judd refused to be quiet. He had courage. He never tired of being specific about sin. Both during the war and after, he continued hammering away with his pacifist philosophy in sermon after sermon, vivid, factual, well documented, eloquent.[36]

In 1845 or 1846, when the dispute with England over the Oregon boundary was being hotly discussed and the Aroostook War over the Maine boundary was still fresh in memory, Judd sought to cool the antagonism against England. In a pair of lengthy, fact-crammed discourses, probably prepared for his Sunday evening lecture series, he reviewed the history of the French Revolution as an object lesson in what happens to those who do not "love their enemies" and "overcome evil with good." Then he declared:

Russia is our great antagonist, not England. . . . It is not possible that England can ever subjugate America, or America invade England; though the two nations may do one another immeasurable injury. Russia occupies the apex of the globe, and like an avalanche, may throw herself down its sides. She commands the heads of both continents. Wherein then is our safety. In the nation's becoming Christian, and acting like a Christian. . . . I suppose that if we or if England insists upon the pound of flesh, we shall probably have war; war with England first, and Russia when her time comes. Now what I would suggest is that we be magnanimous, and for peace sake, concede a little. . . . Is there an individual amongst us, but what, every day of his life, does concede something? And why may not a nation act like an individual.

Whether those words were omitted in delivery is a question. The pages are pinned together. But his pacifist message was also on other pages, and that he did not silence.[37]

In *Richard Edney,* the rule of force is personified in Clover the bully, the villain of the book, and is destroyed in the final scene by a very improbable bolt of lightning from heaven. Judd tells us in an epilogue that he is being allegorical and that there is a "gigantic international Clover," a "Something" that he is presumably smashing with his lightning. As a comment upon the problem of war the scene cannot be taken seriously, and Judd's attempt to mix melodrama, comedy, and allegory does not come off. Clover defies the lightning and challenges "all the fires of heaven" to single combat but inspires in the reader neither interest, pity, anger, nor awe. Clover would sound like King Lear or Ahab if he and his chorus of drinking companions were not so much like Bottom and his comic artisans in *A Midsummer Night's Dream.* Judd, quite simply, was not up to managing a plot or bringing off a climactic scene. Neither did he really know how to end war and slavery, although he knew that he did not like them.

But Judd continued speaking against slavery, war, and other social evils until the end of his life, even in his Fourth of July orations of 1852 in Portland and of 1850 in the Augusta courthouse square, before the assembled fire-clubs of the entire area. His message was consistent: love, universal human brotherhood, and a wise passiveness, or "principled passivity," as he put it. He was against "abusing the South" and the slaveholder, just as he was against the annexation of Texas: he thought both would lead to civil war. "It would sometimes seem as if between the fanaticism of Abolitionists on the one hand, and the infuriated resistance of slaveholders on the other, the ruin of the country was inevitable." Though Judd subscribed to the *National Anti-Slavery Standard,* he could be sarcastic about abolitionist excess: "As regards slaveholders, we might as well hang them all, and done with it. . . . Or, if we do not like that, we may adopt the other alternative, and love them into repentance and reformation." Judd was suspicious of government intervention and force, which he saw as part of the problem not part of the solution. If everybody would change, there would no longer be a problem. "Get right, each of you," he said in his abolition lectures of 1838 in Northampton and Hartford. That was also his cure for the social evil of intemperance. The Sons of Temperance, which operated on the basis of moral suasion, was the only reform society besides the League of Universal Brotherhood that he joined, and demon rum came in for some licks in both *Margaret* and *Richard Edney*; but when prohibition was proposed in Maine, Judd was against it, thinking that it would only create public corruption and private concealment, leading finally to "an exacerbated collision of public sentiment where force shall be repelled by force." His published lecture of 1845 on this subject was prophetic; the Maine prohibition law of 1846, the first in the nation, proved difficult to enforce and was softened in 1851. More effective, he felt, would be a system of coffee houses, after the manner of those recently established in London, some two thousand of them, each one patronized by hundreds of working men in a day, all conversing civilly instead of "brawling or bullying" in a saloon. There they could read newspapers, magazines, and books, on hand for their edification. In *Richard Edney* Judd showed the people of good will going into the slums of Knuckle Lane to get next to the problem, then establishing a public club for all classes, a combination coffee house, reading room, and assembly hall with edifying entertainments. It was a kind of YMCA-YWCA where all could meet on common ground, without the impersonality of delegating interest in the poor to deputies, without the condescension of mere soup societies. Love would get people out of the gutter as force would not, thought Judd. As he stated his philosophy of reform in *Philo,*

> Reform's like catching logs on a swift current,—
> You cannot tow them straightway to the shore,
> But with them down the stream must float a while;
> By yielding draw, and gentle curves bring in.[38]

Judd believed that the root cause of intemperance was a lack of wholesome recreations, that Puritanism was to blame:

> Our Fathers, having discarded everything else, *betook themselves for recreation to the cup....* Our Fathers had no dances, no bowling alleys, no sleigh-rides, no games of goose or back-gammon, no promenades, no systematic holidays, no musical entertainments, no literary or scientific amusements, no pleasures of Art, no Ladies' Fairs, no Tea parties, no Sunday-school celebrations, no rural festivals. . . . Ministers who denounced sports, drank rum; Magistrates, who inflicted penalties for light conduct, drank rum; parents, who whipped their children for playing Saturday nights, drank rum.

Dancing, be it noted, was no novelty in New England, as Judd made clear by including a Thanksgiving ball among the incidents of *Margaret.* The repressive zeal of the Benjamin Tappans was not in evidence in the Westhampton of 1800, and Judd's inclusion of dancing on the list was a mistake.[39] The list of what the forefathers forbade is a good summary of what Judd favored as a program for the improvement of society. "Sunday school celebrations" and "rural festivals" he particularly identified himself with. Although father Judd had regularly fulminated in Northampton about the heathen Christmas observances at the Episcopal church, his son in Augusta was busy trimming the church with greens and conducting his annual Christmas eve service.[40] He wanted more holidays, not less, more of a spirit of celebration in the land; and in *Margaret* he expressed a certain wistfulness about New England's social barrenness, its lack of festivals and folklore, of "fairies in our meadows," of "Whitsuntide given to bearbaiting," of "elves to spirit away our children." "We have," he said, "no traditions, legends, fables, and scarcely a history" (267). He looked forward to the gradual coming of the Golden Day, backward to the Anglo-Saxon forests and Old England. Progress and utilitarian "high calculation" had somehow to be reconciled with wildness, natural exuberance, and the Anglican spirit of celebration. When the Westons wanted to dance their way into Episcopalianism or the Williams family wanted to play parlor games, Sylvester Judd was there to give them his blessing. As Margaret says,

> What relaxes without weakening, is cheerful without frivolity, and offers attraction without danger? Not to the exclusion of other things, our election has fallen on the Dance, a species of recreation enjoined in the Old Testament, and recognized in the New. . . . We praise God in the dances; it is a hymn written with our feet. (450-51)

Not only dancing, but music, literature, and art were included in Judd's prescription for lifting the spirit of the individual and thus the tone of society. Beauty, far from being opposite to morality or subversive of it, was the agency for moral renewal; *Margaret* says, "Beauty is Truth's usher, whereby it is introduced to the heart. No Truth is received till it puts on a beautiful aspect" (448). The Unitarians and the more progressive orthodox preachers encouraged Judd to this view. The Benjamin Tappans and the Enoch Hales were not beautiful, and their world was not Judd's any longer. As opposed to them he was even on the side of Mark Tucker, who taught him that a sermon could sing; or of John Truair, who spoke to him of sacred music; or of Andrews Norton, who vibrated to the verses of Felicia Hemans; or of Andrew Preston Peabody, who reviewed the poetry of uplift for the *North American Review.* With all of these people Judd came from time to time into collision, but all contributed to his conclusion that truth and beauty were reconcilable. As Judd said in *Margaret,* "The Gospels seem to me truth melodized" (448).

The question was whether the smoothness—sensuousness even—of a Mark Tucker's language and the smoothness of Unitarian literary critics like the two Peabodys could be reconciled with the roughness and wildness that Judd reached for in *Margaret.* The opposition was ever between nature and the artificial as well as between solitude and society in romantic aesthetics and romantic morality. In the never-ending struggle between the advocates of beauty on the one side and the advocates of goodness and usefulness on the other, Judd, in *Margaret* at least, concluded that nature, being an expression of God, had the last say. Nature and the voice of folk wisdom spoke with authority, reconciling the apparent conflict between utility and beauty. As Margaret puts it, in a letter,

> The Widow Wright taught me Utility; "Not looks, it's use, child," was her maxim. The hang-bird taught me Caution. Mother Goose's Melodies taught me not to cry when I could not help a thing. But more than this, if we could but see it, there is a waiting for Goodness and Truth in all souls. . . . Then through the world wanders

the spirit of Love, though she be no more than the chipping bird
that builds a nest in the rose-bush, or a butterfly that shimmers
over a dirty pool. (454)

The hang-bird (oriole) teaches Margaret caution, and the
butterfly shimmers over a dirty pool. Just as with Emerson,
who has his moment of ecstasy at the beginning of *Nature*
while "Crossing a bare common, in snow puddles, at twi-
light, under a clouded sky," Margaret sees that nature's
beauty has its dirt and granularity. At its best, *Margaret*
has enough saltness to keep it sweet.

Philo, at its best, also has the roughness of the real to
counteract its sentimental smoothness and perfectionist
message, though the earthiness is not so apparent as in
Margaret, or so fresh. Philo, given a Faustian survey of the
real world by the Angel Gabriel, confronts a host of personified evils. The father of them all is War, whose voice
has tang:

> *Phantasm of War.* Ha! Gabriel, thou art too late. The war
> *Exists*,—thou'lt not blame me for pushing it.
> ·
> 　　　　　　　　　　　　　　　　Work on,
> My daughters; never mind this driveller.
> He's probably a blue light, or some sour
> And disappointed bachelor, that hates
> The sex. Dear Lechery, and sweet Revenge,
> Thou nimble Drunkenness, nice children all,
> Are ye tired? We have a good deal to do.
> Once in, there is no backing out, you know.
> There's Fever, she is really wearing down.
> Come hither, duck; there lies a tender child
> Fresh from Tabasco, where a patriot winged it;—
> We gave the man a medal;—It is warm
> And quivering; apply it to thy chest,—
> 'Twill strengthen thee.

The Devil in *Philo* feeds on war. He is "a travelling merchant of distress" who traffics in other people's tears. He
spends his time "culling hearts" and like a "soap-monger"

turns tears into cosmetics for "the Great Ones." He follows battles and boils down the bodies in his try-works:

> *Philo.* What means this most unearthly stench?
> *The Devil.* 'Tis genuine Christian stench, each pound of it;
> There's not a Turk or Hindoo in the lot.
> I call it fresh; it came in yesterday
> From Vera Cruz.
> . . . .
>   Oregon, somehow, I lost;
> But Mexico is rich, what one might call
> A first-rate speculation.

The Devil may not be nice, but at least he is no hypocrite:

> *"I am not nice!"*—not like your plumed ones, no,
> Who bang dove-bosomed girls, as egg-shells smashed,
> And cackle of the deed, disnatured pullets!

This Devil is really a not unlikable fellow, and Judd, who could find some good in anybody—calling even rumsellers, slaveholders, and generals "men and brothers"—thought he could detect some aptness for improvement in him. With the millennial day advancing on the world, Judd's Devil has had enough of

>   gluttonies,
> And jellied whoredoms; men from rum-shops, pitched
> Into the street.

"I am excited," he shouts to an assembled crowd; "I go for reform." When the Devil turns reformer, the people listen.[41]

But the critics who read *Philo* shuddered. Andrew Preston Peabody, writing for the *North American Review,* which in 1852 he became editor of, doubtless felt constrained by his friendship with Arethusa Hall and by the fact that he had preached at Sylvester Judd's ordination; but he called the scenes with the Devil "the most repulsive portion of the whole poem." Struggling to find something to praise, he singled out the most sentimental and vapid parts: a wholly irrelevant death scene he considered to be superb, an unmemorable hymn to Christ he called "touchingly beautiful," the dull and unconvincing ending he called a "rapt and beatific vision" that was Judd's "most congenial element." But he condemned Judd's use of vulgar, "obsolete, unusual or freshly coined words," such as "muzzy," "soggy," "munch," "mucker," "dowse," "queachy," "peristaltic," and "writhle"—in other words, anything in *Philo* that had life in it or the smell of damp dirt. Indeed, said Peabody, Judd had great "proficiency in the art of sinking":

> He vaults from the kitchen to the clouds, and leaps from the clouds into the gutter; he paints an angel's face over the tavern-bar, and thrusts a Dominie Sampson into the councils of Olympus. . . . Would he confine himself to the ideal, he might win a place second to none on the catalogue of American poets.

With his best called worst and his worst called best, it is no wonder if Judd felt hamstrung and confused. Even Arethusa Hall seemed to be on the side of ideality and gentility and the two Peabodys, A.P. and W.B.O. She wrote Sylvester a letter in which she tried to talk him out of some of his peculiarities of style, and the selections from Judd's works in her biography showed a systematic bias against the "art of sinking" in which Peabody found Judd's proficiency "so thorough."[42]

Judd's language and rough versification, lacking in the expected poetic loftiness and gloss, made critics like Peabody dismiss his experimental efforts. At times Judd's verse sounded uncomfortably close to the way real people talked, as in "never mind this driveller./He's probably a blue light," or "Once in, there is no backing out, you know," or "There's not a Turk or Hindoo in the lot." The critics called such things "prosy," one of the polite terms in their vocabulary of condemnation. As Judd's character Philo says, doubtless with a wink to the reader,

> Our minister is a new hand at rhymes;
> He rolls them off as teamsters bales of cotton;
> Waits Art's more perfect day for the fine tissue.[43]

The "fine tissue" was apparently what Judd tried to create in his next try at poetry, "The White Hills, An American Tragedy," another closet drama like *Philo*. It is a shadowy, Shelleyan work about the evils of Mammon, based on the gold-rush fever of 1849 and set in the context of the scenery and legends of New Hampshire's White Mountains. A mixture of *Faust, Macbeth,* and Hawthorne's "The Great Carbuncle," this unfinished extravaganza is full of midnight soliloquies, fairies, ravens, virtuous maidens rejected, and a whole family of witches, one of whom the protagonist is forced to marry in exchange for help in his quest for the legendary pearl of the mountains. The verse is indeed more resonant and conventionally mellifluous than in *Philo*. Judd apparently had done it again: had responded to criticism by learning how to write even more in the approved, genteel style. We cannot be sure of this, for our only knowledge of this now-lost manuscript is from the excerpts Arethusa Hall chose for her biography of Judd; but it is probable that Judd's new-found tone was consistently maintained, and indeed had to be once he had committed himself to it. The following soliloquy of Normand, after he has given himself over to Mammon and the search for the pearl, has the correct Tennysonian ring:

> The hills gleam, blazing to their crystal core.
> The pale pearl like a globed rainbow burns;
> And my ambition takes a gayer hue.
> Ambition? 'Tis revenge and trick
> Heroic on the temper of the times,
> That makes of gold a god, and penury
> A crime. I will be rich: I'll have estates,
> A seal, blood, quality, and living;
> Some right of way along this crowded world;
> The smiles of art, and thanks of charity.
> Had I the means, I'd do extensive good
> As any man.

Nobody will confuse that with the way real people talk.

Nor does the term "prosy" apply to the following, spoken while Normand waits at midnight for the witch-mother, Vafer, to appear. Shelley's voice can perhaps be heard in the echo:

> Stars, glittering sentinels of sleeping space;
> Thou moon, whose silver lustre blesses earth;
> Ye deep and vaulted mysteries of nature,
> In hill or glade, that keep your hoarded wealth;
> Silence, that hushes up the universe,—
> Ye are but parts of what I am, or types
> Of what I shall be. Life and hope exalt
> My venturous step, and crown the lonesome hour.

Overtones of Wordsworth can be heard later in the same speech:

> An unseen nook breathes sassafras and mint,
> And scent of fern; and here are phosphor-sticks,
> Gleaming like fiery reptiles in my path.
> I used, a boy, to gather them, and loved
> The woods, and tangled crevices, and dark
> And wizard ravines, when others feared.
> I'll not fear now. Toss a pebble down this chasm;
> See if 'twill waken her, and haste my hour.[44]

If Judd could learn to write smooth verse like that in only two or three years of practice, under the tutelage of Andrew Preston Peabody, there's no telling what he might have done by-and-by, had he kept on taking lessons in the art of rising.

In *Philo*, in contrast, Judd was still slamming words around in a "general mash" like that of the sled-race scene in *Margaret*. The Genie of the Earth speaks to Philo about the creation, relying not on Genesis but on geology:

> In those old times, before your race was known,
> It was no joggle, but a general mash,
> And all the elements were by the ears;
> No coast-lifting, but a slam of continents;
> America did tackle Africa,

> Asia dowsed Europe, islands strangled straits;
> And dark it was, so dark you could not see
> Your hand before your face.

And Judd's metaphors in *Philo* often run along the following lines: "She's simple as a kitten in a palace"; "My habits, as a pot of flowers, I set/In the warm rain of thy correction"; "Tears trilled, and clicked, as water in a cave"; "Those bumpkin eyes grew liquid as a girl's"; and "Reform is a cold shower-bath,/Till one gets used to it."[45]

Judd lacked the genius to achieve what Robert Frost would later do in the way of suffusing common speech and common things with beauty and at the same time forming them into artistically controlled lyrics, narratives, and philosophical dramas. But Judd had an idea that that was the way to go, and in *Philo* at least he was still trying. The pity is that, unlike the great artists, who usually develop from the smooth and conventional toward the rough and original, Judd's development was in the opposite direction, doubtless in response to sandpapering critics. He had long since shown in his workaday discourses that he could write perfectly correct and conventional prose. Emersonian richness and density of rhetoric was no longer in his sermons, although he still crammed them with facts and ideas; his more startling diction he reserved for his books and perhaps an occasional letter. He could adapt his language to the occasion and sound like a proper Unitarian gentleman when he had a mind to. He could be smooth.

But the apostle of love and light, the smooth Mr. Judd, at times revealed an abrasive back side to his tongue. With all the good will in the world, he could be snappish, as in the following letter to the *National Anti-Slavery Standard:*

Augusta, Me., Sept. 29, 1851

Dear Sir,

I received sometime since the enclosed bill. Both indignation and inability prevented me from answering it. I have now cooled down so far as to be able to send it back. First, I doubt if I owe you so much (seven dollars). Second, if I do, I owe it not, for you have no right to let arrearages accumulate at such a rate. You ought to forfeit them by your own negligence.

What can a poor country clergyman do? Obliged to take, support, patronize, or whatever it be all the literature, religion, and morality there is in the country, and ever and anon bills like the enclosed coming in upon him—it is enough to make a mud-turtle jump.

Yours truly
S. Judd[46]

In defending some people, Judd found, he was thrown into conflict with others. The ideal and the real often seemed disconcertingly out of harmony. In 1847 he came to the defense of a well-known doctor, named Coolidge, accused of murder and convicted. He even preached a sermon on the subject. Judd was not only interested in abolishing capital punishment and in moving from punishment of criminals to reform of criminals but was, like many others, convinced that Coolidge was innocent. But when William A. Drew, Augusta's Universalist minister and the editor of the widely read newspaper *The Gospel Banner,* made public comments against Coolidge, Judd turned on Drew with something distressingly like a snarl: "Drew has come out against Dr. Coolidge, both like a madman and a fool," he said in a letter to his wife Jane. Drew had taken Judd publicly to task a few months earlier for his "Desecration of Thanksgiving," as he headlined the article in *The Gospel Banner* of December 4, 1847, criticizing Judd's refusal to read the governor's Thanksgiving proclamation. Although he did not say it in his article, Drew doubtless did not like Judd's antiwar position, as we might infer from the fact that Drew was on the committee to welcome President Polk to Augusta for the Fourth of July celebration of 1847, which had jingoistic overtones in that war year. Reuel Williams, who had "fearlessly opposed the Annexation of Texas, and predicted that it would result in a dissolution of the Union or a protracted civil war" was nonetheless a good Democrat and feted the President in a formal breakfast, attended by large numbers. Sylvester Judd, pointedly, was not there.[47] Judd's best friend was the other Universalist minister, J.W. Hanson of nearby Hallowell; and Drew and Judd continued in enough public amity to cooperate on church programs; but we can assume that their relationship was not warm.

It was this Sylvester Judd, regarded as nettlesome and perhaps a bit odd in his individualism,[48] though full of sweetness and light, who wanted to draw all the warring sects of Augusta together in peace, who proposed a kind of Augusta council of churches. With a positive genius for bad timing, Judd proposed, just three weeks after his controversial lecture on the Revolutionary War, that a union meeting of all the ministers and congregations in Augusta be held to promote harmony and understanding among them. Only the Episcopalians, Universalists, and Free-Will Baptists accepted the invitation. The Congregationalists and Methodists declined. Although Judd became "the leading spirit" in the movement later to bring together in one organization the Unitarian churches in Maine,[49] and although he succeeded in Augusta in getting some of the different sects together in occasional meetings and outdoor Sunday school festivals, he did not get very far in healing the essential split between Unitarians and Congregationalists. In an age when Benjamin Tappan and his orthodox parishioners could not even reconcile themselves to dancing in private homes, an age when religious division was increasing rather than diminishing, this Judd with his newfangledness was a well-meaning but not very successful man. Judd longed to reunite the broken circle, to return to simplicity, to the village he had fled from, where there had been one church and one political party, but the gate leading backward was barred.

Fortunately, in confronting the evils of backbiting, snobbery, and social strife, in himself and others, Judd knew how to laugh as well as to denounce. His chapter in *Richard Edney* satirizing politics is somewhere between Swift and Dickens. The Dogbanians (dog haters) have a rivalry with the Catapults (cat haters). The Catapults, like so many Know-Nothings or Dorus Clarkes,

> allowed, indeed, the usefulness of the cat as rat-catcher and hearth-rug companion; but their aversion chiefly vented itself against so many foreign cats, and the endless multiplication of cats. Foreign cats, they said, injured the utility of our own cats; spoiled their habits. . . .

This game of Phumbics, or politics, excites such great feelings that it cannot be discussed from the pulpit: "one Clergyman gave great offence . . . by reading a portion of Scripture, in which the exhortation occurs, Beware of dogs. It was said he emphasized the words, and uttered them with a peculiar snarl of the voice, whereby the friends of that race were aggrieved."[50]

Judd's parishioners, though sometimes restive under his tongue-lash and not always able to laugh at his satire or respond to such oddities as his Thanksgiving lamentations, nonetheless recognized that they were well served. His church was growing, and seventy-five years later people looked back on his period as the "golden age" of Unitarianism in Augusta.[51] Even the dross of Judd's more prosaic sermons—after his early eloquence was redirected into his literary productions—had a richness, a concreteness, a relevance to the real world that made the sermons of lesser men—like Enoch Hale and Solomon Williams, whose congregations were a dozen times or more the size of Judd's—seem vague, pallid, and irrelevant. After Judd's death, when his church had difficulty holding a minister, though served temporarily by Judd's friend from Boston, Robert Waterston, Judd's sermons were dusted off and read a second or third time from the pulpit. Judd had been gradually winning his way back to respectability. After his minor critical success with *Margaret,* Augusta had to take note that its odd, individualistic, Unitarian minister was one of its famous citizens, the author of most consequence in the area, perhaps in the whole state of Maine. The town learned to put up with Judd's tactlessness, his whimsies, his sweetness and light, his nervousness and awkwardness in society, his nosy note-taking, his capacity for being irritated and for being irritating. At times his face glowed, and hearts around him melted.

No politician, Judd nonetheless managed to make his peace with the politicians. In 1844 he was reinstated as one of the chaplains for the state legislature. In 1850 he preached a reconciling sermon on "The True Dignity of Politics" that mollified his critics. The legislature, pleased, ordered a thousand copies printed "for the use of the House." The sermon, like those in *The Church,* was actually among the more prosaic, less interesting ones. What was inspired, eloquent, or abrasive in Judd's sermons did not get printed. Judd was learning to accept the real world, in part, where political compromise was the art of the possible. In 1840, in a sermon, Judd had called politics the art of deception; now he said, "Office is honorable; it is dignified, and I had almost said religious."[52] In the world one learns limitation, and sometimes makes a peace with deception.

For Sylvester Judd, death was the ultimate peace. He had been looking for death all his life—"Twenty four. Shall I live to record Twenty five. Hope I may."—but of late he had neglected to keep these records, and when death came it took him by surprise.[53] Endings have a way of coming swiftly. There was the irony of the uncompleted work, "The White Hills," which lacked only a final scene or two. There was the irony, finally, of the undelivered speech, which was to have been the most important one in Judd's career, a plea for a child-centered church in which membership was a right of birth.[54] Judd was on his way to deliver the address to an audience of Unitarians in Boston when a cold night and damp sheets in a hotel near Augusta led to his fatal illness. The speech was to have been the climax of Judd's campaign to open the church, to unite all the people, a campaign that he had waged intensively but with minimal success for many years. Ironically, Judd's own Christ Church in Augusta waited until the day of Judd's burial to pass a resolution supporting his views on The Birthright Church, the domestic millennium that he had so often advocated to them, and it was not until three months later that Reuel Williams astounded and delighted his son Joseph by marching down the center aisle to receive for the first time the sacraments of baptism and communion that Sylvester Judd had ardently and vainly urged him to receive.[55] Robert Waterston presided over the occasion. It was a living memorial to the man whose name would be inscribed prominently in stone on the wall of the little church, to one side of the pulpit.

Judd's views on the subject of church membership did not differ greatly from those of the Episcopalians, with whom he had been maintaining cordial relations. Judd's idea of birthright membership also resembled the practice of the Quakers, with whom Judd had much in common, but unlike them and unlike some of his fellow Unitarians, he could not accept the term "meeting" to describe the fellowship of Christians. Judd's religion embraced universal mankind—even Mohammedans, Hindoos, and William A. Drew—but he was mystically attracted to tradition, the dark backward and abysm of time, and he liked to read about Episcopalianism, and insisted on the mystical communion of The Church. Judd wanted the church to be a symbol of unity. His goal was to get the children into the church, to remove the lingering Puritan prejudice, which the Unitarians shared in part, against admitting the "unconverted" to the communion table, although for many Unitarians the prejudice was well on the way to becoming one against the sacraments themselves. As an infant, Judd had waited four years for baptism. Then he had suffered through years of uncertainty before daring to announce his conversion and approach the communion table. Judd wanted to make sure that never again would children hover, unbaptized and unhouseled, on the brink of terror.

Now Judd himself was balanced on that final edge to try his wings. Fourteen years earlier he had stretched them, a Uriel, ready for celestial flight to the home in the sun from which he had fallen. In the ecstasy of 1839 he had been only too ready to exchange earth for heaven: "To an inhabitant of the sun, there is not a dark spot on the face of the universe." Now, he was not prepared. Told he was dying, Judd's last thoughts were of his children. "He broke out in piercing tones of anguish, 'Oh, my God! I love thee . . . my *wife* and *children,—I love you,—how can I! how can I!'*" A few moments after, he became calm. Not realizing how near death was, he asked that his children wait until the next day to come in to him for a good-by. He added, "'Cover me up warm. . . . I'm doing well.'"[56] They were his last words. The date was January 26, 1853. Judd was thirty-nine years old.

At the end of the rainbow was the sun. It was setting. Judd's life had been a long, slow Sunday, but too brief by half.

The fishes swam away with the sun, and plunged down the cataract of light that falls over the other side of the earth; and the broad massive clouds grew darker and grimmer, and extended themselves, like huge-breasted lions couchant which the Master had told her about, to watch all night near the gate of the sun. (120)

Deep in the woods a woodpecker rapped and rattled over among the chestnuts. It was January. The sun that presided over Sunday was gone. It had never been closer or so far away.

Notes,

Bibliography,

Index

Notes

The chief source for facts of Judd's life and for his letters and journals is Arethusa Hall, *Life and Character of the Rev. Sylvester Judd* (Boston: Crosby, Nichols, 1854), cited hereafter as "Hall." For the journal of Judd's father the chief source is *Memorabilia: From the Journals of Sylvester Judd, of Northampton, Mass., 1809-1860,* ed. Arethusa Hall (Northampton: Privately printed, 1882), hereafter cited as *Memorabilia.* Material from these sources is not specifically cited when its chronological position in these books makes its location obvious. Quotations from *Margaret* after the first one are indicated parenthetically in the text, e.g. (310-14). I have regularly used the first edition of *Margaret* because I feel the revised edition of 1851 was bowdlerized by Judd in response to criticism.

When no citation is given for a Judd manuscript, the manuscript is located at the Houghton Library, Harvard University, in the collection marked 55M-2.

Introduction

1. *Margaret. A Tale of the Real and Ideal, Blight and Bloom; Including Sketches of a Place Not Before Described, Called Mons Christi* (Boston: Jordan and Wiley, 1845).

2. Sylvester Judd, *Richard Edney and the Governor's Family. A Rus-Urban Tale, Simple and Popular, Yet Cultured and Noble, of Morals, Sentiment, and Life, Practically Treated and Pleasantly Illustrated, Containing, also, Hints on Being Good and Doing Good* (Boston: Phillips, Sampson & Co., 1850). The title is probably a light-hearted poke at the critics who had criticized *Margaret* for its vulgarity.

3. Nathaniel Hawthorne, letter to R. Monckton Milnes, November 13, 1854. Typed copy shown to me by Norman Holmes Pearson.

Chapter 1. Golden Westhampton

1. Dorus Clarke, *"Saying the Catechism" Seventy-five Years Ago and the Historical Results* (Boston: Lee & Shepard, 1879), pp. 42-43. Quotations from Clarke are from this pamphlet unless indicated otherwise.

2. *Memorial of the Reunion of the Natives of Westhampton, Mass., September 5, 1866* (Waltham, Mass.: Free Press, 1866), p. 65; hereafter cited as *Westhampton Reunion*. Clarke here says much of what he said in his speech of 1878.

3. Ibid., p. 38.

4. Nathaniel Bartlett Sylvester, *History of the Connecticut Valley in Massachusetts, with Illustrations and Biographical Sketches of Some of its Prominent Men and Pioneers* (Philadelphia: Louis H. Everts, 1879), I, 296.

5. Enoch Hale Papers, Yale Divinity School Library; for the weather records see the Judd Manuscript, Forbes Library, Northampton, Mass., Miscellaneous Vol. X.

6. Quoted from the journal, in Robert L. Young, "Enoch Hale: The Biography of a New England Country Pastor," Forbes Library.

7. Sylvester, I, 288, 300.

8. Young, p. 100.

9. Sylvester, I, 203, 272, 310, 335, 353, 396, 415.

Chapter 2. Return into Time

1. *Memorabilia*, p. 9.

2. Young, p. 100.

3. *Memorabilia*, p. 15.

4. [Arethusa Hall], "Sathurea, The Story of a Life," Judd Papers, 55M-1, Houghton Library, Harvard University.

5. "Sathurea," pp. 38-39. Also see Arethusa Hall, "Autobiography," *Arethusa Hall, A Memorial*, ed. Francis Ellingwood Abbot (Cambridge, Mass.: Privately printed, 1892), which contains a more reticent version of the story told in "Sathurea."

6. *Westhampton Reunion*, p. 28.

7. Hall, p. 13.

8. *The Speech of His Excellency Governor Strong, Delivered before the Legislature of Massachusetts, October 16, 1812, with the Documents, which Accompanied the Same* (Boston: Russell and Cutler, 1812).

9. *Margaret,* pp. 310-14. References to *Margaret* (1st edition) are hereafter indicated parenthetically in the text, e.g. (310-14).

10. Young, p. 100.

11. For example, see the letter from the New Haven churches to the Northampton church of April 4, 1821, copied into the First Church, Northampton, records, II, 46-50.

12. "Sathurea."

13. Church Records, Westhampton, Massachusetts.

14. Hale, Journal, entry for Oct. 25, 1816.

15. Nathan Hale, letter to Sylvester Judd, February 27, 1820, Judd Manuscript (A. Personal), Forbes Library, Northampton, Mass. This collection is cited hereafter as "Judd Manuscript."

16. Sylvester Judd II, Journal of trip to Ohio, Judd Papers, 55M-1.

17. *Memorabilia,* pp. 58-59.

18. Chauncey Parkman Judd, brother of the novelist, spoke at the Westhampton reunion of 1866 and characterized the period of his childhood as a "golden age" when "the wilderness blossomed as the rose." (*Westhampton Reunion,* p. 29.)

Chapter 3. The Village as Utopia

1. For a full treatment of this concept, see Charles L. Sanford, *The Quest for Paradise: Europe and the American Moral Imagination* (Urbana, Ill.: University of Illinois Press, 1961), which enlarges on his earlier articles, beginning with "The Garden of America," *Modern Review* (Calcutta, India), XCII (July, 1952), 23-32.

2. Timothy Dwight, *Travels in New-England and New-York* (New Haven: T. Dwight, 1821-22), I, 302.

3. *Letters of James Russell Lowell,* ed. Charles Eliot Norton (New York: Harper and Bros., 1894), I, 106. Letter to C.F. Briggs of Feb. 18, 1846.

4. Hall, p. 14.

Chapter 4. Let Us Spend One Day

1. *Westhampton Reunion,* p. 51.

2. Apphia Judd and Sylvester Judd II, letters to Arethusa Hall, January 16, 1822, December 9, 1823, Judd Papers, 55M-1; *Memorabilia,* p. 66; Hall, "Autobiography," p. 19.

3. *Westhampton Reunion,* p. 56.

4. Hall, p. 4.

5. Letter received from Mrs. Sylvester Judd Beach, Feb. 2, 1961.

6. *Memorabilia,* p. 60.

7. Sidney E. Mead, *Nathaniel William Taylor, 1786-1858: A Connecticut Liberal* (Chicago: University of Chicago Press, 1942), p. 235.

8. Hall, "Autobiography," p. 17.

9. *Report of the Westhampton Sesquicentennial Exercises, August 18-19, 1928* (Privately printed, 1928), p. 17.

10. Olive Cleaveland Clarke, *Things That I Remember at Ninety-Five* (Privately printed, 1881), p. 5.

11. *Westhampton Reunion*, p. 35.

12. Judd Manuscript, Forbes Library, "Miscellaneous" Vol. X, 176; First Parish, Northampton, *Meeting Houses and Ministers from 1635 to 1878. Containing a Description of the New Meeting House, Together with the Dedication Sermon, Delivered Sunday, May 5, 1878* (Northampton: Gazette Printing Co., 1878), p. 32; *Confession of Faith, and Catalogue of Members, Jan. 1, 1832* (Northampton: Privately printed, 1832).

13. Dorus Clarke, pp. 11-12.

14. *Westhampton Reunion*, p. 7.

15. Ibid., pp. 58, 64, 65.

16. Letter to C.F. Briggs, Feb. 18, 1846, in *Letters of James Russell Lowell*, I, 106.

17. *Westhampton Reunion*, p. 51.

18. Enoch Hale, *The Personality and Divinity of the Spirit* (Northampton: Butler, 1799), p. 105.

19. Enoch Hale, *A Sermon Preached before the Hampshire Missionary Society, at Their Annual Meeting the Fourth Thursday in August, 1804, in Northampton* (Northampton: William Butler, 1804), pp. 14-15.

20. *Asking Amiss and Not Receiving. A Sermon, Preached in Westhampton, on a Day of Fasting and Prayer in Massachusetts, April 5, A.D. 1804* (Northampton, The Hive Office, 1804), p. 12.

21. *Memorabilia*, p. 9.

22. "Shakespeare's American Fable," *The Massachusetts Review*, II (Autumn, 1960), 48.

23. Perry Miller, *The New England Mind: From Colony to Province* (Cambridge, Mass.: Harvard University Press, 1953).

24. Hall, p. 11.

25. Ibid., pp. 11-12, 16.

26. Inference drawn from various sources, especially from entries by C. Parkman Judd for Aug. 18-29, 1843, in the Judd Manuscript "Notebooks" of S. Judd II. Excerpts from these Notebooks are contained in *Memorabilia*. See below, p. 305.

27. Westhampton Church records.

28. The Training Day scene in *Margaret* contains a brief incident in which Margaret throws herself between her friend and the lash (p. 96).

29. *Margaret,* p. 107. Judd's ability to juxtapose the nuns and squads of dogs in adjacent sentences illustrates his ability to combine the sensibility of Lydia Sigourney or Lydia Maria Child with that of Mark Twain.

30. Hall, "Autobiography," pp. 16-17.

31. Ralph Waldo Emerson, "An Address Delivered before the Senior Class in Divinity College, Cambridge, Sunday Evening, July 15, 1838," *Complete Works,* ed. Edward Waldo Emerson (Centenary Edition; Boston: Houghton Mifflin Co., 1903), I, 129.

32. Judd Manuscript, "Miscellaneous" Vols. XIV, X.

33. Hall, "Autobiography," p. 17.

Chapter 5. Northampton in the 1820's

1. *Memorabilia,* pp. 67-68.

2. *Westhampton Reunion,* p. 60; *Margaret,* p. 136.

3. Ralph Waldo Emerson, manuscript journal DO (1852), Houghton Library, Harvard University; Hall, pp. 522, 531. Judd's birthday records are on a loose page of the journal in my possession. These annual reports on his state of being are more terse and earthbound each year, as in the following entry, made a year after his marriage: "1842. July 23. Twenty nine. My life is. Jane reminded me of the time. She gave me a boquet mignionette, sweet pea, and geranium. We sat together alone at the breakfast table. Butter and Coffee poor." (Here, as elsewhere, I have followed the policy of not indicating the writer's errors by "sic.") Emerson quotation adapted to my context.

4. *Memorabilia,* p. 57.

5. *The Northampton Book: Chapters from 300 Years in the Life of a New England Town, 1654-1954,* ed. Lawrence E. Wikander *et al.* (Northampton, 1954), p. 86.

6. Thomas Belsham, *American Unitarianism: or, A Brief History of "The Progress and Present State of the Unitarian Churches in America." Compiled from Documents and Information Communicated by the Rev. James Freeman, D.D. and William Wells Jun. Esq. of Boston, and from Other Unitarian Gentlemen in this Country. By Rev. Thomas Belsham. Extracted from his "Memoirs of the Life of the Reverend Theophilus Lindsey," printed in London, 1812, and Now Published for the Benefit of the Christian Churches in this Country, without Note or Alteration.* (Boston: N. Willis, 1815); "Unitarian Christianity. Discourse at the Ordination of the Rev. Jared Sparks. Baltimore, 1819," *Works,* 17th ed. (Boston: American Unitarian Association, 1866), III, 59-103.

7. Bernard Whitman, *Two Letters to the Reverend Moses Stuart: on the Subject of Religious Liberty.* (Boston: Gray and Bowen, 1830);

"Review of Letters on Religious Liberty," *The Spirit of the Pilgrims*, IV (March, 1831), 117-80.

8. Whitman, p. 37.

9. Ibid., p. 32.

10. First Church, Northampton, records, entry for April 4, 1821.

11. Whitman, p. 43; Enoch Hale Diary, entry for February 6, 1821.

12. John P. Manwell, *A History of the Hampshire Association of Congregational Churches and Ministers* (Amherst, Mass.: The Newel Press, 1941), pp. 27-28; Enoch Hale Diary, entry for January 29, 1822.

13. Westhampton Church records, May 4, 1821, May 3, 1822; First Church, Northampton, records, November 18, 1821; Manwell, p. 27.

14. Westhampton Church records, May 3, 1822.

15. Ibid., October 16, 1822, May 19, 1825.

16. First Church, Northampton, records, October 5, 1825.

17. *Memorabilia*, p. 57.

18. *Hampshire Gazette, Centennial Edition*, September 6, 1886, p. 2. Hereafter cited as *Centennial Gazette; Northampton Book*, p. 377.

19. Hall, "Sathurea," p. 42.

20. Undated letter, Forbes Library. Note the pedantic insistence on the original spelling of Hawthorne's name.

21. *Hampshire Gazette*, Feb. 23, 1825.

22. Susan I. Lesley, *Recollections of My Mother*, 2nd ed. (Boston, 1886).

23. *Hampshire Gazette*, July 20, 1831.

24. *Centennial Gazette*, p. 2.

25. *Hampshire Gazette*, August 26, 1829; Letter to Arethusa Hall, August 16, 1826, Judd Papers, 55M-1; *Memorabilia*, p. 80.

26. *Centennial Gazette*, p. 32; E.P. Bridgeman, article in *Hampshire Gazette & Courier*, April 5, 1902. (Article describes cattle shows of period c. 1835-1840.)

27. *Northampton Book*, pp. 174, 162; *Northampton Courier*, Feb. 2, 1831; *Hampshire Gazette*, July 17, 1822; *Centennial Gazette*, pp. 29, 34.

28. Olive Cleaveland Clarke, p. 12; Henry S. Gere, *Reminiscences of Old Northampton: Sketches of the Town as It Appeared from 1840 to 1850* ([Northampton: Privately printed], 1902), pp. 127-32; Sylvester, I, 204-05; *Hampshire Gazette & Courier*, May 7, 1902.

29. October 1, 1823, Bancroft Papers, Massachusetts Historical Society.

30. Judd Manuscript, "Miscellaneous," X, 177.

31. Sylvester, I, 205; *Centennial Gazette*, p. 14; *Hampshire Gazette & Courier*, April 28, 1902.

32. Lesley, p. 89.

33. Constance M. Rourke, *Trumpets of Jubilee: Henry Ward Beecher, Harriet Beecher Stowe, Lyman Beecher, Horace Greeley, P.T. Barnum* (New York: Harcourt, Brace & Co., 1927), p. 17.

34. Her letters are rather haphazard in such matters as spelling and punctuation (Judd Papers, 55M-1).

35. Hall, "Sathurea," p. 56; *Centennial Gazette*, p. 2; S. Judd II, letter to Arethusa Hall, Dec. 9, 1823, and Family Reminiscences folder, Judd Papers, 55M-1; Hall, p. 441.

36. Hall, "Sathurea," p. 56.

37. *Centennial Gazette*, p. 24; Lesley, pp. 216-17.

38. Hall, "Sathurea," p. 57.

39. Hall, p. 26.

40. *Memorabilia*, pp. 60, 82.

41. Lesley, pp. 85, 56; Gere, p. 89; Lesley, p. 86.

42. *Richard Edney*, p. 239.

43. Sylvester, I, 166, 192; *Centennial Gazette*, p. 29; *Centennial Gazette*, p. 12; *Memorabilia*, p. 74.

44. Alfred Starkweather, in *Hampshire Gazette & Courier*, March 11, 1902; *Memorabilia*, p. 79.

45. *Centennial Gazette*, pp. 21, 29.

46. Hall, "Autobiography," p. 42; Hall, p. 19.

47. Hall, pp. 19, 446, 467.

48. Hall, p. 18; Hall, "Autobiography," p. 19.

49. "School Reminiscences," *Gazette & Courier* (Northampton), August 15, 1865, article marked "1825."

50. Hall, pp. 11, 12, 446.

51. *Centennial Gazette*, pp. 24, 16. Bancroft's biographer, however, does not mention Bancroft's being elected: Russell B. Nye, *George Bancroft: Brahmin Rebel* (New York: Alfred A. Knopf, 1944).

52. S. Judd II, Judd Manuscript, Notebooks, passim.

53. Lesley, pp. 208, 225.

54. S. Judd II, Judd Manuscript, Notebook, entry for Nov. 13, 1834; *Centennial Gazette*, p. 29.

55. First Church, Northampton, records, Feb. 24, 1824; Unsigned manuscript, dated November 1895, shown to me by Mrs. Thomas M. Shepherd, Northampton; Nathaniel Lauriat, "The History of Unitarianism in Northampton 1824-1954," typescript, Forbes Library, Northampton; *A Statement of Facts, in Relation to the Call and Installation of the Rev. Mark Tucker, over the Society in Northampton, Together with his Correspondence on the Subject of Exchanges* (Northampton: T.W. Shepard, 1824).

56. Sylvester, I, 205.

57. Ibid., pp. 210, 214.

58. Hall, "Sathurea," p. 66.

59. Hall, pp. 16-17.

60. John Todd, "Statistics of the First Church in Northampton, Mass., and of the Several Churches which Have Colonized From It," *The Pulpit–Its Influence upon Society. A Sermon, Delivered at the Dedication of the Edwards Church, in Northampton, Mass., December 25, 1833* (Northampton: J.H. Butler, 1834), p. 61.

61. Letters to Arethusa Hall, August 18, 1826, July 3, 1826, Judd Papers, 55M-1.

62. *Centennial Gazette*, p. 29.

63. *The Value of Sanctuary Privileges, Exhibited in a Sermon, Delivered in Granby, West Parish, at the Dedication of the New Meeting House, April 20, 1825* (Northampton: T.W. Shepard, 1825), p. 4.

64. Hall, p. 21.

65. Solomon Williams, *Three Sermons, Preached at Northampton, One on the 30th of March–the Other Two on the Annual State Fast, April 4, 1805.* (Northampton: William Butler, 1805), pp. 36-38.

66. Hall, p. 21.

67. Letter to Edward Everett, Northampton, July 27, 1826, Bancroft Papers, Massachusetts Historical Society.

68. Letter of Levi Shepherd to Mrs. Aneas Munson, Northampton, April 5, 1816, Northampton Historical Society.

69. Letter to Arethusa Hall, August 18, 1826, Judd Papers, 55M-1.

70. [F.N. Kneeland], *Northampton: The Meadow City* (Northampton: F.N. Kneeland & L.P. Bryant, 1894), p. 73. See *Hampshire Gazette*, July 17, 1822, for father Judd's attitude towards the custom of toasts. On Bancroft, see Nye, p. 87, and Bancroft's letter to Edward Everett, July 27, 1826.

71. First Church, Northampton, records, letter by Mark Tucker, July 29, 1827; records, Feb. 20, 1828.

72. Letter of Mrs. Apphia Judd to Arethusa Hall, April 13, 1827, Judd Papers, 55M-1.

73. Ibid.; Letters by S. Judd II to Arethusa Hall, May 30, 1827, August 16, 1826, Sept. 3, 1829, May 30, 1827, Judd Papers, 55M-1; Hall, p. 25.

74. Letter of Mrs. Apphia Judd to Arethusa Hall, August 7, 1828, Judd Papers, 55M-1.

75. Ibid.; Hall, pp. 31, 21.

76. Enoch Hale diary, 1828.

77. John Truair, *Call from the Ocean, or An Appeal to the Patriot and the Christian, in Behalf of Seamen.* (New York: American Seamen's Friend Society, 1826).

78. Truair, *Sacred Music. An Address Delivered at Westhampton, May 23, 1827* (Northampton: H. Ferry & Co., 1827), p. 7.

79. Truair, *Salvation the Gift of God to a Lost World. A Discourse Delivered at Westhampton, November 29, 1832, Being the Day of Public Thanksgiving* (Northampton: John Metcalf, Printer, 1833), pp. 20-21, 24.

80. *Call from the Ocean,* in Judd's "Sermon" volume in a collection of Judd's books, Lithgow Library, Augusta, Maine. Other books of Judd's with his markings are at the Houghton Library, Harvard University.

81. Westhampton Church records. Truair's side of the case is told in his pamphlet *An Appeal to the Churches of Christ, and to the Public, on a Document from the Hampshire Central Association Withdrawing Ministerial Fellowship from the Author* (Northampton, 1829).

82. Westhampton Church records, Sept. 18, 1829.

83. Truair, *An Appeal to the Churches of Christ.*

84. Letter from John Truair to Asahel Hathaway, Westhampton, March 22, 1831, in Harvard Divinity School's copy of *An Appeal to the Churches of Christ* (manuscript letter, not attached to book).

85. Westhampton Church records. Truair, in *An Appeal to the Churches of Christ,* seems to admit by his silence that the opposition party has some evidence impugning his character.

86. S. Judd II, letter to Arethusa Hall, Oct. 8, 1830, Judd Papers, 55M-1.

87. S. Judd II, letter to Arethusa Hall, March 8, 1830, Judd Papers, 55M-1.

88. S. Judd II, letter to Arethusa Hall, Oct. 8, 1830; Horace B. Chapin, *Love of the Gift, Not Love to the Giver. A Thanksgiving Sermon Delivered at Lewiston Falls, November 28, 1839* (Portland, Maine, 1840), p. 27.

89. Caroline Healy Dall, "Transcendentalism in New England: A Lecture Delivered before the Society for Philosophical Enquiry, Washington, D.C., May 7, 1895," *Journal of Speculative Philosophy,* XXIII, No. 1. (Reprinted Boston, Mass., 1897).

Chapter 6.   The River and the Rainbow

1. Letter to Arethusa Hall, October 8, 1830, Judd Papers, 55M-1.

2. Horace B. Chapin, *Women Forbidden to Speak in the Church* (Northampton, 1837).

3. Martin L. Williston, "Reminiscences from the Life and Character of Deacon John Payson Williston," Northampton Historical Society.

4. *Memorabilia,* pp. 90, 99, 129; Hall, pp. 22, 25.

5. "The Deception. Fragment of a Domestic Drama, in four acts." The progressive changes in Judd's handwriting make it possible, usually, to date a manuscript as closely as two or three years. Judd's manuscripts, other than letters, are all in the Judd Papers, 55M-2, Houghton Library, Harvard University, and are not cited hereafter.

6. Hall, p. 26.

7. "Children," delivered January 3, 1838, quoted with minor changes in Hall, p. 410. Here, as elsewhere, I follow the manuscript.

8. Untitled manuscript, place of delivery and date inferred from internal evidence.

9. Nye, p. 91. Bancroft's article of January, 1831, in the *North American Review* was his first espousal of Jacksonian views on a concrete issue.

10. Ray Allen Billington, *The Protestant Crusade 1800-1860: A Study of the Origins of American Nativism.* (New York: Rinehart & Co., 1938), pp. 70, 73.

11. Hall, "Autobiography," p. 33.

12. Judd's journal, July 29, 1839, in Hall, p. 162.

13. Rourke, p. 46.

14. Statement based on inspection of *Northampton Courier* and *Hampshire Gazette* for 1830-1831.

15. *Minutes of the General Assembly of the Presbyterian Church in the U.S.A.* (Philadelphia, 1831), p. 206.

16. Westhampton Church Records.

17. Hall, p. 29. Only a few of the manuscripts quoted in Hall have been preserved. Mrs. Sylvester Judd Beach told me in June 1955 that it was her impression that her trunk of Judd papers had been destroyed. She did, however, allow me to look for whatever I could find, a treasure search which turned up the manuscripts referred to as the Judd Papers, 55M-1 collection, which she gave to me for my use, with the understanding that I would take them to Harvard University as a gift in memory of her late husband. The trunk which had been thrown out was marked "A.H.," according to Mrs. Beach.

18. Hall, pp. 150-52, 139, 65, 55, 47, 45.

19. Ibid., p. 31. Judd's Journal, March 12, 1842, mentions the names of "Louize" and "Margarette" as "old Friends," and records that Judd's wife, who had been reading his old letters, "asked me the other day if I was sorry I did not marry Sarah Dwight, Elizabeth Gaylord, Louisa Payson."

"Louisa S. Payson, daughter of the celebrated Dr. Payson of Portland, and afterwards wife of Professor Hopkins of Williamstown, was an intimate friend of Margarette, and was in Andover several weeks," recorded Arethusa Hall, in a passage of her autobiography (pp. 43-

44), describing her intimate and lifelong friendship with Margarette
Woods of Andover, Massachusetts, who married the Rev. E.A. Law-
rence in 1839 while Arethusa was visiting the Woods family of An-
dover. Whether Judd's mysterious correspondent of 1838-39 (see
Chapter 9) was Louisa Payson, or one of the others, or none of them,
I leave to the reader to speculate about.

20. The address on the rights of women, dated 1832, Summer
Term, says, concerning the slaves, "It is lack of privilege that makes
them thus, and it is this same deprivation of opportunity that makes
woman no more than she is." But this cannot be construed as abolitionist sentiment. Judd's study of sacred music in Westhampton is
mentioned in Judd's obituary in *The Age* (Augusta), February 10,
1853, p. 1, col. 2, which sounds like Arethusa Hall's writing.

Chapter 7. Yale

1. S. Judd II, Judd Manuscript, Notebook, Jan. 19, 1836, April
4, 1839. Father Judd provided about half of the $400 loaned to
Sylvester for his four years at Yale. Sylvester earned the balance by
teaching and vacation jobs (Hall, pp. 33, 69).

2. Letter to his mother, Nov. 28, 1837, in Hall, p. 471.

3. John Mitchell, *Reminiscences of Scenes and Characters in Col-
lege* (New Haven: A.H. Maltby, 1847), p. 119; Timothy Dwight (1828-
1916), *Memories of Yale Life and Men, 1845-1899* (New York: Dodd,
Mead and Co., 1903), p. 43; *History of the City of New Haven to the
Present Time, by an Association of Writers*, ed. Edward E. Atwater
(New York: W.W. Munsell & Co., 1887), p. 178.

4. *Noah Porter: A Memorial by Friends*, ed. George S. Merriam
(New York: C. Scribner's Sons, 1893), pp. 17-18.

5. Ralph Gabriel, *Religion and Learning at Yale: The Church of
Christ in the College and University, 1757-1957* (New Haven: Yale
Univ., 1958), pp. 135, 112.

6. Dwight, *Memories of Yale Life and Men, 1845-1899*, p. 78.

7. Mitchell, pp. 179-187.

8. Mitchell, p. 116.

9. C.C. Cox, *Poem Read at the Social Reunion of the Yale Alumni Association, Washington, D.C., Febr. 22d, 1875.* (Washington:
Gibson Bros., 1875), pp. 7-8.

10. Hall, p. 69; *Memorabilia*, pp. 73, 33.

11. Mitchell, p. 115. It is possible that this practice had changed
by 1832, however.

12. S. Judd II, Judd Manuscript, Notebook, entries for June 11,
1835, October 3, 1835.

13. Hall, p. 64.

14. Gilbert Barnes, *The Antislavery Impulse, 1830-1844* (New York: D. Appleton-Century Co., 1933), p. 6.

15. Sidney Mead, *Nathaniel William Taylor, 1768-1858: A Connecticut Liberal* (Chicago: University of Chicago Press, 1942), p. 108, quoting Taylor.

16. Letter, "To——," July 6, 1839, in Hall, p. 160.

17. S. Judd II, Judd Manuscript, Notebook, entries for July 2, 1833, August 15, 1835, Jan. 10, 1836, Dec. 2, 1837; Hall, p. 51.

18. S. Judd II, Judd Manuscript, Notebook, entries for June 13, 1833, and Dec. 24, 1833; Stanley M. Vogel, *German Literary Influences on the American Transcendentalists* (New Haven: Yale U. Press, 1955), p. 13. Judd's later library also included Goethe's *Wilhelm Meister.*

19. Hall, pp. 435-36.

20. Hall, pp. 51, 509, 108.

21. *Two Centuries of Christian Activities at Yale,* ed., James B. Reynolds, Samuel H. Fisher, Henry B. Wright (New York: G.P. Putnam's Sons, 1901), pp. 86-88.

22. Quoted in Gabriel, p. 64.

23. Records of the Brothers in Unity, entry for March 31, 1836. Yale University Archives.

24. See Perry Miller, *The Raven and the Whale; The War of Words and Wits in the Era of Poe and Melville* (New York: Harcourt, Brace, 1956).

25. Gabriel, p. 105.

26. Vogel, p. 27; Baldwin, pp. 226-28.

27. Untitled, undated essay on theme, "There is nothing new." Approximate dating based on handwriting.

28. Dwight, *Memories of Yale Life and Men, 1845-1899,* p. 76.

29. Ibid., p. 106.

30. *Richard Edney,* p. 247.

31. *The Yale Literary Magazine,* I (June, 1836), 129-31, 155-61. Identified as Judd's work by Yale archives.

32. Hall, pp. 346-47, 23-24, 30.

33. Vivian C. Hopkins, *Prodigal Puritan: A Life of Delia Bacon* (Cambridge, Mass.: Harvard University Press, 1959), p. 52.

34. *Proceedings of the Class of 1836 at Their First General Meeting* (New Haven: Palladiam Press, 1839).

35. Hall, p. 100.

Chapter 8. Unitarianism vs. Orthodoxy

1. *Memorabilia,* p. 109.

2. This collection was shown to me by Mrs. Sylvester Judd Beach.

3. *A Sermon in Commemoration of the Fiftieth Anniversary of*

the Ordination, Feb. 25th, 1807, of the Author, Rev. Charles Wellington, as Pastor of the First Congregational Church and Society in Templeton, Mass. (Boston: Crosby, Nichols & Co., 1857), pp. 20, 17.

4. Edwin G. Adams, *An Historical Discourse in Commemoration of the One Hundredth Anniversary of the Formation of First Congregational Church in Templeton, Massachusetts. With an Appendix, Embracing a Survey of the Municipal Affairs of the Town* (Boston: Crosby, Nichols, & Co., 1857), p. 141.

5. S. Judd II, Judd Manuscript, Notebook, entry for July 26, 1837.

6. Letter to S.F. Lyman, Cambridge, Sept. 30, 1837, Judd Papers, 55M-1.

7. John P. Manwell, *A History of the Hampshire Association of Congregational Churches and Ministers* (Amherst, Mass.: The Newel Press, 1941), p. 35.

8. S. Judd, *A Young Man's Account of His Conversion from Calvinism. A Statement of Facts.* (American Unitarian Association Tracts, 1st Series, No. 128; Boston: James Munroe & Co., March, 1838), pp. 8, 7; also see Hall, p. 119.

9. Gabriel, p. 115; also see Gabriel's discussion of Paley, pp. 109-113.

10. Leonard Woods, *Letters to Unitarians and Reply to Dr. Ware. Second ed. with an Appendix* (Andover, Mass.: Mark Newman, 1822). Henry Ware, *Letters Addressed to Trinitarians and Calvinists, Occasioned by Dr. Woods' Letters to Unitarians* (Cambridge, Mass.: Hilliard and Metcalf, 1820).

11. Ware, p. 18.

12. Woods, *A Reply to Dr. Ware's Letters to Trinitarians and Calvinists* (Andover, Mass.: Flagg and Gould, 1821), pp. 18-27.

13. *A Young Man's Account of His Conversion*, p. 21, also quoted in Hall, p. 111.

14. Hall, p. 70; *Memorabilia*, p. 129.

15. Mead, pp. 108-09.

16. "Cardiagraphy," in Hall, p. 82.

17. Manwell, p. 35.

18. Hall, pp. 74, 76; S. Judd II, Notebook, entries for April 22, 1837 and May 1, 1835.

19. *Reminiscences and Letters of Caroline C. Briggs*, ed. George S. Merriam (Boston: Houghton, Mifflin & Co., 1897), p. 11.

20. Letter of Lydia M. Child to Caroline Weston, Northampton, July 27, 1838, Department of Rare Books and Manuscripts, Boston Public Library; used by courtesy of the Trustees of the Boston Public Library.

21. Hall, "Autobiography," pp. 41-42.

22. Whitman, pp. 77, 68, 126.

23. *A Young Man's Account of His Conversion*, pp. 13-14.

24. Hall, p. 104; *Memorabilia*, pp. 85-97, quotation on p. 90; S. Judd II, Notebook, entry for Nov. 14, 1836.

25. Hall, "Autobiography," p. 42.

26. Judd to Arethusa Hall, Cambridge, June 3, 1838, in Hall, p. 133.

Chapter 9. Harvard, Emerson, and Judd

1. Alexander H. Everett, Review of Cousin, *North American Review*, XXIX (July, 1829), 67-123, in Perry Miller, *The Transcendentalists, An Anthology* (Cambridge, Mass.: Harvard U., 1950), p. 33.

2. S. Judd II, Judd Manuscript, Notebook, entry for Nov. 15, 1838; Brooks, p. 183; Andrews Norton, *A Discourse on the Latest Form of Infidelity; Delivered at the Request of the "Association of the Alumni of the Cambridge Theological School," on the 19th of July, 1839.* (Cambridge: John Owen, 1839). Judd's copy of this pamphlet, still containing the leaf, is at the Kennebec Historical Society.

3. *The Northampton Book*, pp. 105-06; *Memorabilia*, pp. 107, 111; Charles A. Sheffield (ed.), *The History of Florence, Massachusetts* (Florence, Mass., 1895), p. 101.

4. S. Judd II, Judd Manuscript, Notebook, Aug. 27, 1834, Aug. 24, 1835. Prior to 1834 father Judd had never been to Amherst (Aug. 26, 1834).

5. *The Harvard Divinity School: Its Place in Harvard University and in American Culture*, ed. George H. Williams (Boston: Beacon Press, 1954), p. 23; Andrew P. Peabody, *Harvard Reminiscences* (Boston: Ticknor & Co., 1888), p. 99; Brooks, p. 39; Samuel Eliot Morison, *Three Centuries of Harvard. 1636-1936* (Cambridge, Mass.: Harvard U. Press, 1936), p. 253; *Harvard Divinity School*, p. 40; Bliss Perry, *The Praise of Folly and Other Papers* (Boston: Houghton Mifflin, 1923), p. 87.

6. Perry, pp. 93-96.

7. Edward B. Hall, *Memoir of Mary L. Ware, Wife of Henry Ware, Jr.* (Boston: American Unitarian Association, 1874), p. 291.

8. "Likeness to God," 1828, in Miller, *The Transcendentalists*, p. 23.

9. *Margaret*, pp. 295-306, 100-01, 54-55, 40-41.

10. Lawrence Buell, *Literary Transcendentalism: Style and Vision in the American Renaissance* (Ithaca: Cornell University Press, 1973), pp. 93-94, 97; F.O. Matthiessen, *American Renaissance: Art and Expression in the Age of Emerson and Whitman* (New York: Oxford University Press, 1941), pp. 38-40.

11. The quotations from "The American Scholar" in this chapter are located in Emerson's *Works,* I, 87, 115, 91, 85, 106, 103, 115, 110-11, 98, 85.

12. Arethusa Hall's insertion.

13. Hall, pp. 158-59, 165-66; S. Judd II, Judd Manuscript, Notebook, Dec. 2, 1837, March 14, 1839.

14. Mircea Eliade, "The Yearning for Paradise in Primitive Tradition," *The Making of Myth,* ed. Richard M. Ohmann (New York: G.P. Putnam's Sons, 1962), pp. 84-97.

15. *Margaret,* pp. 388, 460, 387.

16. Prefatory "Note" to *Margaret* (Revised ed.), p. iv; also, see below, p. 315.

17. *Richard Edney,* p. 308.

Chapter 10. Controversy at the Divinity School

1. Emerson, *Works,* X, 552.

2. Daniel Walker Howe, *The Unitarian Conscience: Harvard Moral Philosophy, 1805-1861* (Cambridge: Harvard University Press, 1970), pp. 16, 192.

3. Hall, p. 347.

4. Ibid., p. 162.

5. *Philo,* pp. 183-84.

6. Ibid., pp. 187-88, 166-67.

7. Hall, pp. 107, 140-41.

8. S. Judd II, Judd Manuscript, Notebook, entry made by C. Parkman Judd for Aug. 29, 1843; Hall, p. 449. William Ellery Channing II, like Judd, compiled his own dictionary of obsolete and unusual words, notes Lawrence Buell in his discussion of the transcendentalists' fondness for words and catalogues. Transcendentalists delighted in "strings of images for their own sake": Emerson vibrated to "'bare lists of words'."; Theodore Parker had "a passion for weaving bits and bushels of arcane information into his sermons and his conversation"; Thoreau "was a passionate collector of facts, sayings, and names." Buell's chapter on what he calls the "catalogue rhetoric" of the transcendentalists can be applied equally to Judd. As Buell says, the catalogue was "the closest verbal approximation they were able to achieve to the boundless vitality of nature" (pp. 169, 187).

9. Judd's notebooks are in the Judd Papers, 55M-2.

10. *Works,* I, 94.

11. *North American Review,* LXII (Jan., 1846), 118.

12. Hall, pp. 351, 435-36.

13. Judd to his mother, Cambridge, Feb. 13, 1838, Judd Papers 55M-1.

14. S. Judd II to Peninnah Judd, Northampton, Nov. 14, 1847, Judd Papers, 55M-1. Father Judd apologized for having made fun of a gift of tea brought to him by his son-in-law, Joseph Williams.

15. Hall, pp. 162, 106; S. Judd II, Judd Manuscript, Notebook, entry for April 4, 1839. Judd later repaid this interest-free loan, from Edmund Dwight, although he was not required to do so.

16. S. Judd II, Notebook, entries for July 21, 1838, Feb. 27, 1840, Jan. 3, 1838, Feb. 26, 1840. The abolitionist lecture is dated, in accordance with Judd's custom, as delivered in Northampton, Aug. 19, 1838, and in Hartford, Aug. 11, 1838.

17. Judd to ——, Cambridge, July 6, 1839, in Hall, p. 157.

18. Judd to Arethusa Hall, Cambridge, Sept. 7, 1837, in Hall, p. 115.

19. Judd to his mother, Feb. 13, 1838, Judd Papers, 55M-1.

20. Judd to ——, Cambridge, April 10, 1839, in Hall, p. 146.

21. Hall, p. 109; Judd to S.F. Lyman, Esq. (son of Judge Joseph Lyman), Cambridge, Sept. 30, 1837, Judd Papers, 55M-1.

22. Conrad Wright, "Emerson, Barzillai Frost, and the Divinity School Address," *Harvard Theological Review*, XLIX (Jan., 1956), 19-43.

23. *The Harvard Divinity School*, pp. 49, 51; Emerson, *Journals* (Boston, 1909-14), V, 34.

24. Howe, pp. 16, 151-73.

25. "The American Scholar," *Works*, I, 89.

26. Judd to S.F. Lyman, Sept. 30, 1837, Judd Papers, 55M-1.

27. *The Harvard Divinity School*, p. 57; Ralph Rusk, *The Life of Ralph Waldo Emerson* (New York: Charles Scribner's Sons, 1949), p. 136.

28. Howe, pp. 106-08, 110.

29. *The Harvard Divinity School*, pp. 56, 64.

30. Channing's *Lecture on War* (Boston: Dutton and Wentworth, 1839) is the longest, most eloquent, most nearly pacifist of his three pamphlets; Henry Ware, Jr., *The Promise of Universal Peace; A Sermon, Preached in the Chapel of Harvard University, Lord's Day, Dec. 15, 1833* (Boston: Russell Odiorne, & Metcalf, 1834).

31. Records of the Harvard University Library; one of Judd's early sermons was called "The Indwelling Christ," Aug. 2, 1840.

32. "No mob, no tumult. Laus Deo," reported father Judd (Judd Manuscript, Notebook, Jan. 13, 1836, May 12, 1836).

33. Ibid., Jan. 30, 1837.

34. "Records of the Theological School," May 25, 1838, Harvard University Archives; "Records of the Philanthropic Society in the Theological School of Harvard University," pp. 116-18.

35. Morison, p. 255; Howe, p. 282.

36. Lydia M. Child to Caroline Weston, Northampton, March 7,

1839, Department of Rare Books and Manuscripts, Boston Public Library.

37. Sermon XXVI, "The Reformer," Augusta, Nov. 15, 1840.

38. Child to Weston, Northampton, July 27, 1838, Boston Public Library.

39. Rusk, p. 268.

40. *The Letters of Ralph Waldo Emerson,* ed. Ralph L. Rusk (New York: Columbia Univ. Press, 1939), II, 147.

41. *Works,* I, 119.

42. *The Personality of the Deity. A Sermon, Preached in the Chapel of Harvard University, September 23, 1838* (Boston: James Munroe & Co., 1838), p. 13. Judd owned a copy of this sermon.

43. Miller, *The Transcendentalists,* p. 195.

44. Octavius Brooks Frothingham, *Recollections and Impressions, 1822-1890* (New York: G.P. Putnam's Sons, 1891), p. 31. German rationalism, says Frothingham, was an "ever-present spectre" at Harvard in the 1840's.

45. Hall, "Autobiography," p. 42; S. Judd II, Judd Manuscript, Notebook, entry for Aug. 8, 1839.

46. Clarence H. Faust, "The Background of the Unitarian Opposition to Transcendentalism," *Modern Philology,* XXXV (Feb., 1938), 297-324.

47. *A Young Man's Account of His Conversion;* Hall, p. 172.

48. *The Harvard Divinity School,* pp. 155, 159, quoted from the "Records of the Theological School," Harvard University.

49. Andrews Norton, *A Discourse on the Latest Form of Infidelity: Delivered at the Request of the "Association of the Alumni of the Cambridge Theological School," on the 19th of July, 1839. With Notes.* (Cambridge: John Owen, 1839); George Ripley, *"The Latest Form of Infidelity" Examined. A Letter to Mr. Andrews Norton.* (Boston: James Munroe & Co., 1839); Andrews Norton, *Remarks on a Pamphlet Entitled "'The Latest Form of Infidelity' Examined."* (Cambridge: John Owen, 1839).

50. *Works,* I, 129, 144.

51. Ripley, p. 55, quoting Luther, *Works* (Walch's Ed.), XI, 1338.

52. Norton, *A Discourse on the Latest Form of Infidelity,* p. 11; Ripley, pp. 155-59; *The Harvard Divinity School,* p. 50.

53. Howe, p. 37.

54. Ibid., pp. 78-81, 86, 90.

55. Horace Bushnell, *God in Christ* (Hartford, 1849), pp. 189, 191.

56. Hall, "Autobiography," p. 54.

57. Howe, p. 117.

58. *Lectures on Revivals of Religion* (1835; rpt. New York: Fleming H. Revell, 1868), pp. 12-14.

59. *The Church: In a Series of Discourses* (Boston: Crosby, Nichols, 1854), pp. 208, 211.

60. Howe, p. 169.

61. Hall, p. 404.

62. *God in Christ*, pp. 49, 73, 69.

63. *Transcendentalism in New England: A History* (1876; rpt. New York: Harper, 1959), pp. 382-83.

64. Judd, Journal entry for November 8, 1841.

65. Letter to Alexander Ireland, October 6, 1846, quoted in Moncure D. Conway, *Autobiography, Memories and Experiences of Moncure Daniel Conway* (Boston: Houghton, Mifflin, 1904) I, 179.

66. William Hutchison, *The Transcendentalist Ministers: Church Reform in the New England Renaissance* (New Haven: Yale University Press, 1959), p. 32.

67. Dickinson to Higginson, April 25, 1862, letter number 261 in *The Letters of Emily Dickinson*, ed. Thomas H. Johnson and Theodora W. Ward (Cambridge: Harvard University Press); Hale to Judd, Jan. 10, 1850, Judd Papers, 55M-2.

68. William Irving Bartlett, *Jones Very: Emerson's "Brave Saint"* (Durham, N.C.: Duke University Press, 1942), p. 56, quoting Emerson's Journal for Oct. 30, 1838; Rusk, pp. 255-56.

69. Hall, pp. 345-46.

70. The note is headed "Bro. Very, Sept 22, 1839," Judd Papers, 55M-1.

71. Francis B. Dedmond, *Sylvester Judd* (Boston: Twayne Publishers, 1980), p. 35.

72. "Records of the Theological School," p. 105.

73. *The Journals and Miscellaneous Notebooks of Ralph Waldo Emerson*, ed. A.W. Plumstead and Harrison Hayford, VII (Cambridge: Harvard University Press, 1969), 65, entry for September 8, 1838. Emerson's comment must, of course, be seen in tension with his celebration of "the near, the low, the common," in other passages.

Chapter 11. The End of the Rainbow: Augusta, Maine

1. James W. North, *The History of Augusta, from the Earliest Settlement to the Present Time* (Augusta: Clapp & North, 1870), pp. 584, 586, 569, 512-15; *Centennial Gazette*, p. 15.

2. P. 282.

3. *The Letters of John Fairfield*, ed. Arthur G. Staples (Lewiston, Maine: Lewiston Journal Co., 1922), pp. 294, 304, 306, etc.; Hall, p. 109; North, pp. 462-65.

4. Judd's sermon of November 1, 1840, marks the beginning of his concern with the problem of the communion.

5. Letter of Joseph Williams to Reuel Williams, Cambridge, Mass., Sept. 1, 1834, Williams Papers, Maine Historical Society, Portland, Maine.

6. Anonymous typescript, shown to me by Richard Hamlen, Schenectady, New York; guest book shown to me by John T.G. Nichols, Marblehead, Massachusetts.

7. Pp. 272, 275.

8. Letter of S. Judd III to his father, Feb. 16, 1841, Judd Papers, 55M-1.

9. By "orthodox," as throughout this book, I mean Congregational. Francis Dedmond, in borrowing from me several facts and judgments on this and the preceding page, incorrectly attributes to me his statement that Mrs. Williams was an Episcopalian.

10. Letter of Judd to his mother, Feb. 16, 1841, in Judd Papers, 55M-1; various letters in Williams Papers, Maine Historical Society; letters of Judd to Arethusa Hall, in Judd Papers, 55M-1; Judd's journal for 1841-42.

11. *Scenes in a Vestry: Being an Account of the Late Controversy in the South Parish Congregational Church at Augusta* (Augusta, 1841); Edward S. Drown, "There Was War in Heaven," *New England Quarterly,* IV (January, 1931), 30-53; Ralph Waldo Emerson, letter to F.H. Hedge, Sept. 1, 1842, in *Letters,* III, 85, 58.

12. Letter to Apphia Judd Williams, Nov. 28, 1842, Judd Papers, 55M-1.

13. General Henry Sewall diary, shown to me by Joseph Mellen, Bowdoinham, Maine.

14. Hall, p. 176.

15. *The Age* (Augusta, Maine), 10 Feb. 1853, p. 1, col. 3.

16. Joel Myerson, "Frederic Henry Hedge and the Failure of Transcendentalism," *Harvard Library Bulletin,* XXIII (October, 1975), 396-410; Hall, "Autobiography," p. 53.

17. Manuscript shown to me by Henry Fuller, York, Maine.

18. See their letters, Williams Papers, Maine Historical Society.

19. Letter of John Fairfield to his wife, Augusta, October 4, 1840, in *The Letters of John Fairfield,* p. 294.

20. Letters of Feb. 18, 1841, and Feb. 25, 1841, Judd Papers, 55M-1.

21. Letters both dated Feb. 16, 1841, Judd Papers, 55M-1.

22. Above, p. 213.

23. Letter of August 28, 1841, in Hall, p. 490; entry of April 15, 1841, in Hall, p. 490; Sylvester Judd III, Journal entry for Sept. 6, 1841.

24. Personal interview with Miriam Titcomb of Augusta, Maine, June, 1959.

25. Sylvester Judd II, Judd Manuscript, Notebook, entry for

August 29, 1843, made by Chauncey Parkman Judd.

26. "Sylvester Judd," *Fraser's Magazine for Town and Country,* No. 451 (July, 1867), 60.

27. *Arethusa Hall: A Memorial,* pp. 145, 156-67. The removal of the stone cross when the house passed out of family hands in the twentieth century caused much comment in Augusta, as did the destruction of the Williams mansion to make way for a bridge approach.

28. *Richard Edney,* pp. 281, 282-83. Arguing in defense of *Richard Edney* that it was addressed to a younger audience than was commonly supposed, Edward Everett Hale wrote: "The newspaper critics wondered what he wrote 'Richard Edney' for. He did not write it for them. He did not write it for reputation. He wrote it for country boys who have occasion to go to seek their living in large towns. It was just like him, that he wrote to his publishers to have part of the edition bound in 'red cambric,' that it might work its way, in cheap auction-rooms, into the hands of those for whom he made it" ["Life and Character of Sylvester Judd," *Christian Examiner,* LVIII (January, 1855), 74].

29. Hall, p. 303.

30. *Philo,* p. 232.

31. Above, p. 151.

32. Sanford, p. 18.

33. *Memorabilia,* pp. 128-30. The part torn out begins with "'well,' says father, 'you know but little about my disease.'"

34. Hall, p. 191; letter by Judd's mother to Arethusa Hall, May 1, 1842, Judd Papers, 55M-1. Judd's journal entry of March 14, the day after the lecture, reads thus: "In the midst of the War sermon difficulties. I preached it last night to a full house. Some members of the Legislature left. Jane was not there. Poor girl. She stayed at Mothers, her poor heart in a volcanic state. I loved her and petted her; and still thought I was doing my duty. We came home, made a fire, agitated, went to bed. She expected I should be shot. She said she felt like Lovejoys wife. We did not get to sleep for a long time. This morning, before breakfast Joseph came in quite agitated, said they were going to dismiss me from the State house. To night the documents came. ordered that Rev Mr Judd be dismissed as chaplain. I would be calm. I do but right. I have the approbation of my conscience and Christ. and what do I care besides."

35. Judd to Samuel Fessenden, Sept. 15, 1847, in Samuel Fessenden Papers, Maine Historical Society; *The Christian Citizen,* Sept. 11, 1847, p. 146, Nov. 13, 1847, p. 182, Dec. 18, 1847, p. 202, Feb. 23, 1850, p. 29.

36. The legislator, William Chick, gave a detailed summary of a Judd sermon in his letter but passed over a sermon of Benjamin Tappan with the comment: "in the P M I attended the Rev Dr

Tappans Cutch [sic] the exercise here was very good they sung Naomi
Marlow and Hamburg but not so well as we can in Amherst" (letter
to Stephen Osgood, December 30, 1844, shown to me by Jennie
Cochrane of Hallowell, Maine).

37. Sermon Bxxxiii-xxxiv, p. 71. In this discourse Judd gives his
views on every issue from immigration and slavery to labor-capital
strife, but shows a tendency to a scattershot approach and simplistic
solutions to complex problems. On labor-capital strife, for example,
here is his entire statement: "There is strife between labor and capital. Let both parties treat one another fairly; that is all we can say;
let both adopt the Christian principle of doing as they would be
done by; and all will come out well in the end, and not otherwise;
labor will soon become Capital, and old Capital when he retires from
business, will be glad to see his children, labor, take his place on the
active stage."

38. Ibid., pp. 62-71; Hall, pp. 294, 303-08; Judd to *National
Anti-Slavery Standard,* April 16, 1849, Sydney Howard Gay Papers,
Rare Book and Manuscript Library, Columbia University (a letter
in which Judd speaks rather testily about the unannounced rise in
subscription price: "You wait till more than a year expires, and then,
plump, comes your bill. You abuse the clergy, but the worst sort of
abuse is an unforeseen Bill"); Sylvester Judd, *A Discourse Touching
the Causes and Remedies of Intemperance. Preached February 2,
1845* (Augusta: Wm. T. Johnson, 1845), p. 37, excerpts in Hall, pp.
312-18; *Richard Edney,* pp. 292-306; *Philo,* p. 134.

39. *Intemperance,* p. 14. Sylvester Judd II noted that dancing
was common at weddings, quiltings, huskings, on election day, the
day after Thanksgiving, etc., usually with a Negro fiddler (Judd Manuscript, "Miscellaneous," XIV, 228-29). Apparently the revival
movement after 1800 changed things, for during the revival of 1819
the church in Northampton cautioned the faithful against dancing.

40. Hall, p. 330.

41. *Philo,* pp. 38-39, 165, 89, 94, 164, 91-92, 166; Sylvester
Judd, *Intemperance,* p. 38.

42. *North American Review,* LXX (April, 1850), 434, 436-40;
Hall to Judd, April 5, 1851, Judd Papers, 55M-2; *Arethusa Hall: A
Memorial,* p. 136. Edward Everett Hale, in contrast, was enthusiastic
about *Philo.* Hale's secretary, Abigail W. Clark, later penned a note
on the typed copy of one of Hale's letters to Frederic Greenleaf that
"E.E.H. used to say that they really seriously expected 'Philo' was to
convert the world. A.W.C." In the letter, Hale had written, about
Judd, "He had been hurt that people said they could not understand it [*Philo*]—and so wrote me the most glorious letter of eight
pages, telling all about his notion of Christ's second coming" [Feb.
3, 1850, E.E. Hale Papers, The New York State Library, Albany,

printed without Clark's note in Edward E. Hale, Jr., *Life and Letters
of Edward Everett Hale* (Boston: Little, Brown, 1917), I, 216]. To
his mother Hale wrote "I *think* <u>Philo</u> glorious." Judd had sent Hale
the first copy of *Philo,* along with the comment that "If I belong to
a clique it is one of which you and your sisters are members, and *I
know of no others*" (letters by Hale to his mother and to Frederic
Greenleaf, both dated December 27, 1849, in E.E. Hale Papers). In
1855 Hale wrote about Judd in the *Christian Examiner:* "Certain
people were troubled about 'Philo,' for fear it compromised his
reputation. He did not care whether it did or not. They were worried because it was arranged on the machinery of Festus and Faust.
Of course it was. But it was written, not to make a reputation, and
with great indifference as to machinery, to show what is meant by
'the second coming of Christ'; and we venture the suggestion, that
any course of criticism on that subject is incomplete without a reference to this book, as a monograph upon it. With just the same
spirit, he had in his mind a course of books for children, which he
was anxious to write and publish, because he thought there was need
of them" ["Life and Character of Sylvester Judd," *Christian Examiner,* LVIII (January, 1855), 74].

43. *Philo,* p. 19.
44. Hall, pp. 382, 388-89.
45. *Philo,* pp. 177, 142, 144, 130, 131, 158.
46. Sylvester Judd to [*National Anti-Slavery Standard*], September 29, 1851, Sydney Howard Gay Papers, Rare Book and Manuscript Library, Columbia University; also see footnote 38, above.
47. Sylvester Judd to Jane Judd, April 30, 1848, Judd Papers,
55M-1; letter of Helen Gilman to John T. Gilman, July 4, 1847,
shown to me by John T.G. Nichols of Marblehead, Mass.; Lewiston,
Maine, *Evening Journal,* August 26, 1902; John A. Poor, *Memoir
of Hon. Reuel Williams* (privately printed for Maine Historical Society, 1864), p. 37.
48. R.P. Cutler, *A Sermon Preached at Park Street Church, Portland, Sunday, Jan. 30, 1853, Occasioned by the Death of Rev. Sylvester Judd.* (Portland: J.H. Little, 1853), p. 21. Cutler concedes in
his eulogy that "Upon a short acquaintance, however, he was not
likely to be understood, his peculiarities intercepted one's vision,
and unless the eye looked through them upon the substantial qualities of his character, he was in danger of being underrated."
49. Hall, pp. 197-99; John C. Perkins, *Unitarianism in Maine,*
Church Exchange Tracts, Number 3 (Portland, 1900), p. 11.
50. *Richard Edney,* pp. 148-49.
51. Sylvester Judd, *Intemperance,* pp. 38-39; Leslie C. Corn-
ish, *Centennial Services, All Souls Church (Unitarian) 1826-1926,*
p. 19 (in church library). Note that the name Judd insisted on,

"Christ Church," became later "All Souls Church."

52. *The True Dignity of Politics. A Sermon: by the Rev. Sylvester Judd, Preached in Christ Church, Augusta, May 26, 1850* (Augusta: William T. Johnson, Printer to the State, 1850), p. 18.

53. See above, p. 95.

54. S. Judd III, *The Birthright Church: A Discourse by the Late Rev. Sylvester Judd, of Augusta, Maine* (Augusta: William H. Simpson, Printer, 1854).

55. Letter of Joseph H. Williams to Helen Gilman, May 2, 1853, Williams Collection, Maine Historical Society. The cause of Judd's fatal illness was reported to me by Mrs. Sylvester Judd Beach in a personal interview, August, 1959.

56. Hall, p. 520.

Bibliography

The Judd Papers in the Houghton Library, Harvard University, contain all but a handful of the extant manuscripts by Sylvester Judd III. Judd's manuscript sermons, lectures, essays, plays, poems, notes, reviews of reading are all contained in the sixteen boxes marked 55M-2 of this collection; they are not specifically cited in my notes. The remaining two boxes, marked 55M-1, contain letters by Judd and his immediate family, plus Arethusa Hall's autobiographical "Sathurea" and Sylvester Judd II's journal of a trip to Ohio in 1819. Citations are given in the notes for letters in the 55M-1 collection. The reader should assume that Judd's letters and journal entries not cited in the notes are to be found chronologically arranged in Arethusa Hall's *Life and Character of the Rev. Sylvester Judd,* a book which is the only source for most of Judd's letters and journals. The only Judd journal extant, so far as I know, is for the years 1841-42; it was given to me by Judd's granddaughter, Jeannette Whipple, in microfilm form. A few Judd letters are in the collections of the Massachusetts Historical Society, the Boston Public Library, the Maine Historical Society, the University of Virginia, the Chicago Historical Society, the New York Historical Society, the Historical Society of Pennsylvania, the University of Iowa, and Columbia University—from one to four letters in each library.

The Reuel Williams Papers at the Maine Historical Society contain letters of various members of the Reuel Williams family. Except for family letters in the 55M-1 boxes at Houghton Library, virtually all of Sylvester Judd II's papers, referred to as the "Judd Manuscript," are at the Forbes Library, Northampton, Massachusetts. This huge collection consists primarily of his notes on local history, plus observations of the change of seasons, with journal entries of a more personal nature scattered among the botanical observations that increasingly occupied his attention. The Enoch Hale Papers are in the Yale Divinity School library. A diary of Jane E. Judd for the year 1852 was shown to me by Elizabeth Judd Micoleau, Judd's granddaughter; it is not very lengthy or informative. Other manuscript collections used are cited in the notes, above.

SELECTED MEMOIRS, REMINISCENCES, PUBLISHED LETTERS AND JOURNALS

Abbot, Francis Ellingwood, ed. *Arethusa Hall: A Memorial.* Cambridge: John Wilson and Son, 1892. "Privately Printed for the Family." Contains Arethusa Hall's "Autobiography," etc.

Clarke, Dorus. *"Saying the Catechism," Seventy-five Years Ago and the Historical Results.* Boston: Lee and Shepard, 1879.

Cutler, R.P. *A Sermon Preached at Park Street Church, Portland, Sunday, Jan. 30, 1853, Occasioned by the Death of Rev. Sylvester Judd.* Portland: H.J. Little & Co., 1853.

Hall, Arethusa. *Life and Character of the Rev. Sylvester Judd.* Boston: Crosby, Nichols & Co., 1854. Reprinted Boston: D.C. Colesworthy, 1857; reprinted Port Washington, N.Y.: Kennikat Press, 1971.

Hall, Arethusa, ed. *Memorabilia: From the Journals of Sylvester Judd, of Northampton, Mass. 1809-1860.* Northampton: Private edition, 1882.

Memorial of the Reunion of the Natives of Westhampton, Mass., September 5, 1866. Waltham, Mass.: Office of the Free Press, 1866.

Poor, John A. *Memoir of Hon. Reuel Williams.* Prepared for the Maine Historical Society: Privately printed, 1864.

WORKS BY SYLVESTER JUDD (1813-1853),
Chronologically Arranged

"Truth." *The Yale Literary Magazine,* I (June, 1836), 129-31.

"The Outlaw and His Daughter." *The Yale Literary Magazine,* I (June, 1836), 155-61. These works from *The Yale Literary Magazine* identified as Judd's by Yale Archives.

A Young Man's Account of His Conversion from Calvinism. A Statement of Facts. American Unitarian Association Tracts, First Series, No. 128. Boston: James Munroe & Co., March, 1838.

The Little Coat: Concerning Religious Education. Unitarian Sunday-School Society Tract Series, No. 14. Boston: n.d.

The Beautiful Zion. A Sermon . . . Preached July 4, 1841. Augusta: Severance & Dorr, Printers, 1841.

A Moral Review of the Revolutionary War, or Some of the Evils of that Event Considered. A Discourse Delivered at the Unitarian Church, Augusta, Sabbath Evening, March 13th, 1842. With an Introductory Address, and Notes. Hallowell: Glazier, Masters & Smith, Printers, 1842.

Letter to the editor. *Christian Register,* XXI (July 9, 1842), 109.

A Discourse Touching the Causes and Remedies of Intemperance. Preached February 2, 1845. Augusta: Wm. T. Johnson, Printer, 1845.

Margaret. A Tale of the Real and Ideal, Blight and Bloom; Including Sketches of a Place Not Before Described, Called Mons Christi. Boston: Jordan and Wiley, 1845. Revised Edition in two volumes, Boston: Phillips, Sampson, and Company, 1851; reprinted 1857. One-volume edition of revised version issued in Boston by Roberts Brothers, 1871; reprinted in 1882 and 1891, and by The Gregg Press in 1968. Edition in Library of Favorite Authors Series, London: Ward, Lock, & Co., 1874.

"Worth of the Soul." In *Sermons on Christian Communion, Designed to Promote the Growth of the Religious Affections, by Living Ministers.* Ed. Thomas R. Sullivan. Boston: William Crosby and H.P. Nichols, 1848, pp. 24-37.

Philo: An Evangeliad. By the Author of 'Margaret; A Tale of the Real and Ideal.' Boston: Phillips, Sampson, and Company, 1850.

The True Dignity of Politics. A Sermon: By the Rev. Sylvester Judd, Preached in Christ Church, Augusta, May 26, 1850. Augusta: William T. Johnson, Printer to the State, 1850.

Richard Edney and the Governor's Family. A Rus-Urban Tale, Simple and Popular, Yet Cultured and Noble, of Morals, Sentiment, and Life, Practically Treated and Pleasantly Illustrated Containing, Also, Hints on Being Good and Doing Good. By the Author of "Margaret," and "Philo." Boston: Phillips, Sampson & Company, 1850. Reprinted Boston: Roberts Brothers, 1880.

The Birthright Church: A Discourse by the Late Rev. Sylvester Judd . . . Designed for "Thursday Lecture" in Boston, Jan. 6, 1853. Ed. J.H. Williams. Boston: Crosby, Nichols, and Company, 1853. Reprinted Augusta: William H. Simpson, 1854, for the Association of the Unitarian Church of Maine.

The Church: In a Series of Discourses. Boston: Crosby, Nichols and Company, 1854. Reprinted Boston: D.C. Colesworthy, 1857.

"The Dramatic Element in the Bible." *Atlantic Monthly,* IV (August, 1859), 137-53.

SELECTED REVIEWS AND CRITICAL WORKS,
Chronologically Arranged

"Mr. Judd's Discourse on the Moral Effects of the Revolutionary War." *Christian Register,* XXI (May 14, 1842), 79.

[Huntington, Frederic D.] Rev. of *Margaret. Christian Examiner,* XXXIX (November, 1845), 418-20.

[Ossoli], S. Margaret Fuller. *Papers on Literature and Art.* 2 vols. London: Wiley & Putnam, 1846; rpt. New York: AMS Press, 1972, II, 137.

[Peabody, William B.O.] Rev. of *Margaret. North American Review,* LXII (January, 1846), 102-41.

[Clapp, Dexter]. Rev. of *Margaret. Southern Quarterly Review,* IX (April, 1846), 507-22.

[Lowell, James Russell]. "Longfellow's *Kavanagh:* Nationality in Literature." *North American Review,* LXIX (July, 1849), 209.

[Peabody, Andrew Preston]. Rev. of *Philo. North American Review,* LXX (April, 1850), 433-43.

[Clapp, Dexter]. Rev. of *Philo. Christian Examiner,* XLVIII (May, 1850), 499-500.

Rev. of *Richard Edney and the Governor's Family. Literary World,* VII (December, 1850), 452-53.

Rev. of *Richard Edney and the Governor's Family. Knickerbocker Magazine,* XXXVII (January, 1851), 72-75.

[Morison, J.H.] Rev. of *Richard Edney and the Governor's Family. Christian Examiner,* L (January, 1851), 140-42.

[Abbot, A.W.] Rev. of *Richard Edney and the Governor's Family. North American Review,* LXXII (April, 1851), 493-505.

Obituary of Sylvester Judd. *Christian Examiner,* LIV (March, 1853), 346-49.

——. *New York Quarterly,* II (July, 1853), 278-312.

Hale, E[dward] E[verett]. "Judd's Discourses on the Church." *Christian Examiner,* LVI (May, 1854), 428-45.

——. "Life and Character of Sylvester Judd." *Christian Examiner,* LVIII (January, 1855), 63-75.

[Morison, J.H.] Rev. of *Life and Character of the Rev. Sylvester Judd. North American Review,* LXXX (April, 1855), 420-39.

D[uyckinck], E[vert] A. Introduction to *Compositions in Outline by Felix O.C. Darley from Judd's* Margaret. New York: Redfield, 1856.

[Osgood, S.] "The Real and the Ideal in New England." *North American Review,* LXXXIV (April, 1857), 535-59.

"Sylvester Judd." *Fraser's Magazine for Town and Country,* LXXVI (July, 1867), 45-60.

Hale, Percy. "Sylvester Judd's *Margaret."* *Yale Literary Magazine,* XL (1875), 471-75.

Keith, Elmer D. "A Forgotten Yale Author." *Yale Literary Magazine,* LXXIV (1908), 113-20.

Van Doren, Carl. *The American Novel.* New York: Macmillan Company, 1921.

Brooks, Van Wyck. *The Flowering of New England: 1815-1865.* New York: E.P. Dutton, 1936.

Fenn, William Wallace. "Rev. Sylvester Judd and the Birthright Church 1813-53." *Proceedings of the Unitarian Historical Society,* VI (1938), 13-30.

Brockway, Philip Judd. "Sylvester Judd: Novelist of Transcendentalism." *New England Quarterly,* XIII (December, 1940), 654-77.

——. *Sylvester Judd (1813-1853): Novelist of Transcendentalism.* University of Maine Studies, Second Series, No. 53. Orono, Maine: University of Maine Press, 1941, in *Maine Bulletin,* XLIII (April, 1941).

Matthiessen, F.O. *American Renaissance: Art and Expression in the Age of Emerson and Whitman.* New York: Oxford University Press, 1941. Comments that Melville read *Margaret* and perhaps borrowed from it in *Pierre.*

Parrington, Vernon L., Jr. *American Dreams: A Study of American Utopias.* Providence: Brown University Press, 1947.

Loomis, C. Grant. "Sylvester Judd's New England Lore." *Journal of American Folklore,* LX (April, 1947), 151-58.

Cameron, Kenneth W. "The Episcopal Church in the Romanticism of Sylvester Judd." *Emerson Society Quarterly,* No. 34 (First Quarter, 1964), 100-01.

Hathaway, Richard D. "The Lapse of Uriel: The Conversions of Sylvester Judd (1813-1853)." Diss. Western Reserve 1964.

King, Donald R. "Emerson's 'Divinity School Address' and Judd's *Margaret."* *Emerson Society Quarterly,* No. 47 (Second Quarter, 1967), 3-7.

Shurr, William H. "Sylvester Judd and G.M. Hopkins' Margaret." *Victorian Poetry,* XI (1973), 337-39.

Ronda, Bruce A. "Sylvester Judd's *Margaret:* Open Spirits and Hidden Hearts." *American Transcendental Quarterly,* XXXIX (1978), 217-29. This and the chapter on Judd in the Parrington book are the most substantial modern studies of Judd of less than book length.

Dedmond, Francis B. *Sylvester Judd.* Boston: Twayne Publishers, 1980.

Index

356